30/8/13
4/5/15

D0531233

WGC

Please renew or return items by the date
shown on your receipt

www.hertsdirect.org/libraries

Renewals and   0300 123 4049
enquiries:

Textphone for hearing   0300 123 4041
or speech impaired

Hertfordshire

To my godchildren: Francesca, Alexander, Elijah, and Rumi

The Compact Guide to
Christian History

LION

Stephen Backhouse

A Lion Book
an imprint of
Lion Hudson plc
Wilkinson House, Jordan Hill Road,
Oxford OX2 8DR, England
www.lionhudson.com
ISBN 978 0 7459 5506 3

Distributed by:
UK: Marston Book Services, PO Box 269,
Abingdon, Oxon, OX14 4YN
USA: Trafalgar Square Publishing, 814
N. Franklin Street, Chicago, IL 60610
USA Christian Market: Kregel Publications,
PO Box 2607, Grand Rapids, MI 49501
First edition 2011
10 9 8 7 6 5 4 3 2 1 0

A catalogue record for this book is available
from the British Library
Typeset in 9.5/11 Bodoni SvtyTwo ITC TT
Printed and bound in China

Acknowledgments:

Many people helped along the way during this
project. Thanks are due to my colleagues at
St Mellitus College, London, and the
University of Oxford, as well as the librarians
of the Oxford Theology Faculty. I am
especially grateful to Kate Kirkpatrick,
Miranda Powell, and to Elizabeth Lock of
Lion Hudson, and to my wife, Clare.

Contents

Introduction 6

1 The Second Century 11
2 The Third Century 18
3 The Fourth Century 25
4 The Fifth Century 33
5 The Sixth Century 39
6 The Seventh Century 47
7 The Eighth Century 53
8 The Ninth Century 61
9 The Tenth Century 68
10 The Eleventh Century 74
11 The Twelfth Century 83
12 The Thirteenth Century 93

13 The Fourteenth Century 104
14 The Fifteenth Century 114
15 The Sixteenth Century 124
16 The Seventeenth Century 135
17 The Eighteenth Century 147
18 The Nineteenth Century 161
19 The Twentieth Century 178
20 Epilogue 194
    Suggested reading 195
    Glossary 196
    Index 199
    Acknowledgments 208

Introduction

Once upon a time in first-century Roman-occupied Palestine, an itinerant Jewish teacher began to attract attention for his surprising statements about God, his radical approach to religion and politics, and his healing care for the poor, lonely, and sick. His message offended the ruling authorities and he was executed. Shortly thereafter, his followers began to claim that their leader was not dead but had been raised to life. What is more, they began to make startling claims about the divine nature of this man whose influence continued to animate their growing communities. It began to dawn on these people that the man, Jesus, was not only God's "Messiah" or "Christ" – a saviour awaited by the Jews who was expected to bring God's kingdom on earth – he was also, in some mysterious way, God himself in human form.

Jesus Christ's main message was that the kingdom of God was not only near, it was *here*. His followers taught that, through Jesus, forgiveness of sin, reconciliation with God, and membership of this kingdom was open to all. Citizenship of this kingdom came with its own set of freedoms, rights, and responsibilities: a new spiritual reality that had practical, social consequences. It is belief in the God who became humankind and in the values of his kingdom that provides the twin drives for the new movement that came to be known as Christianity.

Christians have not always been true to their founder, and the societies they produce have not always expressed the best of their values. Yet time and again Christianity has inspired heroic men and women to work against their own best interests and against the common sense of their culture in the service of others. Christendom's kings have started wars and its merchants have traded in exploitation while its peacemakers have brought down tyrannies and its scientists have cured diseases. Acts of deepest folly can be found alongside work of the highest wisdom: the same century that saw the first crusades also saw the creation of the first universities and hospitals in the modern tradition. Christendom's thinkers provided the foundation for the philosophical ideas that continue to shape modern life. Its artists, writers, and musicians created many of the world's cultural treasures. From the start, the various communities of Christ have displayed a vibrancy, originality, stubbornness, flexibility, ferocity, and gentleness unparalleled in history.

In telling the story of Christianity, certain themes can be traced throughout the centuries. One recurring motif is that of martyrdom. Christianity began with a crucifixion, and persecution of Christ's followers remains a constant reality worldwide. Indeed, more people have been killed for their Christian faith in the modern

Throughout the text, boxes like this one invite you to take a closer look at some of the notable people, places or events in Christian history. Words in **bold** are further explained in the glossary at the end of the book.

Opposite: Mosaic of Christ as Lord of All, from Cefalu Cathedral, Sicily.

age than at any other time in history. The reality of martyrdom is closely related to another common theme: that of the ambiguous relationship between Christians and their nations. From Constantine to Charlemagne, Kublai Khan to King Henry VIII, from Russian tsars to US presidents, the story of Christendom is, in many ways, the story of the state seeking to control, manage, or harness the power of Christianity. Another key theme is thus that of internal restoration. Whenever Christian institutions have become too much like the world around them, reform movements are never far away. Historically, it has often been Christians who prove to be the fiercest critics of Christendom.

Christianity is the most diffuse religion on earth. Its followers are widespread, its ideas profound, and its implications far-reaching. For this reason Christianity has provoked dissent as much as it has inspired emulation, and hence a history of Christianity is also a history of the modern world itself. The whole history of Christianity can never be told: the full story lies in the day-to-day lives of men and (mostly) women who lived the faith and transmitted it to others, keeping traditions and customs alive that would shape future generations. While not a total history, this book provides a guide through the whirlwind of extraordinary people, ideas, events of war, and pursuits of peace that have shaped the main contours of Christian thought and practice throughout the world.

The earliest Christians

Almost all of the information that we have about the earliest Christians comes from their documents and letters collected together as the New Testament. Thus the historical study of the first church is necessarily a matter for biblical scholars. The subject has attracted much attention and debate over the years, especially in the area of dating the Gospels. Most scholars propose dates ranging from before c. AD 70 to the late 90s.

c.40–44

"Christians" (meaning "Christ's ones") is first used in Antioch, probably as a pejorative term.
Christianity develops as a contentious movement within Judaism. Stephen becomes the first Christian martyr.
The apostle Peter is imprisoned and questioned by the Judean king, Herod Agrippa.
Peter is possibly in Rome.
After his conversion experience, Saul of Tarsus adopts the name Paul and ceases persecuting Christians.

c.58

Paul writes his epistle to the Romans to a church already well established in Rome.

c.59–61

Paul is in Rome.

c.30

Crucifixion of Jesus, called by his Jewish disciples the *Christ* (meaning "Messiah" or "anointed one") takes place. Shortly thereafter the disciples begin to claim publicly that Jesus has risen to life, and that this resurrection is a sign of the present reality and future hope of the kingdom of God. Their message is met with resistance in Jerusalem but also attracts many followers to the way of Christ.

The Crucifixion, from predella, Altarpiece of San Martino.

c.47–57

The apostle Paul is active in Arabia, Tarsus, Cyprus, central Asia Minor, Macedonia, Corinth, Ephesus, and elsewhere preaching primarily to non-Jewish people (Gentiles). Jerusalem and Antioch are major bases for the movement. The word *ekklesia* ("church", meaning an assembly of political or religious significance) is in common usage.

Paul Preaching at Athens, from the Sistine Chapel.

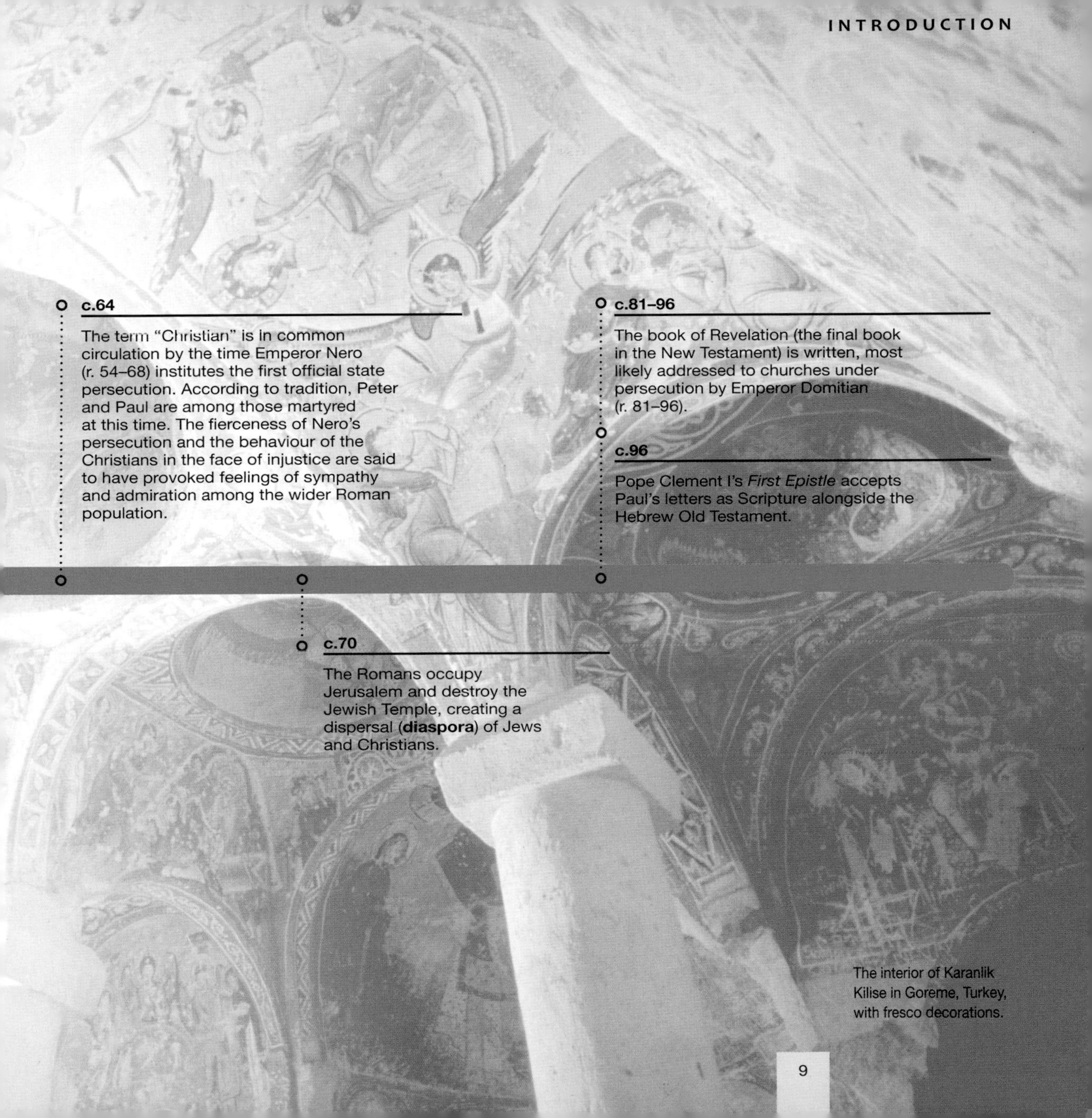

c.64

The term "Christian" is in common circulation by the time Emperor Nero (r. 54–68) institutes the first official state persecution. According to tradition, Peter and Paul are among those martyred at this time. The fierceness of Nero's persecution and the behaviour of the Christians in the face of injustice are said to have provoked feelings of sympathy and admiration among the wider Roman population.

c.81–96

The book of Revelation (the final book in the New Testament) is written, most likely addressed to churches under persecution by Emperor Domitian (r. 81–96).

c.96

Pope Clement I's *First Epistle* accepts Paul's letters as Scripture alongside the Hebrew Old Testament.

c.70

The Romans occupy Jerusalem and destroy the Jewish Temple, creating a dispersal (**diaspora**) of Jews and Christians.

The interior of Karanlik Kilise in Goreme, Turkey, with fresco decorations.

In order to escape persecution, the early Christians often worshipped in rooms and tunnels carved from the underground, much like these catacombs at Kom al-Shuqafa, Alexandria.

The Second Century

As the first generations of Christians passed away, the followers of Christ in the second century found themselves having to deal with the issue of legitimate authority. Who best preserved the message of Jesus and his apostles? Some groups radically diverged from the original teaching, spreading ideas that continue to affect Christianity to the present day. Others explored the depths of Christian thought, finding ways to communicate the new theology to a largely hostile world. Indeed, persecution and martyrdom form the backdrop to Christianity's development throughout this era.

Bust of Emperor Trajan.

Obstinate atheists

By 100 Trajan (r. 98–117) had been Roman emperor for two years. In 111 he received the first of a series of letters from Pliny the Younger (c.62 – c.115), the governor of Bithynia (in modern Turkey). Pliny was concerned about a new, "obstinate", religious group active in his region. These people refused to incorporate local gods into their worship, he said, and they did not partake in the cult of the emperor. Although they were good citizens in other respects, this refusal to treat the emperor as a god was worrying. Since they did not worship any of the publicly available deities, these Christians were deemed to be atheists. And atheists are an unstable, subversive element in any society that requires displays of civic religion for its smooth running. Trajan counselled that care should be taken over prosecution and that anonymous accusations of Christianity should not be accepted; however, he advised Pliny not to tolerate this obstinate religion.

The Way

For this subversive sect was growing. By the opening of the century, of the known world's estimated population of 60 million, approximately 7,500 belonged to "the Way" of Christ. Their communities were dotted throughout the Roman empire and beyond. By 115 there were reports that Christianity had reached Edessa, outside the empire's eastern border. The Christians met regularly in the houses of richer church members – textile merchants, Roman soldiers, and other professionals. Organized under a network of deacons and bishops, they communicated with each other through travelling preachers and a robust exchange of letters, written instructions, and histories about their Jewish founder, Jesus Christ. Yet despite all this it was clear that not everyone agreed on what it meant to be "Christian".

Legitimate authority

One of the most prominent church leaders of the time was Pope Clement I (r. 88–97). Clement was the third man to hold the office of **bishop** of Rome after the apostle Peter, and his writings offer a window into the issues faced by the Christian church of his day. His *First Epistle to the Corinthians* (written c.96) addresses fierce intra-church factionalism, demanding the reinstatement of **presbyters** who had been deposed and calling for a return to obedience to legitimate church authorities.

Legitimate authority was a key issue for the early church. For Ignatius, bishop of Antioch (c.50 – c.107), unity under the care of proper authority was essential. It is probably from Ignatius that we first have the idea of a **Catholic** ("universal") church. Ignatius insisted that without the presence of a bishop, both marriage and the **eucharist** were invalid. These practices were important because, for Ignatius, *bodies* were important. Marriage affirms sex and birth, families, and hospitality. The eucharist is a celebration of the life of Christ which was both divine and human. With his affirmation of the physical and material, Ignatius shared with other church leaders a concern to counter the most potent of the contemporary rival claims to Christian authority and authenticity: **Gnosticism.**

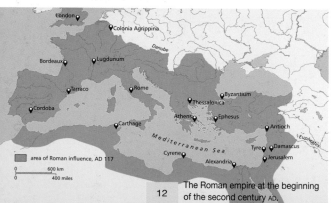

Clement I, one of the first popes of Rome after the apostle Peter.

area of Roman influence, AD 117

0 600 km
0 400 miles

London
Colonia Agrippina
Danube
Bordeaux
Lugdunum
Tarraco
Rome
Byzantium
Cordoba
Thessalonica
Carthage
Athens
Ephesus
Mediterranean Sea
Antioch
Euphrates
Tyre
Damascus
Cyrene
Jerusalem
Alexandria

The Roman empire at the beginning of the second century AD.

Gnosticism

Flourishing in Alexandria and Egypt since the first decades of the second century, Gnostic groups claimed to have secret knowledge (or *gnosis*) handed down from the apostles, beyond what was freely available in the Gospels and epistles. They also made a distinction between the material and the spiritual worlds. Gnosticism demonizes matter, claiming that the world was created by an evil god (the *Demiurge*) and that the (secret) message of Christ is the only way to escape from it into the pure, spiritual realm. There are many bewildering variations within Gnosticism, but all tend to share two main features. The first is that, because the Jews worship a Creator God, Gnostics seek to purge all Jewish influence from their own thought. The other main feature is that Gnostics are unwilling and unable to affirm the bodily **incarnation** of Jesus Christ. They argue instead for **docetism**: the view that Jesus only appeared to be human.

Marcion (c.85 – c.160)

The Gnostic Marcion of Sinope was declared a heretic and **excommunicated** from the church in Rome in 144. Marcion denied that Christ was born of a woman or that his body was material. He rejected the Hebrew Scriptures as irrelevant to the new revelation of Christ, and he dismissed the original apostles as being too Jewish to understand Jesus correctly. The debate with Marcion catalysed Christian thinking about the relationship between the Old and New Testaments, and paved the way for the eventual formation of the biblical canon.

The Shepherd of Hermas

Hermas was a freed slave who later became a rich merchant before losing his fortune. It is possible that he was a contemporary of Clement; however, some scholars date his work between 140 and 155. In any case, *The Shepherd* combines mystical visions with practical teaching, emphasizing that even sins committed after **baptism** can be forgiven. The work was so popular and so influential that churches in the East considered it as part of Scripture in the second and third centuries.

The Temple of Esna, a second-century shrine located on the banks of the Nile in Egypt.

Apologetics

The claims of Christianity were a challenge to Greek and Roman philosophy. Aristides of Athens (died c.140) is thought to have written the first Christian *Apology*, reportedly presented to Emperor Hadrian (r. 117–38) in 125. Aristides helped to set the pattern for much Christian apologetics by attempting to prove the existence of God. He also addressed the limits of other world-views, demonstrating how Christianity meets moral and intellectual demands that other systems do not address.

Opposite: The remains of the Arch of Marcus Aurelius, Tripoli, Libya, dating from AD 163.

Below: Justin Martyr taught the connection between philosophy and theology. He was killed for his faith.

Justin Martyr

Another early apologist, Justin (c.100 – c.165), was the first writer systematically to combine the claims of faith and reason. Born into a pagan family, Justin converted to Christianity in 130, after which he embarked on a teaching career in Ephesus, later starting a school in Rome. His *First Apology*

(c.155) was written for the emperor Antoninus Pius (r. 138–61) and argues that Christianity is the most rational philosophy. His *Second Apology* addresses the Roman senate, again attempting to refute rationalist objections to Christian life and thought. Although his writings would later become foundational works of Christian literature, they were not immediately successful in convincing pagan Rome, and Justin was martyred by beheading some time around 165.

Martyrdom of Polycarp

Justin's fate at the hands of the state was not unusual. Ignatius was martyred in Rome in 107. By 124 official persecutions had increased under the emperor Hadrian, leading to the execution of Pope Telesphorus (r. 125–36). Also sometimes active in Rome, but known primarily as the bishop of Smyrna, was Polycarp (c.69 – c.156). A leading member of the second-century church, Polycarp was said to have been appointed bishop by the original apostles, and his *Epistle to the Philippians* (c.116) provides insight into early Christian use of apostolic literature. But *Martyrdom of Polycarp*, a book recounting Polycarp's trial, and death by burning and stabbing, perhaps had a more lasting influence on the Christianity of the second and third centuries.

The cult of martyrs

The story of Polycarp's last days became the standard for other martyr accounts, known as *Acta*. These emphasized both the painful details of the martyr's execution and the holy, Christ-like way in which the martyr went to his or her death. The common practice of venerating martyrs' bones began with Polycarp, too, when his preserved remains formed the focus of an annual event celebrating the anniversary of his martyrdom. This was the beginning of the "cult of martyrs", in which some Christians enthusiastically embraced persecution and many more revered the martyrs as attaining heights of spiritual perfection.

Stoic persecution

After Polycarp's death a campaign of intense persecution of Christians took place under Emperor Marcus Aurelius (r. 161–80). Many Christians had hoped that Aurelius, a Stoic philosopher, would give their religion a fair hearing, and apologists such as Justin addressed books to him. Yet Aurelius remained convinced that Christianity was an internal threat to Roman society. Rome at this time was troubled by wars, invasion by the Parthians (163–66), repeated attacks from northern Germanic tribes (166–80), a plague (166–67), and revolts in Syria and Egypt (175). In these times of unrest, superstitious populations were keen to find someone to blame, and often it was the "atheistic" Christians who drew their anger. Aurelius allowed his regional rulers to step up their attacks on local Christian groups.

Martyrs of Lyons

One such attack happened in Lyons in 177 when the governor executed all Christians who did not recant. The purge resulted in the capture and public execution of some forty-eight people, including the ninety-year-old bishop Pothinus (c.87–177), who was starved and then stoned to death.

Blandina

A slave girl, Blandina was one of the martyrs of Lyons in 177. Although frail and weak after a period of starvation, she is said to have endured tortures that left even her tormentors tired and in need of rest. When she was tied to a pole as bait for wild animals, Blandina's fellow Christians took heart, seeing in her "him who was crucified for them". Finally, Blandina was scourged, burnt, and thrown bound into a ring where she was trampled to death by a bull. Her story is recounted in *The Letter of the Churches of Vienne and Lyons*, collected by Eusebius of Caesarea (c.260–341).

The first Catholic

The church was in disarray until the election of Irenaeus (c.130 – c.200) as the new bishop of Lyons in 178. Irenaeus is widely considered to be the first great Catholic writer and pastor. He mediated disputes between the Eastern and Western churches and developed strong ties with Gaelic-speaking barbarian tribes. His rule of apostolic origin asserted that it was bishops, and not scholars or preachers, who had primary authority in the church, because their office had been inherited from the original disciples. He upheld the Old Testament as Scripture, defended the four Gospels as a canon, and developed a list of the writings that would eventually become accepted as the New Testament. Irenaeus is primarily known for his battle with Gnosticism, and his most important work is called *Against Heresies* (c.185).

Right: Tertullian, the premier North African theologian, is considered to be the father of Latin Christianity.

Marcia (died 193)

Christians fared slightly better under Emperor Commodus (r. 180–92) than they did under his father. This is due in large part to the influence of Commodus's concubine Marcia. She sought to assist Christians and used her position at court to bring them favour. In one instance, Marcia ensured the release of some Christians sentenced to penal slavery in Sardinia, including Callistus, a future **pope** (r. 217–22).

Carthage

Persecution was widespread, and not confined to the Western reaches of the Roman empire. One of the earliest African Christian documents is the Acts of the Scillitan martyrs. Five women and seven men were executed at Scillium, near Carthage, in 180 on charges related to the accusation that as Christians they owed allegiance to a Lord who was higher than emperors or kings. Accounts suggest that the martyrs enjoyed popular local support: North Africa was a major centre of Christianity. Christians in Carthage were not allowed to own land in the city, but they had established a graveyard outside the boundaries, and the Carthaginian church was prominent in Christian life and thought. The African Church Father Tertullian (c.160 – c.225) grew up in Carthage, and joined the church there after his conversion from paganism. Writing in Latin, rather than the traditional Greek, Tertullian was a master of communication aimed at sophisticated Roman audiences.

Church Fathers

Tertullian's *Apology* (c.197) marks the high point of second-century writing, and is considered to be the source of the Latin Christian literary tradition. Cyprian (see chapter 2) called Tertullian his "master", as did Augustine (see chapter 3): together these three North Africans are considered to be the fathers of the Western churches.

Alexandria

In the Egyptian metropolis of Alexandria, Christianity seems to have emerged out of the strong Jewish community, perhaps at the instigation of Mark the evangelist. Alexandria was known as a centre of religious ferment, and many cults jostled for attention. Much of Alexandrian Christian culture was strongly influenced

Opposite: Patio of a Roman villa, Odeon Quarter, Carthage, Tunisia.

by Gnosticism and it is probable that the Gnostic texts *Epistle of Barnabas*, *The Gospel of the Egyptians*, and *The Gospel to the Hebrews* all emerged from there. Orthodox Christianity also had a presence, represented most strongly by Clement of Alexandria (c.150 – c.215).

The first theologian

Said to have come originally from Athens, Clement became head of the catechetical school in the city in 190. The school taught Christianity as the true philosophy to advanced scholars, but also trained new converts (catechumens) in preparation for full acceptance into the church. A flavour of their education can be seen from the trilogy of texts produced by Clement during his time as head of the school. *The Exhortation to the Greeks*, *The Instructor*, and *The Miscellanies* engage with pagan Greek philosophy on the one hand and Gnostic Christian thought on the other. The books are not concerned simply with theory and often stress the moral discipline and duties that follow from Christian claims. For this reason Clement is sometimes regarded as the first self-conscious theologian and ethicist.

Clement was forced to flee his school, and many other Christians from Alexandria and Carthage also fled, because of a rash of local discrimination campaigns that flourished under the new, African-born emperor, Septimius Severus (r. 193–211), during a period of persecution that began at the close of the century in 199.

Easter

The early church was faced with a problem. Should Easter be celebrated according to the time of Passover in the lunar Jewish calendar, or is the solar, Gentile, "Julian" calendar more appropriate (see chapter 15, **Calendars**)? The older traditions of Asia Minor celebrated the Christian **paschal** according to the Jewish date for Passover (called *Quartodeciman* because it fell on the fourteenth day after the spring full moon). The Gentile Roman Christians preferred to celebrate Easter on the Sunday following the spring equinox. This conflict mattered because it touched on the centrality of the resurrection of Jesus for Christian belief. Furthermore, as well as representing the division that had existed between Jewish and Gentile Christians since the earliest days of Christianity (see, for example, Galatians 2:1–21), the conflict highlighted the emerging differences between East and West. Sensing a challenge to Roman authority, the African pope Victor I (r. 189–98) excommunicated the Quartodecimans, a move opposed by Irenaeus of Lyons. The search for a uniform method for establishing the calendar date of Easter was picked up again at the First Council of Nicea in 325, but even today the date of Easter varies between Eastern and Western traditions.

The Third Century

Persecutions continued throughout the third century, leading to the creation of both martyrs and apostates. Problems of order and authority were heightened by the rise of major heretical movements that would shape Christian thought for centuries to come. Despite these troubles, the third century saw the activity of some of the most prominent Church Fathers, and Christianity expanded further into the deserts and cities of the Roman empire and beyond.

Authority of martyrs

As part of a campaign to consolidate power throughout his empire, Emperor Septimius Severus banned conversion to Judaism or Christianity. Caught up in the wave of new persecutions in 203 was a group of catechumens in Carthage. *The Passion of Perpetua and Felicitas* describes the martyrdom of two women in this group, the nobly born Perpetua and the slave-girl Felicitas. The document is important because it provides first-hand accounts of prison life, and also offers an insight into the lives of Christian women in the third century – who, like Perpetua, often assumed leadership roles within house-church communities.

The *Passion* also sheds light on internal church conflicts of the day. Questions of official authority, as well as debate over

Above: Perpetua, noblewoman, church leader, and Christian martyr. Mosaic from Archiepiscopal Cathedral, Ravenna, c. 500.

the role that the new martyrs were having in shaping Christian belief, are evident from the text – in one scene a vision of the martyred Perpetua is depicted as resolving a dispute between a presbyter and his bishop. The unknown editor was a Montanist, and the book argues that, through martyrs such as these, the work of the Holy Spirit was continuing in ways as significant as those recounted in the Scriptures.

Montanism

Founded by Montanus c.170, the prophetic movement that took his name flourished in the early third century. Montanists were famous for their strict asceticism and their claim that they received direct revelations from God. Women held prominent leadership positions, the most famous being the prophets Maximilla and Priscilla. The Montanists do not seem to have been doctrinal heretics, but they clashed with Catholic Christianity over the Montanist belief that spiritual ecstasy overrode the prophet's rational mind. Tertullian became a Montanist in 208.

Far left and right: The Arch of Septimius Severus stands at the entrance of the Roman citadel of Leptis Magna in modern-day Libya. Severus was born here in 146.

Early church order

Different groups of Christians varied as to how much authority they accorded to martyrs, women, and wandering prophets, not to mention deacons, presbyters, and bishops. An example of early attempts to preserve church order and structure comes by way of the Greek theologian Hippolytus (died c.236) and his *Apostolic Tradition* (c.220). Despite facing a large number of converts, Hippolytus opposed relaxing the penitential system by which new catechumens were only allowed to participate in Communion after a rigorous programme of teaching, confession, and discipline. The *Tradition* also reveals the strict hierarchy between **ordinands** and other ministers, and it details the standard rites of baptism and of the eucharist, and other liturgical practices prevalent in the third-century Roman church.

Manichaeism

This was probably the most persistent of the heretical Gnostic movements. There is evidence of Manichaeism in China in the tenth century, as well as continued influence into the medieval and modern eras. The teaching of Mani of Persia (c.216–76) centred on belief in a primal conflict between Light and Darkness. Satan is supposed to have trapped particles of light within each human body, and it was the purpose of religion to release the pure spirit from its corrupt matter. Jesus, Buddha, the prophets, and Mani were all helpers in this task.

Origen, teacher and theologian, was the most prolific author in antiquity.

Origen

It was in this context of both speculative thought and rigid structures within the church that Origen (c.185 – c.251) lived and worked. His father, an Egyptian Christian named Leonidas, was executed under the persecutions of Septimius Severus in 201, and Origen was set to die alongside him until saved by his mother. Following his old teacher Clement, Origen served as head of the catechetical school in Alexandria for twenty-eight years. A Greek Church Father, he was perhaps the most prolific writer of antiquity, with some scholars attributing to him between 800 and 2,000 works. These include the first works of serious biblical textual commentary such as the *Hexapla* (c.230), a parallel translation of the Old Testament written in six languages. Another essential work is *On First Principles*, one of the first systematic theologies in Christian history.

The Decian persecution

Origen died in 251, after suffering imprisonment and torture as one of the final victims of the persecution of Decius. When Emperor Decius came to power in 249 he had intentionally adopted the name "Trajan Decius" in emulation of his predecessor's success at defending pagan Rome against the "atheists". The Decian campaign was the first empire-wide persecution, and the bloodiest yet for Christians. When Decius was struck down in battle in 251, many Christians took this as a judgment from God and rejoiced. The persecution campaign may have been short, but the consequences were far-reaching, for while the Decian persecution had produced many martyrs, it had created many more apostates.

Lapsed Christians

After the period of intense persecution, by 251 the seat of the bishop of Rome had been vacant for fourteen months. Cornelius was elected pope and he served for two years before his death in 253. Cornelius was faced with the problem of what to do with all the members of his flock who had given in to persecution. For one thing, it was unclear what counted as a lapse. Did giving over Christian Scriptures and letters to the authorities count as **apostasy**? What about those who publicly renounced Christ but privately continued to worship? Were people who fled persecution just as culpable as those who recanted their faith under pain of torture? Faced with such difficulties, Cornelius adopted a lenient position toward apostates, welcoming them back into the church.

The Basilica of Sacre Coeur built in the nineteenth century, Montmartre, Paris. It marks the place of the martyrdom of Denys (Dionysius), the first bishop of Paris, who was executed here c.250.

Martyrdom of St Denys, patron saint of France. Denys is seen receiving his last Holy Communion on the left, and on the right, is being decapitated.

Novatian

Cornelius was opposed by the presbyter and theologian Novatian (c.200–58), who took a much more rigorous stance. Novatian did not allow any concessions to be made to lapsed Christians. Eventually consecrated bishop as a direct rival to Cornelius, Novatian established a separate church for those who refused to allow apostates back into the fold. He himself was martyred in 258 following the renewed campaign of Emperor Valerian.

Novatianists

The schismatic movement founded by Novatian continued well into the fifth century. Rigorous in their denunciation of Christians who compromised their faith, the group was doctrinally orthodox, although they remained excommunicated from the Roman church.

Cyprian

The effects of apostasy were also being felt in North Africa. Cyprian (c.200–58) had been a pagan philosopher before converting to Christianity c.246 and becoming bishop of Carthage two years later. He fled the Decian persecutions in 249 and only returned to his post after Decius's death in 251; a move that was viewed with suspicion by his opponents, many of whom had stayed to face persecution.

The problem of rebaptism

Cyprian was opposed to the lenient treatment of the lapsed or those who had purchased their way out of persecution, but he did allow for them to return to the church after a period of penance. The excommunication of the Novatianists had given rise to another, related problem. Were baptisms conducted by schismatics valid? Cyprian thought not, and in 255 demanded that anyone baptized by a schismatic or heretic be rebaptized in order to enjoy full communion with the true church. This drew criticism from Stephen I (died 257), who had been made pope in 254. Stephen held that as the **sacraments** drew their validity from God, their worth was not dependent on the standing of the priest who administered them. A series of significant letters between the two bishops followed, but the debate was cut short when Stephen died; Cyprian was martyred during Valerian's persecutions a year later.

The first toleration

Emperor of Rome from 253 to 260, Valerian ruled over an empire stricken by civil war and threatened by Persia in the east and barbarian tribes in the north. To placate the Roman gods, Valerian issued edicts in 257 and 258 outlawing and condemning Christian clergy, purging Christians from the upper classes of society and banning Christian assemblies.

To help manage his unwieldy empire, Valerian set up his son Gallienus as his co-emperor, charging him with responsibility for the West. When Valerian was captured by Persian forces in 260, Gallienus (died 268) assumed control of the entire empire. That same year he reversed his father's policy of persecution and issued the first Edict of Toleration of Christianity. The edict restored bishops to their churches, allowed burial in Christian cemeteries, and halted the practice of forcing Christians publicly to worship Roman civic deities. Christians interpreted Valerian's defeat and the actions of Gallienus as God protecting his followers. Although toleration was a welcome relief, Gallienus's edict was not due to conversion on his part. Instead, it was a pragmatic decision to reverse his father's disastrous empire-wide policy; local persecutions continued to occur.

West and East

Valerian's innovation of dividing the Roman empire into Western and Eastern jurisdictions set a precedent that would have lasting consequences for the history of Christianity, with the eventual establishment of the Church of Rome in the West and the Church of Constantinople in the East.

Plague in Carthage

In 252, a severe plague struck the city. The outbreak provoked widespread anti-Christian feeling, prompting church leaders to argue publicly that Christianity does not cause natural catastrophes. At the same time, Cyprian wrote a series of pastoral letters exhorting his fellow Christians to continue to help the dying and provide relief for those affected by the epidemic.

strong Christian community, 3rd century

town with Christian congregations

border of Roman empire, 3rd century

0   600 km

0   400 miles

Map of the church in the third-century Roman empire.

Desert hermits

Sometime around 269 in Egypt, a wealthy Coptic man gave away all his possessions and withdrew to live in the desert. The long-lived Anthony (c.251–356) was not the first hermit to pursue a life of religious solitude, but he was one of the first to do so as a Christian. A major figure in early Egyptian monasticism, Anthony wrote little and spoke only Coptic. Nevertheless, his simple life and reputed wisdom attracted many followers. In 285 Anthony withdrew even further from society, but was found again by others who wished to live as hermits. These **coenobite** communities flourished in the deserts of Egypt and Syria, establishing the monastic way of life within Christianity and helping to lay the foundations for the distinctive Coptic Church of the fourth and fifth centuries.

The Coptic Church would come to date its foundation to 284, the year that the emperor Diocletian came to power. In 303 Diocletian would unleash the Great Persecution, the most organized and extensive campaign against Christians yet seen in the Roman empire.

Dionysius (260–68)

Dionysius became pope in Rome in 260. One of the most important popes of this era, Dionysius helped to restore church order after the ravages of Valerian's persecution. His letters reveal a pastoral concern for the bishops under his care.

Synaxarium

This is a list of saints and their dates of death used by the Oriental Orthodox churches. The large number of martyrs commemorated in such books attests to the severity of Diocletian's persecution of the Coptic Church, a time known as the *Era of Martyrs*.

The desert hermits lived in structures similar to these rooms cut from the rock cliffs in Bilad el-Rum, Siwah Oasis, Egypt.

The Fourth Century

After the first century, the fourth is arguably the most influential period in the history of Christianity. It was then that Christianity became the official religion of the Roman empire; the foundational creeds were formulated; the biblical canon was finalized; major monastic movements were established; and the main traditions of the Christian church were shaped. The Four Doctors of the Church – Gregory the Great, Ambrose, Augustine, and Jerome – were also active at this time.

The Era of Martyrs

Valerius Diocletianus was emperor of Rome from 284 to 305. The time of Christian trial under his reign is known by Western churches as the Great Persecution, and by the Eastern tradition as the Era of Martyrs. In 303 and 304 Emperor Diocletian ordered that all churches should be torn down, Bibles burned, and clergy tortured. Diocletian abdicated in 305 but the persecutions continued until 312.

Alban

The first known British martyr, Alban, is traditionally thought to have died c.304 during the Great Persecution. Alban was a pagan who converted to Christianity when he offered shelter to a missionary and volunteered to die in the priest's place.

Emperor Diocletian is depicted along with three other rulers: Maximian, Galerius, and Constantius. A Roman Syrian work of the fourth century, the statue now adorns the Basilica of St Marco in Venice.

Catherine of Alexandria, by Carlo Crivelli (1435/40–95).

Catherine of Alexandria (c.285 – c.305)

According to tradition, Catherine was a scholar and virgin martyred in Alexandria c.305. Celebrated in the East and West, Catherine was a popular object of devotion in the Middle Ages. Her symbol is a spiked wheel: the instrument of torture upon which she was killed.

The Donatist movement

In 311 Caecilian (died c.345) was made bishop of Carthage. The Great Persecution had hit North Africa hard, with many Christians exiled or killed, and many more, known as *traditores*, forced to hand over their writings and holy texts to be burned by the authorities.

One such *traditor* had consecrated Caecilian. As a result, the rigorist church party claimed that Caecilian's position was invalid. Eventually, a bishop named Donatus Magnus (died 355) was consecrated as his rival, lending the schismatic group its name.

The debate was not a new one for Christianity. What makes the Donatist controversy singular is that it was the first to attract intervention from the new emperor.

Emperor Constantine

The son of Constantius Chlorus and Helena, Constantine (r. 306–37) was proclaimed emperor during a campaign in York in 306. However, it was not until 312 and the battle of Milvian Bridge that Constantine was able to secure the throne along with his co-emperor Licinius (r.308–24).

Before entering the fray, Constantine is reputed to have had a vision of the cross of Christ leading his soldiers into battle, and he consequently adopted the *labarum* as his military standard. Constantine's victory

Background: *Fireworks*, with a Catherine wheel at the centre. Museo di Roma, Rome, Italy.

soon led to toleration of the church, which in turn would lead to the promotion of Christianity to become the dominant religion of Rome.

Labarum

Constantine's symbol was a Christian monogram incorporating the Greek letters X and P; the first two letters of the Greek for "Christ" (*ΧΡΙΣΤΟΣ*).

Ecclesiastical History

Bishop Eusebius of Caesarea (c.265 – c.339) completed the first major work of Christian history in 325. His *History* is invaluable, as it preserves documents and stories found nowhere else.

The Edict of Milan

In 313 Licinius and Constantine met at Milan and took a decision that has since come to be called the Edict of Milan. The policy gave legal standing to Christian churches, granting toleration to all religions in the empire and bringing an end to the Great Persecution.

Although toleration at this time did not officially grant Christianity favoured status, it is clear that Constantine took a great interest in the Christian religion. Constantine's strategy of political consolidation was mirrored in his approach to Christianity, and he sought to bind the church to the state.

Helena (c.255 – c.330)

The mother of the emperor Constantine, Helena held a prominent position of authority in the Roman empire. She was a passionate supporter of Christianity and led a significant excursion to the Holy Land in 326 where she founded major churches on the Mount of Olives and in Bethlehem. Helena is also known for collecting relics and is fabled to have acquired pieces of the cross.

Emperor Constantine is depicted alongside his celebrated mother Helena. Sixteenth-century fresco, Moldovita Monastery, Romania.

Constantinian building projects

313

Construction begins on the Church of St John Lateran in Rome. Built on imperial property, it signalled Constantine's attitude toward Christianity.

320

Construction begins on the first Church of St Peter's, the largest basilica in Rome.

325

The Church of the Nativity is founded in Bethlehem.

326

Building begins on the Church of the Holy Sepulchre in Jerusalem. The building would have a significant influence on later church architecture.

328

Byzantium is given the new name Constantinople and made capital of the empire. A series of Christian public building-works ensue.

Council of Arles

Constantine's first opportunity to involve himself in church affairs came when the Donatists invited him to arbitrate in their dispute with Pope Miltiades (r. 311–14) in 313. The following year, in partnership with Pope Sylvester I (r. 314–35), the emperor summoned the Council of Arles to deal with the problem. In 316 Constantine found against the Donatists. A campaign of coercion against them lasted until 321 and thus, for the first time in history, the church and the state collaborated in the suppression of **heresy**.

Armenia

By 314 King Tiridates III (286–330) had been converted by Gregory the Illuminator (c.240 – c.328), making Armenia the first kingdom officially to adopt Christianity as its national religion. Gregory was an Armenian by birth who returned from exile in Caesarea to his native homeland as a missionary. After Tiridates' conversion, Gregory formed the Armenian church, instituting a system of religious hierarchy following the Greek model. Armenia would become the base for missions to the neighbouring kingdoms of Georgia and Albania.

Arianism – Christ is not God

The controversy over Donatism revolved around leaders who had fallen short of the Christian ideal and asked questions about the nature of the church. At the same time as this controversy was raging, a debate about the person of Christ and the nature of God was also in full swing. Significantly, the problem of Arianism would also attract Constantine's intervention.

An Alexandrian priest, Arius (c.250 – c.336) preached that Christ was not God, but (following John 1:3) was made by God to be the instrument through which the world was created. This teaching had consequences for the Christian doctrines of the **Trinity**, of creation, and of Jesus' role in redemption, and it was condemned by the church in 320. Nevertheless, Arius continued to attract followers, causing dissension within the Christian community.

Nicene Creed

In an effort to quell the unrest, in 325 Constantine called the Council of Nicea (modern-day Iznik in Turkey). Over 300 bishops were present (mostly from the East), and the council settled on a formulation of **orthodoxy**. This first Nicene Creed affirmed the bodily incarnation and stressed that the Son was "begotten, *not made*". On the advice of his bishops, Constantine also inserted the crucial term *homoousios* to describe the relation between the Son and the Father. A Greek technical phrase which means "of one substance", it marks a significant development in Christian thought.

Athanasius (c.296–373)

The most prominent champion of orthodoxy against Arianism, Athanasius became bishop of Alexandria in 328. Because of its strong affirmation of the incarnation and the Trinity, the fifth-century "Athanasian Creed" used by **Catholics** and some **Protestants** shares his name: "We worship one God in Trinity, and Trinity in unity; neither confounding the persons, nor dividing the substance."

Desert monks

While complex debates raged at the centre of Christendom, a life of Christian simplicity was flourishing at its edges.

There is evidence of early monasticism in Syria and the East. However, it was the *Life of St Anthony* (written by Athanasius c.357) that had the most effect on the Christian monastic movement. In Egypt and North Africa, coenobite desert communities included Cellia, Wâdi n' Natrûn and Scete (still a site of Coptic monasteries). It was in these three communities that the "sayings of the Desert Fathers" were preserved. One Desert Father, Pachomius (292–346), created the communal rule that would become the predominant pattern for most monastic movements. Another pre-eminent figure in Coptic Christianity was Shenoutte (334–450), a strict coenobite, council theologian, and author.

Eastern monks

Basil the Great was born in Pontus about 329 and died in Caesarea 379. He had lived for a time as a monk in Syria and Egypt, and was able to put what he learned there to use when he founded a new Greek monastic order. Written 358–64, Basil's monastic rule emphasized *koinobios* (living in community) over and against the solitary life of the **anchorite**. This form of community life rejected harsh asceticism in favour of a life of prayer, **liturgy**, charity, and useful labour. It became the template for subsequent Slavonic and Greek monastic orders, and Basil is considered a Doctor of the Church.

Western monks

The father of monasticism in Gaul (modern France), Martin of Tours (c.335 – c.400), founded its first monastery at Ligugé, near Poitiers, in 361. Martin wrote no rule, but his simple living attracted many people to the community. When Martin reluctantly became bishop of Tours in 372 the monastery relocated to Marmoutier.

Also significant was Jerome (c.342 – c.420). After training in the Antioch desert, Jerome

Left: A depiction of Arius. His heretical ideas prompted Constantine's intervention and led to the formulation of the Nicene Creed.

returned to his native Italy as a champion of monasticism. Women were especially attracted to his message of ascetic discipline, which offered an alternative way to live faithfully apart from the roles usually open to daughters, wives, and mothers. Around 386 Jerome settled at a monastery at Bethlehem, one of four institutions founded by the widow Paula (347–404) and her daughter Eustochium.

Gothic bishop

Bishop Ulfilas (c.311–83) travelled to evangelize the Teutonic tribes of northern Europe (see chapter 4, **Germanic peoples**) in 341. Many converted to Christianity under his influence, and Ulfilas translated the entire Bible into Gothic. But Ulfilas was a follower of Arius, and Arianism would remain a troublesome factor in Gothic relations with the Western empire until the Catholic conversion of Clovis, King of the Franks, in 496.

India

There is much legend but little written evidence of early Indian Christian activity. Traditionally the introduction of Christianity to India is attributed to the first-century missionary efforts of the apostle Thomas. The Persian *Chronicle of Seert* reports that Bishop David of Basra instituted a mission to India c.300. A Persian bishop "from India" attended the Council of Nicea in 325. Contested reports say that the merchant Thomas of Cana and Joseph, bishop of Edessa, travelled to Malabar in c.345 in aid of the native church there. Around this same time Emperor Constantius is reported to have sent a missionary named Theophilus. The early documentary evidence for Malabar Christians (also called Syrian or Saint Thomas Christians) suggests Nestorian influence from the sixth century.

The biblical canon

The Doctor of the Church Jerome is primarily known for his work as a biblical scholar. Jerome argued that the Christian Old Testament should follow the Hebrew **canon** and exclude the books of the **Apocrypha**.

The development of the Christian canon of Scriptures was a long-running process. By c.130 Christian communities had largely agreed on the core texts of the Hebrew Scriptures and by c.220 were treating the four Gospels and thirteen Pauline epistles as their New Testament, on a par with the Old. Yet this was not the end of the issue.

The first clear evidence of the complete New Testament canon, and indeed the earliest mention of the term "canonized" (*kanonizomena*), comes from Athanasius's list of the twenty-seven books of the New Testament in his *Easter* or *Festal Letter* of 367. Pope Damasus I (r. 366–83) instituted a council in c.382 which settled the complete list of Old and New Testament books known in the present age. Damasus's secretary during this council was Jerome, and it was here that he was charged with revising the biblical texts, a task he began in 386. Over his lifetime Jerome would translate most of the Bible into Latin. These texts would eventually be collected as the "Vulgate Bible" and become the most widely read Bible in Western Christendom.

Augustine (354–430)

Aurelius Augustinus is considered to be the greatest of the Church Doctors and the most influential thinker in the history of Western Christianity. Born into a North African Christian family, Augustine lived a dissolute life until joining the Manichees (see chapter 2) in 373. The influence of his mother Monica (died 387) and the preaching of Bishop Ambrose of Milan (c.340–97) returned him to mainstream Christianity in 386. By popular acclaim Augustine was made bishop of Hippo (modern-day Annaba, in Algeria) in 395. Augustine was a prolific author, and his most famous works include the autobiographical *Confessions* (387), *The Trinity* (399–419) and *City of God* (412–26; see chapter 4).

Original sin

In response to the British monk Pelagius (active in Rome c.383–410) Augustine refined his conception of "**original sin**". Pelagianism preached the possibility of sinlessness and spiritual perfection. Against this Augustine developed the idea of inherited guilt, and taught that in order to obey God, man needs divine grace.

A Christian empire

Julian, a pagan, was emperor of Rome from 361 to 363. He attempted to restore the old temples and rituals, exiled Christian clergy and closed churches. But he was the last of the non-Christian Roman emperors.

Theodosius I (r. 379–95) was a staunch supporter of orthodox Christianity, which had until then been the privileged – but not established – religion of the Roman empire. In 380 Theodosius issued an edict that made Christianity the official religion and deviation from Nicea illegal. In 381 Theodosius called the First Council of Constantinople, which placed the bishop of Constantinople second in honour to the pope, outlawed Arian congregations, and confiscated property held by heretical groups. Many pagan temples were destroyed or forcibly converted into churches.

The Council of Nicea as depicted in this eighteenth-century icon from the Novgorod School.

Within not above

In 390, Theodosius killed over 7,000 citizens of Thessalonica in retribution for a seditious riot. An outraged Bishop Ambrose castigated the emperor for his harshness. Theodosius publicly acknowledged his guilt and submitted to **penance**. This marked the first time in history that an imperial power had bowed to the authority of the church, demonstrating the strength of Ambrose's famous maxim: "The emperor indeed is within the church, not above the church."

John Chrysostom (c.344–407)

A celebrated preacher, John's epithet *Chrysostom* means "golden-mouthed". John was made **patriarch** of Constantinople in 398 but his zeal for church reform soon led him to clash with the empress Eudoxia and clergymen loyal to her. At the **Synod** of Oak in 403 John was condemned on spurious charges and banished. But even in exile, John remained enormously popular with both the Eastern and Western churches.

Ambrose

One of the four Doctors of the Western church and originally from Gaul, Ambrose became bishop of Milan in 374. He wrote *On the Duties of the Clergy,* a compendium of ethical teaching for priests. Ambrose's emphasis on emulating the Virgin Mary makes him one of the earliest supporters of Marian devotion.

East and West

Theodosius was the last emperor to rule over a united empire. Upon his death in 395 one son, Arcadius (r. 395–408), became emperor of the East; the other son, Honorius (r. 395–423), took the West. The Roman world would never be united again, and the West would soon splinter further under barbarian pressure.

Map of Western Europe in the last days of Rome.

LYONS ■ MILAN ■
BORDEAUX ■ *Rhône* VISIGOTHS *Danube* ABASGIANS LAZICA IBERIA
SARAGOSSA ■ *Ebro* *Corsica* ROME ■ Black Sea ARMENIANS
Tagus TOLEDO ■ *Sardinia* NAPLES ■ THESSALONICA ■ CONSTANTINOPLE ■ NICAEA ■ CAESAREA ■
CORDOBA ■ *Balearic Islands* CARTHAGE ■ *Sicily* ATHENS ■ EPHESUS ■ EDESSA ■ NISIBIS ■ PERSIAN EMPIRE
SYRACUSE ■ Cyprus ANTIOCH ■ *Euphrates* CTESIPHON ■
Mediterranean Sea *Crete* DAMASCUS ■
B E R B E R S CYRENE ■ ALEXANDRIA ■ JERUSALEM ■
Nile A R A B S

Roman empire, 4th century
Slavs
Mongols
Persians
Arabs
Georgians
Teutons
→ Visigoth invasion route, 395–418

0 ___ 600 km
0 ___ 400 miles

The Fifth Century

The story of Christianity in the fifth century saw the beginning of the long-standing historical division between Constantinople and Rome. The theological differences between East and West were exacerbated by the differing political fortunes of both empires, as Rome fell to barbarian invaders and Constantinople enjoyed relative stability. In this era, investigation into the nature of the Trinity and the implications of the incarnation led to major statements of orthodox doctrine, the creation of influential heretical groups, and the start of significant church traditions that persist into the present age.

Eastern and Western churches

By 395 the Roman empire had been divided into East and West, with separate capital cities, ruling families and even languages. As the fifth century opened there was still nominal unity in the church; however, there was a marked drift between the Eastern and Western traditions.

The East, ruled from the city of Constantinople, enjoyed relative unity and stability. In the West the empire was soon to splinter into smaller fragments ruled by Germanic tribes from the north. Rome was growing increasingly untenable as a political capital, and c.404 the imperial residence was moved to Ravenna.

In the fifth century, the city of Constantinople rose to become the centre of Christianity and politics for much of the world.

Armenian literature

Around 400 the monk Mesrob Mashtots (or Maštoc, c.361–440) invented the Armenian alphabet. He continued the mission work of Gregory the Illuminator. Translations of liturgical books, theological texts, and the full Bible soon followed, as well as original works.

The falling fortunes of Rome

Right: Attila, king of the Huns, threatened to overrun the Eastern empire.

Below: Alaric I, king of the Visigoths, was the first Teutonic ruler to successfully invade Rome.

The pope was now the most significant official left in the city and the importance of the church grew. The centrality of Christian Rome was assured under the leadership of popes such as Innocent I (r. 401–17), Celestine I (r. 422–32), and especially Leo the Great (r. 440–61), who was granted authority over the entire Western church by Emperor Valentinian III (r. 425–55).

At the opening of the fifth century, hordes led by the Visigoth King Alaric I (r. 395–410) were ravaging Greece and the Balkans. Alaric first advanced on Italy in 401. In 410 he sacked Rome and occupied it for three days. The event shocked pagans and Christians alike, leading to much blame and recrimination on all sides. While Rome continued to be a centre for Christianity, its economic and political status fell further when it was sacked again by Vandals (see chapter 4, **Germanic peoples**) in 455.

The rise of Constantinople

Apart from continuing small-scale warfare with the Zoroastrian Persian empire, the Eastern empire was comparatively stable. Constantinople was flourishing and the imperial government remained strong. Although also harried by Germanic attacks, Constantinople fared better than Rome, and Emperor Theodosius II (r. 408–50) was able to appease Attila's Hunnic invaders with payments of gold.

The most important patriarch at this time was Cyril, patriarch of Alexandria (c.376–444), who was elected in 412. Cyril had a reputation for precise reasoning and an uncompromising style, and he presided over a number of controversies and key events in the development of Christianity.

Invention of the secular

Prompted by Alaric's occupation of Rome, Augustine wrote *City of God* in defence of Christianity against paganism on the one hand, and against Christian triumphalism on the other. *City of God* argues that the success of the "heavenly city" – the followers of Christ – is independent of the fortunes of the "earthly city". This magisterial work encompasses history, politics, ethics, theology, and the philosophy of space and time. It is often considered to be second only to the Bible in its influence on the development of Christian civilization. Its notion that all human institutions (including the church) occupy the "secular" sphere, and that only God can determine membership of the "sacred", has been as influential as it has been misunderstood in the history of church and state relations.

Mary, bearer of God

From the Greek *theos* (God) and *tikto* (to bear), the term *Theotokos* was a popular term for the Virgin Mary, mother of Jesus and "God-bearer".

A favoured formulation of the Alexandrian school from Origen onwards, the term was important for preserving the **Christology** that emphasized the eternal and divine nature of the "Word become flesh". Cyril of Alexandria was an enthusiastic champion of the term, and *Theotokos* was a central feature of popular Alexandrian piety.

Mary, bearer of man

Nestorius (c.381 – c.451) was made patriarch of Constantinople in 428. As a monk in Antioch, Nestorius had gained a reputation for his vehement style, and shortly after his consecration he caused offence when he preached against the title *Theotokos*. Instead of "God-bearer", Nestorius recommended that Mary be referred to as *Anthropotokos* (man-bearer) or, better, *Christotokos* (Christ-bearer). The resulting major controversy had consequences that endure in the present age.

Nestorius came from the Antiochene school of theology, which was at odds with the Alexandrian tradition. Antioch Christology stressed the humanity of Jesus, and emphasized that Christ's life involved growth, temptation, suffering, and love. These things were seen to be impossible in the context of an Alexandrian Christology which (in its extreme form) supposedly overemphasized the divine nature of Jesus Christ at the expense of the human.

Council of Ephesus

The ensuing controversy was thus as much about ecclesiastical politics as it was about doctrine. When Cyril of Alexandria defended *Theotokos* in his paschal letter of 429 he was also defending the Alexandrian church against infringement from Antioch. Cyril gained the support of Pope Celestine I in Rome in 430, and in 431 the emperor Theodosius II convened the Council of Ephesus to settle the matter.

Cyril opened the council before the Syrian bishops or representatives from Rome had arrived. The council quickly found against Nestorian theology, and Nestorius was excommunicated (he died in exile). The result was a **schism** between Cyril's party (mainly Alexandria and Rome) and the Syrian and Mesopotamian churches. Eventually an agreement between Cyril and John of Antioch (leader of the Syrian churches 429–41) was reached in 433, but the Nestorian rift was widening.

Cyril of Alexandria was one of the most important patriarchs of the early church. Among other doctrines, he promoted the idea that Mary, as mother of Jesus, was the *Theotokos* or "Bearer of God".

Nestorianism

The Nestorian church gradually formed from the Eastern bishops who refused to accept the Council of Ephesus and the compromise of 433. Its patriarchal centre was in Persia, at Seleucia-Ctesiphon (in modern Iraq), with significant schools of Nestorian theology in Edessa and Nisibis (in modern Turkey). In the following centuries the Nestorians would be an active missionary church, with a significant presence in India, China, and Arabia. During Muslim rule, the patriarchal **see** relocated to Baghdad. The Nestorian church was nearly destroyed under Mongol rule in the fourteenth century, but remnant groups survive today.

Above: Courtyard of a Roman house on Mount Coressos, Ephesus, Turkey.

Top right: Sixteenth-century fresco from Galata, Cyprus depicting the Council of Ephesus, which condemned Nestorianism in 431.

Scotland

The first missionary to the Scottish Picts was Ninian (c.360 – c.432). Ninian was consecrated in Rome in 394, but little is known about his mission except that he was based in Whithorn, Galloway, where he founded a church known as *Candida Casa* ("White House").

Ireland

The earliest introduction of Christianity to Ireland is also obscure, but it was probably in the fourth century. Sometime about 431 Pope Celestine I sent Palladius to be Ireland's first bishop. He was joined a few years later by Patrick (probably c.390 – c.460), a British priest who had been enslaved in Ireland. Patrick founded churches in Meath, Ulster, Connaught, and elsewhere and is celebrated as the patron saint of Ireland.

formulated the view that there was only one, divine, nature, with the implication that the life of Christ was "too divine" to be of much moral or spiritual relevance for normal humans.

Council of Chalcedon

Both views had implications for the philosophical questions of human and divine identity, as well as for the Christian doctrines of creation and redemption. In 451 the Eastern emperor Marcian (r. 450–57) convoked the Council of Chalcedon to deal with these issues. Most attending bishops were from the East, but after a two-year delay the Western church accepted most of its decisions, including its Definition of Faith.

The council rejected the formulations of both Nestorius and Eutyches, denying that the humanity of Christ could be separate from his divine person, and also that the two natures were fused into one. The Definition or Creed of Chalcedon set out the existence of one person in two natures, and also affirmed *Theotokos*.

Too human or too divine

The clash between Cyril and Nestorius had opened up much deeper discussions in the church about the nature of God, Christ, and the incarnation. Nestorianism implied that there was a clear divide between the human and divine natures of Christ, to the extent that its critics charged it with doing away with the divine nature altogether. The implication of Nestorian theology was that Jesus was "too human" to allow for the reconciliation with the divine that is so important for Christian thought and practice. In turn, this led some theologians to react the other way. As a corrective to Nestorianism, in 448 Eutyches (c.378–454)

Monophysites

The movement known as Monophysitism came into being as a direct result of the Dyophysite ("two nature") doctrine of Chalcedon. Regional, independent and often isolated from the rest of Christendom, churches that were founded on anti-Chalcedon principles include the Syrian Orthodox Church (also called the Jacobites), the Egyptian Coptic Church, and the Ethiopian (or Abyssinian) Church.

Fall of the West

In the West the empire, ruled from Ravenna, was racked by constant revolutions and imperial intrigues. In 475 the young Romulus Augustus was put in place by his father Orestes (died 476) as a puppet emperor. In 476, taking advantage of the disarray, the Germanic mercenary general Odoacer launched a mutiny and was proclaimed king of Italy (r. 476–93). This event marked the end of the Western Roman empire.

Germanic peoples

The Gothic tribes were divided into Ostrogoths (Eastern Goths) and Visigoths (Western Goths). Other tribes included the Vandals, Lombards, Alans, and Burgundians. Many of these tribes followed Arian Christianity (see chapter 3); this was a source of further conflict as the Germanic peoples gained a foothold in the Catholic empire.

Theatre at Ephesus, Turkey, built third century BC, and rebuilt during the Roman period to house 24,000 spectators.

The first schism

At this time there was also political unrest in the East, contributing to the first significant schism between the Western and Eastern churches.

In 475 the usurper Basiliscus forced the Eastern emperor Zeno to flee Constantinople. Basiliscus was a supporter of Monophysitism, a movement which had nationalist and anti-imperial implications as well as theological ones. When Zeno reclaimed the throne twenty months later he faced an empire divided on regional and religious grounds.

In partnership with Acacius (died 489), patriarch of Constantinople, Zeno drafted a document of union between the Monophysites and orthodox Christians. Acacius's and Zeno's *Decree of Unity* of 482 affirmed the Nicean Creed and condemned Nestorius and Eutyches. However, as a concession to the Monophysites it deliberately did not mention the Definition of Chalcedon. The *Decree of Unity* compromise was accepted by the majority of bishops in the East, but it was completely rejected by Rome. In 484 Pope Felix III (r. 483–92) excommunicated Acacius and was anathematized by him in turn. The schism between Rome and Constantinople would last until 518.

The Sixth Century

The rift between East and West was healed at the beginning of the sixth century. However, this would prove to be temporary as Rome objected to the emperor meddling in theological affairs. While the importance of the Western pope and the Eastern ecumenical patriarch remained, the flourishing church was not confined to these major centres. In this century Christianity spread to India, Sri Lanka and Scotland, and thrived in Ethiopia, Armenia, and Ireland. Untouched by the barbarian wars in mainland Europe, sixth-century Celtic Christians were able to preserve literary, artistic and monastic traditions that would irrevocably alter the future development of Christendom.

The first healing

The first significant schism between the Eastern and Western churches was not healed until the accession of Emperor Justin I (r. 518–27) in Constantinople. Justin revoked the offending *Decree of Unity* and brokered peace between the churches. In this he was advised by his nephew Justinian I (r. 527–65), who took a keen, and educated, interest in theological matters. When Justinian succeeded his uncle, he sought to revive the universal Christian empire of old.

Emperor Justinian

Emperor Justinian I enjoyed much success in his efforts to restore the fortunes of Christianity. In 529 he closed down the

Emperor Justinian depicted in a mosaic from the Emilia Romanga Region, Italy.

The sun rises over the Hagia Sophia in Istanbul (Constantinople). The structure stands on the site of the foundations of a church built by Justinian in 538. Converted into a mosque by the Ottomans in 1453, since 1934 it has been used as a museum.

pagan philosophical schools in Athens and waged a campaign against the Montanists (see chapter 2), the heretical movement still lingering from the second century. Also in 529 Justinian updated and revised the imperial statutes, producing a new code that would become the basis for civil and church law. Justinian commissioned a series of major building works, including Constantinople's most celebrated church, the Hagia Sophia ("Church of the Holy Wisdom": begun 532, completed 538). However, Justinian's continued efforts to solve the problem of Monophysitism finally served to exacerbate – rather than calm – tensions within the church.

Boethius (c.480–524)

The Roman Boethius was a member of the Ostrogothic court at Ravenna. Because he disagreed with Arianism (see chapter 3) he was charged with treason and imprisoned in 522. It was there that Boethius wrote *The Consolations of Philosophy*, a reflection on identity, God, and morality which would become one of the most influential texts in medieval Europe. He was executed in 524.

The three chapters

In 543 Justinian intervened in church affairs when, in an attempt to placate the powerful Monophysite group, he issued an edict condemning the fifth-century writings (or "chapters") of Theodore, bishop of Mopsuestia (c.350–428), Ibas, bishop of Edessa (died 457), and the Syrian bishop of Cyrrhus, Theodoret (c.393 – c.457), all of whom held Nestorian or other Christological positions opposed to Monophysitism. The Eastern patriarchs assented to the edict, but the pope in Rome refused, declaring that the Edict of the Three Chapters went against the Council of Chalcedon.

Theodora (c.500–48)

Crowned alongside Justinian in 527, Theodora was as active and as interested in Christian theology as her husband. Theodora was sympathetic to Monophysitism and sponsored a Monophysite monastery in 531. Under her patronage the Syrian Monophysites established themselves as a separate church under Bishop Jacob Baradaeus (died 578). Theodora's influence raised Vigilius (r. 537–55), a well-known moral reformer, to the papacy – although she would later be disappointed when his support proved inconstant.

Council of Constantinople

Pope Vigilius was forcibly brought to Constantinople by Justinian and reluctantly agreed to uphold the Three Chapters in 548. Western church reaction was fierce, and Vigilius once again rejected Justinian's conciliatory measures. At the Second Council of Constantinople in 553, Vigilius vacillated yet again, this time allowing the council to confirm the edict and defy the Western bishops. Large sections of the Western church, led by northern Italian

clergy, refused to submit to Vigilius, causing a schism with Rome – a church which itself had uncertain relations with Constantinople.

The 553 council demonstrated plainly the distinctions between the early Byzantine church in the East and the Western Roman church. As well as moving the East closer to the Monophysite position, the council also added another title to Mary. Along with *Theotokos* ("God-bearer"), the church also bestowed on her that of *Aeiparthenos* ("ever-virgin"), thus fixing the **dogma** of Mary's perpetual virginity.

The Prophet Muhammad

Muhammad was born In Mecca, western Arabia, in 570.

In 622, Muhammad fled persecution in Mecca to the city of Medina, Saudi Arabia (pictured here). The Hijrah ("flight") marks the beginning of the Muslim calendar.

The first ecumenical patriarch

The relationship between East and West was further troubled when the patriarch of Constantinople, John the Faster (died 595), assumed the title **ecumenical patriarch** in 588. The title has been used by his successors in the Eastern tradition ever since. This claim to universal church primacy was challenged by Pope Pelagius II (r. 579–90) and then Pope Gregory I (r. 590–604).

Pope Gregory did much to expand papal authority in religion and politics, earning his appellation "the Great".

Recared I (586–601)

Recared was king of the Visigoths in Spain. In 586 he renounced his Arian creed and became Catholic. He suppressed Arianism among the Visigoths, and in 589 the Council of Toledo proclaimed Catholic Christianity the official religion of the Spanish kingdom.

Filioque

Latin for "and from the Son". The formula is associated with the Trinitarian doctrine of the "double procession of the Holy Spirit", which states that the Spirit proceeds from the Father *and the Son*. *Filioque* had been in steady use (especially in the West) from the time of the early Church Fathers, but was not officially interpolated into the Nicene Creed until the Council of Toledo in 589. At the time the insertion passed without controversy, but Patriarch Photius (c.820–93) would make the *Filioque* the basis for the Eastern attack on the church of Rome in 864.

Gregory the Great

Gregory became pope in 590. His objections to the title of ecumenical patriarch assumed by John the Faster stemmed from the conviction that Rome was the original see of Peter, and as such it was to Rome that the care of the universal church had been entrusted. As pope, Gregory extended the responsibilities of the papacy more than any of his predecessors.

In 592 he sent papal troops against the Lombards (see chapter 4, **Germanic peoples**) in an effort to stave off their impending invasion of Rome, achieving a temporary respite. When the Lombards did eventually invade in 598 it was Gregory, and not the civil authorities, who administered the peace settlements with the barbarians. This action paved the way for the eventual creation of the Papal States and the establishment of the pope as a temporal power.

Gregory also consolidated papal power in church affairs. His *Pastoral Care* was an influential book detailing the duties of bishops and other clergy. Through his efforts the independent Frankish church was incorporated into Rome. Gregory welcomed the conversion of the Spanish Arian Visigoths and worked closely with Leander, bishop of Seville (c.534 – c.600). Gregory also attempted to align the Celtic church to Rome and he established a major mission to England instituting Augustine (died 604) as first archbishop of Canterbury in 596.

Aethelbert (560–610)

Aethelbert (or Ethelbert) was king of Kent, and was converted by Augustine in 597. Aethelbert's wife, Bertha, was a Frankish Christian, and it is because of her influence that the Roman missionary party was welcomed. Aethelbert and Bertha were enthusiastic supporters of the Roman Christian cause in England, although they failed to reach agreement with the Celtic British church.

Ethiopia

Native Christian culture flourished in other regions relatively independent of Constantinople or Rome. After the Council of Chalcedon in 451, Christianity in Ethiopia became firmly identified with Monophysitism under the influence of Syrian and Egyptian missionary refugees. By the start of the sixth century, the explorer Cosmas Indicopleustes could describe Ethiopia as a "thoroughly Christian country". Between 514 and 542 Christianity thrived under the reign of King Kaleb (c.514 – c.540) in the northern Ethiopian kingdom of Axum. It was during this time that the Bible was translated into Ge'ez (Ethiopic), and a number of patristic writings were preserved (most notably the *Shepherd of Hermas* and texts attributed to Cyril of Alexandria called the *Qerellos*).

Armenia

In Armenia, Christian art and literature flourished after the scholarly innovations of the missionary Mesrob in the previous century. In 555 the Armenian Gregorian Church formally repudiated the Council of Chalcedon, aligning itself with the Monophysite movement, if not embracing full theological Monophysitism. This schism (which remains in effect) was made largely for national, cultural, and political reasons in an effort to avoid the dominance of Constantinople.

Ireland

Irish Christians wrote in Latin and adopted Latin forms of biblical commentary and hagiography. Yet the Christianity of the Celtic fringe in the sixth century was distinct from that of mainland Europe. Following the strong influence of Patrick, Irish Christianity was a religion of powerful rural monasteries, distinct from the urban church culture of Rome or Constantinople. It is from this monastic tradition that the great names of Irish Christianity emerge, including Finnian of Clonard (died 549), Brigid the nun (died c.525), Brendan, celebrated navigator and abbot of Clonfert (484 – c.580), and Comgall, abbot of Bangor (died c.600), whose reputation as a founder of monastic churches was known across Europe.

Untouched by the Germanic barbarian invasions racking the Western empire, Irish monasteries were free to foster learning and study, as well as preserve important texts. It was in Ireland that the earliest forms of the Latin Bible were recovered, as well as the writings of Pelagius, Gregory the Great, and other Latin theologians. From this base, Irish monks and scholars engaged in numerous missionary journeys, evangelizing Scotland and northern England, and reintroducing or reinvigorating Christianity in France and Italy.

The Celtic cross is a distinctive symbol of ancient Scottish and Irish Christianity.

Iona Abbey at sunrise.

Iona

The monk and scholar Columba (c.521–97) founded churches and monasteries in his native Ireland before leaving the country in 563. Columba made the perilous journey to Scotland where he founded the monastic community of Iona. Iona soon became the catalyst for missionary activity to the northern Pictish tribes and the people of Northumbria. A major pillar of Celtic Christianity, the Columban order survived until the **Reformation**. A new community was established in the twentieth century.

The rise of monastic orders

The sixth century saw the formulation of monastic rules and the creation of important monastic orders. During the chaos following the collapse of the Western Roman empire, these communities would play a crucial role in preserving scholarship, social organization, art, liturgy, and Christian theology.

Benedict

Benedict of Nursia (c.480 – c.550) and his sister Scholastica (died c.543) were foundational figures of Western monasticism. Benedict withdrew c.500 from Rome, a city he thought had grown hedonistic and corrupt. Although Benedict was not ordained, he became the focal point for other like-minded ascetics, and a monastic community thrived under Benedict's supervision. Sometime between 525 and 529 the community moved to Monte Cassino in Italy and became the principal monastery of what would become the Benedictine Order (Benedict did not found an order in his lifetime). Around this time, Scholastica also established the convent of Benedictine nuns at nearby Plombariola. Following attacks from the Lombards c.570, the Monte Cassino monastery was forced to relocate to Rome.

The Rule of Benedict

Drawn up c.540, the rule reformed previous monastic rules and provided guidance for the spiritual and administrative direction of monastic life. It became the template for virtually all monastic communities for men and women in Western Christendom.

Columbanus

Born in Ireland, Columbanus (c.543–615) travelled c.590 to Burgundy where he established a monastery at Luxeuil. Monasteries in St Gall, Würzburg, Salzburg, and elsewhere soon followed. The monastic rule was strict and rigorous, and the monks were known for their adherence to Irish Christianity, and for their outspoken attacks on the laxity of the local clergy and governing authorities. As a result Columbanus was expelled from Burgundy in 610, after which he founded a notable monastery at Bobbio, Italy.

Benedict of Nursia prays with his monks. Fresco by Giovanni Antonio Bazzi (1477–1549).

The Seventh Century

Seventh-century Christianity saw the deepening of cultural divisions between East and West. The Eastern empire became identifiably Greek and Byzantine, as Constantinople flowered as a major centre of church activity. In Persia, perpetual war between Zoroastrians and Christians – as well as infighting between the Christian groups themselves – paved the way for the dominance of the new, vigorous religion of the Prophet Muhammad. Elsewhere, Assyrian Christianity took root in China and central Asia. In northern Europe and Britain, the Roman church was both challenged and invigorated by the infusion of Celtic Christianity.

The Bobbio monastery

Expelled from Luxeuil, Abbot Columbanus settled in the small north Italian town of Bobbio in 612. The monastery he founded there would soon become famous as a centre for scholarship and manuscript collecting. Here Columbanus wrote his *Penitential* and the influential *Monastic Rule*. However, as a standard pattern for monastic life and the right ordering of abbeys, this severe rule would eventually be superseded by the more lenient and inclusive rule of Benedict of Nursia.

Celtic Christianity

The outspoken, rigorous Christianity preached by Columbanus that proved so unpalatable to much of Europe was a

Large mosaic floor in the crypt of the Basilica of San Colombano in Bobbio.

Right: Reproduction of the title page of John's Gospel, from the Lindisfarne Gospels.

The Irish monastery at Lindisfarne was an early and important base for the spread of Christianity among the Celts.

product of the Celtic fringe. British, Cornish, Irish, Scottish, and Welsh Christianity were not united under one church leadership, but they did tend to share common characteristics that could be contrasted with different mainland traditions. The differences were largely cultural rather than doctrinal. Since the withdrawal of the Roman empire in the fifth century, the Celtic peoples had operated independently of foreign control. One consequence for Celtic Christianity was that its energy was spent largely in the creation of autonomous monasteries rather than in conformity to the structure and authority of a central church. The Celts followed their own calendar and celebrated Easter on a different day from the rest of Christendom. (The southern Irish church was urged to conform over Easter by Pope Honorius I [r. 625–38]. The northern churches, including Iona, held out until c.768.) The Celts made different demands on their monks, for example over the practice of **tonsuring**. Celtic Christianity was more rural than urban: vernacular Christian poetry reveals an emphasis on the natural world, and Celtic saints were often portrayed as communing with nature and animals.

Anglo-Saxon Christianity

The Anglo-Saxons in seventh-century England operated under the influence of two Christian traditions.

In the south, Augustine and King Aethelbert of Kent founded Roman monasteries and churches at Canterbury in 597. In 601 Pope Gregory the Great sent Paulinus (died 644) to assist Augustine's mission. By 625 Paulinus had converted King Edwin of Northumbria (r. 616–32) and had become the first bishop of York. In 604 the priest Justus (died 627) was appointed bishop of Rochester, and Mellitus (died 624) was made the first bishop of London. A succession of pagan Saxon kings hostile to Christianity forced Mellitus and Justus to flee to Gaul c.617, but they were soon invited back by the king of Kent.

Celtic Christian churches across what is now Scotland and northern England. In 664 many of Lindisfarne's Celtic monks relocated to the Iona monastery. Their move was prompted by the increasing Romanization of Christianity and their displeasure at being forced to conform to Roman discipline after the Synod of Whitby.

Synod of Whitby

In 663 the problem of the two strands of Christianity came to a head when the Northumbrian king Oswy (r. 642–70) realized that, as a Celtic Christian, he would be celebrating Easter on a different date from his wife, Queen Eanfleda, who followed the Roman rite practised in Kent. Oswy convened a synod at Hilda's Abbey in Whitby. Representatives from both traditions argued their case, and the king eventually ruled in favour of the Roman party. The decision to turn to Rome was unpopular with some members of the Celtic church, but it served to align Anglo-Saxon Christianity with the mainstream of Christendom and marked a turning point in the history of Christianity in England. The decision paved the way for significant structural reforms under the direction of Theodore of Tarsus (602–90), who, as archbishop of Canterbury, introduced strong church hierarchy and the Roman parish system.

Lindisfarne Gospels

The illustrated manuscript now known as the Lindisfarne Gospels was created at the monastery between 696 and 698. The book is an important indicator of the preservation of biblical translations throughout Christendom.

The Lindisfarne community

In the northern regions, the Irish missionary Aidan (died 651) established a monastery at Lindisfarne and was consecrated bishop there in 635. With Lindisfarne as their base, Aidan and his successor Finan (died 661) established

Hilda (614–80)

Hilda was a Northumbrian princess who was baptized by Paulinus in 627. In 659 she founded a double monastery for men and women, located on the cliffs of Streanshalch (modern-day Whitby, Yorkshire). As abbess, Hilda defended the Celtic customs, but she accepted the decision of the Synod of Whitby in 664. Under her care, the abbey became a celebrated centre for scholarship, literature, and theology.

Chinese Christianity

There are legendary accounts that the apostle Thomas travelled to China as well as India. The first historical evidence for the presence of Christianity in China comes from the Sian-fu (or Hsi-an-fu) Stone. This monument was erected in 781 and recounts the arrival in 635 of a missionary named Alopen. This may possibly be a version of the name Abraham. Alopen came from the Church of the East (or Assyrian Church) and settled in the T'ang dynasty capital, where he was welcomed and saw some missionary success. There was Buddhist reaction against the mission c.698, but Assyrian Chinese Christianity would remain in some form until the tenth century (some accounts suggest possibly as late as the fourteenth century). However, as the Chinese church did not have a Bible or contact with the wider communion, the religion did not flourish and **syncretism** with Buddhism was likely.

Above and below: The Sian-Fu stone is preserved in a group known as the Forest of Stone Tablets. Xian, China.

Byzantine Christianity

While Rome and the Western regions were struggling to align their Christianity, Constantinople in the East was becoming a consolidated church power, even while it suffered multiple attacks from Visigoths in the west and Persians and Muslims in the south.

Emperor Heraclius

Although during the reign of Heraclius (610–41) the empire was harassed by many invading armies, his reign marks an era of revival for the Eastern church when its culture became distinctly Greek and Byzantine.

During the period 620–29 the Visigoths gained complete control of Spain, driving out Heraclius' armies. At the same time, the Byzantine army was gaining ground previously lost to the Persians, who had made successful advances in 611. In 627 Heraclius won back Nineveh; and Egypt was under Byzantine rule in 629, the same year that Heraclius regained control of Jerusalem and expelled the Jews living there.

Church of the East

The Assyrian Church of the East does not follow the teachings of Nestorius, although it is opposed to the Definition of Chalcedon. Originally centred in Mesopotamia (modern-day Iraq), the "Church of the East" operated largely independently of the great councils of Rome and Constantinople. It emphasized monastic life and missionary activity and was active throughout central and east Asia and India. Long persecuted by the Zoroastrian Persians, the Christians were treated better by the Muslim Arabs after the conquests of 651.

The one activity of Christ

In their territorial skirmishes with the Eastern empire, the Persians were greatly assisted by the fact that the Christian populations of the contested regions were not themselves united.

From 624, in an effort to rally the Monophysites with the orthodox Chalcedonian church of Constantinople, Heraclius attempted to create a Christological formula acceptable to both sides. In 633, together with Sergius, patriarch of Constantinople (died 638), Heraclius promoted the nuanced teaching called "Monoenergism": that Christ had two natures but one mode of "activity" – that of the divine Word. The solution was rejected as heretical by many churchmen, including Sophronius of Jerusalem (c.560–638).

The one will of Christ

In 634 Sergius wrote to Pope Honorius I in Rome seeking assistance. Honorius' suggestion resulted in the *Ecthesis*, a statement of faith drawn up by Sergius that replaced mention of the "activity" of Christ with his one "will" (Monothelitism). Although the *Ecthesis* was initially accepted by Eastern church councils in 638 and 639, it was repeatedly condemned by Pope Honorius's successors in the West, including Pope Martin I (r. 649–55), who was exiled to the Crimea for his refusal to adopt Monothelitism. When Martin died in 655 he became the last pope to be venerated as a martyr.

Two natures

The Monothelite solution had had the opposite of its intended effect of promoting good relations between the traditions. To keep the peace the emperor disowned the teaching, and it was finally pronounced a heresy at the Third Council of Constantinople (Sixth General Council, 680–81), making two natures and two wills in Christ a matter of orthodox faith.

Detail of *Knights in Combat from the Battle of Heraclius Against Khosrow II*, by Piero della Francesca.

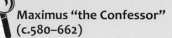

Maximus "the Confessor" (c.580–662)

Maximus was a Greek theologian who opposed Monothelitism and was eventually banished in 653 when he would not agree to the settlement. His prolific writings and influential teachings focused on the origin of evil from man's unreasonable sensuality and the defeat of that evil through the incarnation.

Muslim advance

At the same time as doctrinal battles were being fought in the city churches, Byzantium's frontier war with the Persian empire had weakened both sides, opening the way for the rapid expansion of the new Muslim Arab army. In 636 the Arabs won a significant victory over the Byzantine army at Yarmuk. By 638 Jerusalem was under Muslim control and some Jewish families were allowed to return. As the Arabs advanced further Constantinople lost Antioch (638), Edessa (641), and Alexandria (643), marking the end of Byzantine rule in Egypt. In 653 Muslim Arabs conquered Armenia and between 673 and 678 Constantinople was forced to fend off a Muslim siege by land and sea. The event marked the high point of Arab threat to the capital city.

The Quinisext Council – away from Rome

Arab conquests had made the empire weaker, but the loss of Alexandria, Antioch, and other cities to the Muslims meant that the church of Constantinople grew in stature and importance. In 692 the Eastern bishops met in synod in order to complete the work of the Fifth (553) and Sixth (680–81; see above) General Councils. The Quinisext ("Fifth-Sixth") Council met in the palace of the emperor Justinian II, and its findings were strongly pro-Constantinople. Many of the 102 canons produced there were directed against the Roman church, including attacks on the Western practice of clerical celibacy. Neither the pope nor any other Western representative was present at the council, and they did not approve of its conclusions.

End of Christian North Africa

Between 697 and 698 Carthage was under Muslim Arab control. The mass exodus of the Greek and Roman population from the city marked the end of Byzantine rule in North Africa.

The Greek theologian Maximus "the Confessor" is depicted preaching outside the city walls.

Charles Martel, king of the Franks. Christianity spread throughout the Germanic peoples under his reign; however, his leadership also brought the church into disarray.

The Eighth Century

The iconoclastic controversy racked the East for the best part of the eighth century and beyond, laying the groundwork for the final schism between Constantinople and Rome. The Western church asserted political power with the creation of the Papal States, and the once culturally dominant Christians in North Africa and the Middle East adjusted to life under Muslim rule. In the north, Celtic Christians faced the Viking threat even as the conversion of Germanic pagan tribes continued apace. Here also was witnessed the rise of the Frankish king Charlemagne, whose Catholic renaissance would eventually give rise to the new Holy Roman Empire.

East icons

The Jewish and Muslim religions strictly forbade the use of images in the worship of God. Manichaeism (see chapter 2) held that all matter was evil. Monophysites emphasized the divine nature of Christ at the expense of his human nature. In the face of so much hostility to images and objects, Christianity in this era generally strongly emphasized the veneration of icons.

But the popular practice of icon veneration was challenged by Emperor Leo III (r. 717–41). Leo earned his reputation for breaking the Muslim siege of Constantinople in 718. An often excessive cult of devotion had grown up around some icons, and Leo thought that icons also formed the main obstacle to the conversion of Jews and Muslims, and contributed to the hostility directed at Christendom. In 726 Leo issued an edict declaring that the

Opposite: The Empress Irene was the first woman to rule the Eastern empire. She was deeply interested in theological matters.

veneration of icons was idolatrous, and he ordered all images to be destroyed in an iconoclastic purge.

Iconoclasm

The edict was not welcomed by many, and monks became the core group defending icons. The driving force of resistance to the iconoclastic movement was Patriarch Germanus (c.640 – c.733), although he was aided by many Greek theologians, such as John of Damascus (c.655 – c.750), who wrote three influential discourses in favour of icons. After Leo had Germanus deposed in 730, a systematic movement of persecution, seizure, and destruction followed throughout the Eastern empire.

Illuminated manuscript page depicting the coronation of Emperor Charlemagne by Pope Leo III at St Peter's, Rome.

The culture of icons was not strong in Roman Christianity, but the popes were alarmed by the emperor's tendency to pronounce on matters of theology. They too opposed Leo from 727 onwards. When the Synod of Rome, led by Pope Gregory III (r. 732–41), denounced the iconoclasts in 731, Leo retaliated by removing papal jurisdiction from the imperial territories in southern Italy and seizing other Italian territories belonging to the papacy.

Synod of Hieria

When Leo's son Constantine V (r. 741–75) became emperor, he had to put down a pro-icon rebellion before securing his power. In 753 he instituted the Synod of Hieria, which affirmed Leo's edicts that icon veneration was heretical and idolatrous. Many orthodox clergy accepted the ruling, but monks often refused and were martyred when they resisted the suppression of their monasteries. As the synod had no representatives from Antioch, Alexandria, Jerusalem, or Rome its decrees were not considered to be representative of the wider church.

Empress Irene

Iconoclasm abated somewhat when Constantine's son Leo IV was emperor between 775 and 780. After Leo died, his wife, Empress Irene (r. 797–802), attempted to reverse the iconoclastic policy of her predecessors. Irene was the first woman to rule the Eastern empire and she was zealous in putting down challengers to her reign, including her own son, Constantine VI. Irene's support of icons also drew violent opposition, as the army was led by anti-icon forces.

For Christianity, Irene's reign marks a time of conciliation between the pro-icon Eastern members of the Synod of Hieria and the wider church. Working together with Tarasius, patriarch of Constantinople (died 806), and Pope Hadrian I (r. 772–95), Irene called the Second Council of Nicea in 787.

Second Nicene Council

Over 300 bishops gathered at the council, including representatives from all the parties that had been absent at Hieria. Their first attempt at meeting was blocked by the iconoclast army, but when the council convened a second time they reversed the decrees of Hieria. Veneration of icons was defined as a matter of respect and admiration that was not in itself idolatrous. Absolute adoration, on the other hand, was reserved only for God.

Nicea is also important in that it passed a number of disciplinary measures intended to reform the church. **Simony** was condemned, as was the practice of priests living outside their diocese without permission. Clerics were encouraged to live a simple life. The foundation of new double monasteries (where men and women lived together in the same enclosure) was forbidden in order to preserve propriety.

Continued antagonism

Although icons were officially restored throughout the empire, iconoclastic sentiments did not disappear, and remained especially strong in the army. In 790 the imperial army rebelled and established Constantine VI as emperor. His reign until 797 was unpopular and short-lived, but it paved the way for the accession of his fellow iconoclast Emperor Leo V "the Armenian" (r. 813–20) and for the second great iconoclastic controversy of the following century.

Christendom and Islam

711

Moorish era begins in Spain.

725–831

Having survived the Muslim domination of Egypt and North Africa begun a century earlier (c.650), Coptic Christianity experiences unrest and internal divisions that aid the consolidation of Islam in the region.

732

The Muslim advance into France is halted at the Battle of Poitiers.

782

Muslim armies advance on the Bosporus. Peace is bought by a heavy tribute from Constantinople.

Papal States

Leo III's confiscation of papal land in the 730s highlights the source of much of the Western church's power at this time. By the eighth century, the papacy controlled land throughout Italy, as well as in Sicily, Gaul, Illyria, Corsica, and Sardinia.

The emergence of the Western church as a temporal power brought it into conflict with other powers seeking political and economic gain. In 754 Rome was besieged by the Lombard king Aistulf (r. 749–56). Initially Pope Stephen II (r. 752–57) sought protection from Byzantium, but this was not forthcoming. So Stephen turned to the Frankish king Pepin "the Short" (r. 751–68) for assistance. In 756, after defeating the Lombards, Pepin donated significant regions of Venetia and Istria to the pope and firmly established Ravenna and Rome under church authority. The accumulation of secure lands free from the authority of the emperor in the East marked the creation of the Papal States.

Donation of Constantine

Written toward the end of the eighth century, the *Donation* purports to record the gift of land and authority from Emperor Constantine I (see chapter 3) to the pope and his successors. Although the document's authenticity was suspected early on in its circulation, in the Middle Ages it was influential as a support for the claims of papal primacy. In the fifteenth century the *Donation* was conclusively proved to be a forgery.

Conversion of Germany

Concerted missionary projects to convert pagan Germanic tribes were underway in the eighth century. The greatest figure during this time was Boniface, the "Apostle of Germany".

Boniface (originally named Wynfrith, c.675–754) was born in Wessex, England. After training as a scholar and monk, Boniface made his first journey to the Frisians in 716. The mission did not thrive and Boniface went to Rome. In 719 Pope Gregory II (r. 715–31) instituted a new mission, returning Boniface to the Rhineland to work with the heathen Frisian and Hessian people. In 722 Boniface was made bishop of Germany. He did not have a fixed see, but was charged with ministering to the whole Germanic frontier. Under Boniface's influence, parishes and monasteries were founded, including Regensburg, Fritzlar, Kitzingen, and Fulda.

The Oak of Thor

Boniface cut down the sacred tree at Geismar (modern-day Fritzlar, Germany) in 723 in front of a hostile crowd. When they saw that Boniface was not struck by lightning, the crowd converted to Christianity and a chapel was built on the spot. The event represents a key turning-point in the acceptance of Christianity in pagan Germany.

Charles Martel

The Franks were the most powerful of the Christianized Germanic peoples. Charles Martel (c.690–741) established his rule over them between 714 and 719. Under Martel, Christianity made further inroads as he waged campaigns against Bavarians, Saxons, and Frisians. The growth of Christianity was secured when Martel repelled the Muslim invaders at Poitiers in 732.

Martel considered himself a champion of Christianity, yet his support was often more opportunistic than constructive, and under his rule the Frankish church fell somewhat into disarray. High church offices were often sold to the highest bidder or given to court favourites for political purposes. Many priests held more than one position, making it impossible for them to devote their full attention to one parish. There had been no Frankish synod or church council for over eighty years and many of the clergy were untrained and ill-disciplined.

This statue in Fulda, Germany commemorates Boniface. He risked much to bring Christianity to the Germanic tribes and was eventually martyred in 754.

Teutonic restoration

Martel had given Boniface protection and support. After Martel's death in 741 Boniface was freer to act as he saw fit to restore the church. A series of reforms quickly followed. The Synods of Germanicum (742) and Soissons (743), and a council of Frankish clergy in 747, did much to deal with errors and abuses in the Teutonic church.

In 746 Boniface was made the first archbishop of Mainz. He was martyred in Frisia in 754, where pagan violence continued until a final revolt in 784. Boniface's body was returned to the abbey he had helped found at Fulda. The site in Hesse soon became a popular pilgrimage destination, increasing the stature and reputation of the church in Germany. In the following century Fulda would become one of the most important centres for Christianity, culture, and learning in all of Europe.

Thecla (died c.790)

In 749 Boniface sent a request back to England for Anglo-Saxon women to be sent in aid of the mission to the Teutons. One of these, Thecla, became abbess of the Benedictine convents of Ochsenfurt and later Kitzingen. Letters sent to her by Boniface reveal the extent to which he relied on her as a fellow labourer, especially in the education and conversion of hostile Teutonic women and their children. Thecla was martyred around 790.

Opposite: Charlemagne receives the scholar Alcuin, with whom he planned a "new Athens" of Christian civilization. Fresco by Victor Schnetz (1787–1870).

Church History of the English People·

Bede (c.673–735) was a celebrated scholar and monk at Jarrow when he wrote his book (completed 731). It was the first ever work on English national and church history.

King Charlemagne

Charlemagne ("Charles the Great", r. 768–814) inherited the powerful Frankish kingdom of his father Pepin and grandfather Martel. When he became the sole king in 771 he set about expanding the empire over other Teutonic peoples, violently incorporating the Saxons under Frankish rule in 772 and defeating the Lombards by 774. Charlemagne fought the Spanish Moors in the south-west of his kingdom and also expanded eastwards, defeating the Asiatic Avar tribes and other pagan Slavic groups.

Carolingian renaissance

As well as military expansion, Charlemagne sought to re-establish a common culture in the West. His revival of learning, language, administration, and theology became known as the Carolingian renaissance. The campaign itself would collapse after the Norse invasions of the ninth century, but it still helped to preserve knowledge and paved the way for later medieval renaissances.

Charlemagne gathered Italian historians and grammarians, Spanish poets, and Irish theologians to his court. He founded

academies in monasteries at Tours
and Fulda among others. Following
the educational system of Boethius,
Charlemagne's schools taught
the seven liberal arts: arithmetic,
astronomy, geometry, grammar,
logic, music, and rhetoric.

Alcuin and the new Athens

Right: Vikings were considered "Kings of the Sea", as in this French engraving *Les rois de la mer en expédition*, after Albert Sebille (1874–1953).

Charlemagne intentionally followed the lead of the old Greco-Roman civilization, although his focus was primarily on creating a literate, educated Christian clergy. In this his chief assistant was the scholar Alcuin (c.735–804), who wrote to him in a letter: "It may be that a new Athens will arise in Francia, and an Athens fairer than of old, for our Athens, ennobled by the teachings of Christ, will surpass the wisdom of the Academy."

Alcuin was invited from York to run the Carolingian palace school of Aachen in 782. There he organized the literary and educational aspects of the renaissance, and assisted Charlemagne's interventions in matters of church discipline and doctrine. Alcuin wrote biblical commentaries and led the scholarly reworking of the Vulgate Bible, correcting many corruptions of translation that had crept in. In 794 Alcuin took part in the Synod of Frankfurt, which did much to align Spanish clergy to the Roman church. He was appointed abbot of St Martin's Abbey in Tours in 796.

Vikings

From 789 constant attacks from Norse Vikings brought chaos to the coastal regions of England and Scotland. Monasteries and churches were sacked for their wealth (including Lindisfarne in 793 and Jarrow in 794), and many people were displaced as a result of the raids. Norsemen would dominate northern Europe in the following century.

Emperor Charlemagne

In Rome, on Christmas Day in the year 800, Pope Leo III (r. 795–816) crowned Charlemagne as emperor. This action, which crystallized Charlemagne's desire to restore the Western empire, caused consternation in the Byzantine East. It would also have ramifications for church unity in East and West, and would eventually lead to the creation of the Holy Roman Empire of medieval Europe.

Map of Western Europe in the eighth century.

Byzantine empire, 8th century
Turks
Mongols
Magyars
Slavs
Celts
Teutons
Latins
Balts
Georgians
Arabs

0 ———— 600 km
0 ———— 400 miles

Istanbul (Constantinople) as seen from the Sea of Marmara.

The Ninth Century

In the ninth century, old conflicts continued, yet the era also witnessed a renewal of conversion among new peoples. Although initially bloody, the second iconoclastic movement would eventually produce a rejuvenated Constantinople. From here, Christianity spread to the eastern frontiers leading to the conversion of the Slavic and other pagan groups.

In the West, the Norse onslaught slowed Charlemagne's renaissance, yet the potential for resurgence remained. As Vikings settled in their newly conquered Christian lands, they too began to adopt Christianity for themselves. The mission to the Scandinavian tribes of the north began at this time.

East

Theodore of Studios

Between 797 and 799 the threat of Muslim raids led the Byzantine abbot Theodore (759–826) to move his monastery from Saccudion in Bithynia to Studios at Constantinople. Under the energetic

Theodore the Studios monks thrived and the monastery became the principal centre for monastic life in the East. Theodore was prolific, writing many influential works and over 600 letters in defence of a strong, independent church. Theodore's austerity and Christian idealism often brought him into conflict with morally lax emperors and the priests who supported them, and he was occasionally sent into exile, prompting several appeals to the papacy as well as to the Byzantine authorities.

Second iconoclasm

After a military coup in 813 Leo V assumed the throne as emperor and

Right: The Empress Theodora is credited with the restoration of icons within Orthodoxy. Mosaic from the Basilica San Vitale, Ravenna, Italy.

61

promptly set about reviving the iconoclastic policies of his predecessor Constantine V. As the most prominent opponent of iconoclasm, Theodore was once again banished in 815. The patriarch Nicephorus (758–828) was deposed and many other monks were imprisoned or killed when they opposed the removal of icons from their churches and buildings.

Leo was assassinated in 820. His successor, Michael II (r. 820–29), continued a milder iconoclasm, prohibiting the worship of images only in the capital city. In 829 his son and successor Theophilus brought back violent opposition to icons – a persecution that only ended with Theophilus's death in 842.

Theophilus's widow Theodora (died c.867) announced an end to iconoclasm and ordered that the icons be restored. She supported the election of the pro-icon monk Methodius (died 847) to the office of patriarch in 843, and a great feast was celebrated in honour of the event.

Feast of Orthodoxy

The feast established to celebrate the defeat of iconoclasm is a major point in the Orthodox calendar. On the first Sunday of Lent, hymns composed by martyrs are chanted during the procession of icons, and a list of heretics, saints, and devout emperors (called the *Synodicon*) is read out in litany.

Right: A national Greek Orthodox shrine of St Photius.

Rejuvenation of the East

The iconoclastic controversies set the stage for the final schism between the Eastern and Western churches. The theological implications of images aroused less interest in the West than did the worrying tendency for Eastern emperors to exert political control over the church, a trend that was largely welcomed, and in principle unopposed, by the Byzantine clergy. In addition, Roman and Byzantine Christianity inhabited very different contexts. The growing vitality of the Papal States in Rome and of the Christian culture of Frankish Europe in the West was matched by a confident Eastern church firmly entwined with the Eastern empire and Greek culture.

Photius and Nicholas

Byzantine court intrigues in 858 resulted in Emperor Michael III (r. 842–67) deposing Ignatius (c.798–877) as patriarch of Constantinople and installing the layman Photius (c.820 – c.895) in his place. Constantinople appealed to Rome for confirmation of the appointment and, under pressure from the emperor, the papal legates approved Photius. Pope Nicholas I (r. 858–67) rejected the decision that had been made in his name, and in 863 he affirmed Ignatius as patriarch and attempted to depose Photius and all his supporters.

The Western intervention caused great offence in the East. The rift was compounded by debates about whether a mission to Bulgaria should be carried out under the auspices of Rome or Constantinople. In 867 Photius (who, supported by Emperor Michael, had remained patriarch despite Nicholas's objections) denounced the presence of Roman missionaries in Bulgaria and officially objected to Latin practices such as inserting the *Filioque* clause into the Nicene Creed. Furthermore, Photius convened a church council which excommunicated Pope Nicholas. A tentative peace between East and West would be established, broken and established again, but the Photian controversy marks a major milestone in the road toward permanent schism.

Encyclical Letter of Photius

Photius's 867 **encyclical** opposing the *Filioque* and other aspects of Roman theology is the first of a series of major statements of Eastern doctrine that would come to be known in the Orthodox Church as the Symbolical Books. The last such statement was written in 1952.

Muslim, Jewish, and Christian conflict

837

Christians and Jews revolt against Moorish rule in Toledo.

846

The Basilica of St Peter's in Rome is sacked by Muslim raiders.

847

Pope Leo IV erects walls around Rome to defend against further raids.

871–79

War continues between Christian and Muslim armies in the East. The Eastern empire is also at war with the Christian Paulicians, who aid the Saracens.

878

Periodic persecution of Christians and Jews occurs under Egyptian Muslim rule of Jerusalem.

Paulicians

This Byzantine sect probably earned its name from the third-century heretical bishop Paul of Samosata (c.200 – c.275). They rejected the Old Testament and professed dualistic belief in a good, spiritual God and an evil God who created material things. As a result of being persecuted between 842 and 857, many Paulicians assisted the Muslims against the Byzantine armies. Popular and widespread, Paulicianism developed into the Bogomil (see chapter 9), Cathar, and Albigensian (see chapter 12) heresies of the medieval period.

Slavic missions

In the ninth century missions to the pagan Bulgarian, Croatian, Serbian, and Czech peoples were largely conducted by the Eastern churches. The Western influence was always present, however, and local kings often prevaricated between Constantinople and Rome.

Croats

Prince Viseslav reigned in the Croatian port city of Nin c.800. A Christian, Viseslav was in power when a Frankish bishopric was established c.803 and the Croatians officially became a Christian people. Inspired by Pope John VIII (r. 872–82), missions to establish Croatian clergy and the Croatian church were organized between 879 and 892.

Czechs and Moravians

Christianity was evident among the Czech peoples from early in the century. In 845, fourteen Czech princes presented themselves before the German king Louis (r. 843–76), in Regensburg, demanding to be baptized. This move, although probably motivated by political and military considerations, would nonetheless have brought considerable changes to the fabric of Czech society as the princes represented the majority of the Czech power base at the time. However, it was the 863 mission of Cyril (826–69) and Methodius (c.815–85) to Greater Moravia that would fully entrench Christianity among the Slavic peoples.

"Apostles to the Slavs"

These Greek brothers from Thessalonica were the era's most celebrated missionaries. Before becoming a monk, Methodius was a governor of a Slavic province in the Byzantine empire. Theologian, linguist, and minister, Cyril was originally called Constantine but changed his name when he became a monk shortly before his death.

Their first mission was to the Khazars in 860. In 862 Emperor Michael III and Patriarch Photius recruited the brothers to lead a mission to the Slavs of Bohemia and Moravia. Cyril and Methodius enjoyed great success preaching in Slavic, translating the liturgy, and organizing church services in the local vernacular. The mission also gained the support of Rome and acted under full papal authority, although

Methodius, Bishop of Moravia and "Apostle to the Slavs". Fourteenth-century fresco from the Monastery of St Mark, Skopje, Macedonia.

Germanic churchmen sometimes resented the Eastern influence.

After Cyril died in a Roman monastery in 869, Methodius was consecrated bishop to the Slavs by Pope Hadrian II (r. 867–72). On his return to Moravia, Methodius was opposed by the German bishops already there, and he was imprisoned by the local Slav prince, Sviatopolk (r. 870–94). Pope John VIII secured his release, and Methodius went on to work in Pannonia and Velehrad (in the modern-day Czech Republic) where he died.

The Cyrillic alphabet

Tradition ascribes the invention of the alphabet used by the Slavonic peoples to Cyril. The vernacular work of Cyril and Methodius opened the way for the rich tradition of Slavonic literature, liturgy, and Scripture translations.

Serbs

Under the influence of Cyril and Methodius, the Serbian prince Mutimir (ruled c.860–91) converted to Christianity and was baptized. From this point the Serbs became an officially Christian people, but the transition was not always easy. Under orders from Emperor Basil I (r. 867–86), Serbs living in the Narenta Valley were forcibly baptized. Serbian Christianization continued until 874, with the country wavering between allegiance to Constantinople and to Rome.

Bulgarians

Christian missionaries had seen some success in Bulgaria from as early as the seventh century. Later concerted missionary efforts led to Boris (r. 852–89), the khan (or king) of Bulgaria, being baptized in 864. As Greek and German Christian missionaries already had some influence in Bulgaria, Boris too prevaricated between Rome and Constantinople. Boris favoured an independent Bulgarian church, and for this reason fell foul of both the patriarch and the pope. Eventually Boris chose Constantinople c.870. In 885 the Bulgarian church received a vernacular liturgy under the auspices of Clement of Ochrid (840–916), a disciple of Cyril and Methodius and founder of the first Slavic university, teaching language and theology. A Bulgarian pagan reaction against forced baptisms led to violent conflicts in 889–93. The rebellion was short-lived, however, and under the rule of the Christian khan Simeon I (r. 893–927) Bulgaria enjoyed a golden age of literature and culture. It was also under Simeon's rule that the Bulgarian church became **autocephalous** – it had its own patriarch – early in the following century.

Opening text of Matthew's Gospel, from the Slavonic Gospels, 1429.

Tsarevets fortress, Veliko Tarnovo, Bulgaria.

West

Persistent Scandinavian raiding undoubtedly unsettled much of society in the West; however, the English and Frankish churches retained a strong influence on the religion, administration, education, and culture of the European peoples.

Louis the Pious

When Charlemagne died, his son Louis (r. 814–40) assumed the empire. Louis took a great interest in mission and monastic reform. In 815 he built a model abbey at Aachen and handed its rule over to Benedict of Aniane (c.750–821). As the founder of a monastery in Languedoc which emphasized manual labour rather than study, Benedict had already earned a reputation as a strict enforcer of the Benedictine Rule. Through regular councils held at the Aachen community in 816, 817, and 818 Benedict enforced the conformity of the surrounding monasteries. He died before the reform scheme could fully take root, and Louis' attempt to achieve monastic unity was further disrupted by the constant Viking raids.

Detail from Charlemagne's sarcophagus, which now resides in Aachen Cathedral, Germany.

Scandinavian missions

Louis did not allow the Scandinavian threat to thwart his attempts at Christian expansion. A royal visit to Denmark led to the conversion and baptism of the Danish chief Harald. Louis followed up this initial missionary endeavour by creating the archbishopric of Hamburg and Bremen, and sending its first archbishop, Anskar (801–65), to establish a church and school in Hedeby (modern-day Schleswig) c.826. Although he saw little success during his missionary career, Anskar would become known as "the Apostle to the North" and would be seen as the foundational influence for Scandinavian Christianity.

Heathen opposition forced Anskar to return to Louis' court in 829, only to be sent out again to Sweden at the request of Björn, a local chief. Anskar founded Sweden's first church at Birka in 830. In 854 he returned to Denmark, acting as a Christian influence on King Erik II (or Horik, r. 854– c.873) of Jutland, and where he opposed the Viking slave trade. Anskar continually faced stiff challenges from the local warlords and populations. After his death Scandinavia collapsed back into paganism, not to resurge until a century later.

Continued Viking attacks

800

In Britain, Vikings attack the shrine of St Andrew.

807

Iona is abandoned as a result of Viking raids.

840

Ireland becomes the centre for Norse trade with Europe. Settled Vikings begin to adopt Christianity.

866

Vikings destroy the Great Library of York.

870

Danish raiders destroy Ely Monastery.

Alfred the Great

For Christianity, the last half of the ninth century in England was a time of culture and learning set against the backdrop of devastating Viking incursions. Alfred "the Great" (r. 871–99), king of Wessex, planned reforms to the parish system and a revival of monasticism, but was thwarted by the crippling cost of defence against the Danish. Instead, Alfred turned to literacy as a way of maintaining the links with wider Christendom and civilization that the pagan raiders threatened to sever. A great work of disseminating and preserving key Latin Christian texts was undertaken. Alfred himself did many of the translations, alongside a team of international scholars that he assembled for the purpose.

Alfred set the pattern for Christian kingship, as well as establishing a high standard of education for clergymen and nobles. He also began the work of Christianizing the Danish invaders. Despite the threat of destruction at the hands of the barbarians, Christianity in the British Isles thrived with his help, and it was in good health on his death.

King Guthrum (died 890)

In 878 this Danish warlord overran Wessex in a surprise attack on Alfred's forces. Alfred's successful counterattack brought Guthrum to terms under a treaty known as the Peace of Wedmore. Guthrum accepted conversion and was baptized under the name Aethelstan. In 880 he withdrew to East Anglia and ruled as a Christian king.

Pilgrimage

The pilgrimage of Santiago de Compostela began in 899 following the purported discovery of the relics of James the apostle in north-west Spain. The shrine of St James remains a major pilgrimage destination for travellers from all over the world.

Bottom left: King Alfred ordered copies of the "Alfred Jewel" to accompany the texts that he sent out around the country. It was probably used as a pointer to aid in reading. Only one Jewel remains and is kept in the Ashmolean Museum, Oxford.

Bottom right: The scallop shell is the symbol of James the apostle. Pilgrims wear a shell to mark their visit to James's shrine at the cathedral of Santiago de Compostela, Spain.

The Tenth Century

In the tenth century the Roman church endured a string of bad popes. Yet even as the centre of Western Christendom suffered, monks living and working on the fringes preserved the ideals and culture of Christianity. In the East, major developments were also due to a thriving monasticism. Monks led the Christianization of the Slavic peoples. Bulgaria especially benefitted from its adoption of Eastern Christianity. The century also witnessed the Christianization of Russia – an event of future great significance. Meanwhile, territorial wars between Christians and Muslims raged on, preparing the ground for the Crusades of the following century and beyond.

West

Disastrous popes

The year 900 saw yet another tenuous renewal of the relationship between Rome and Constantinople. However, reconciliation was hampered by the reputation of the hierarchy of the Western church, which was suffering under a series of corrupt, worldly, or simply incompetent popes.

As the Papal States grew in temporal and economic influence they became more entrenched in the political power games of the day. The office of the papacy had become a desirable acquisition for rival aristocratic Italian families, who jostled to get their own members into the position. The trend began in the previous century with publicly corrupt popes such as Sergius II (r. 844–47) and John VIII, who held office for ten years before becoming the first pope to be assassinated in 882. Other

Domes of St Mark's Basilica in Piazza San Marco or St Mark's Square, Venice, Italy.
On the left are the Prophets and Ascension cupolas; on the right the Pentecost cupola.

mad or bad popes followed, including Stephen VI (r. 896–97), who was strangled after presiding over an infamous synod which condemned the exhumed corpse of his predecessor Formosus (r. 891–96); Leo V (pope for only thirty days before being killed in 903); and his successor (and possibly murderer) Sergius III (r. 904–11). There were also political or ineffectual popes: John X (r. 914–28) and Stephen VIII (r. 939–42) were both deposed and imprisoned.

Pope John XII

The reputation of the papacy reached one of its low points with the career of Pope John XII (r. 955–63). Octavian was the son of Alberic, the ruler of Rome. As part of his consolidation of power, Alberic arranged for his son to be made pope. Octavian was eighteen years old when he took the name John XII.

Octavian became Pope John XII when he was eighteen years old. His time in office marks a low point in the history of the papacy.

John XII's pontificate was marked by worldliness and political intrigues from the beginning. In 962 John enlisted the help of the German king Otto I (r. 936–73) against a rival, King Berengar (r. 950–63), from northern Italy. John offered his fealty to Otto and crowned him Roman emperor. The *Ottonian Privilege*, a legal document detailing their treaty, was based in part on the forged *Donation of Constantine* (see chapter 7) and it gave Otto effective control over the Papal States, putting the authority of the pope under the emperor. John reneged on his agreement, and turned to Berengar and to the Byzantines for help against Otto's troops. This help was not forthcoming, and John was deposed for "immorality" in 963. He returned to Rome a year later, but died suddenly under mysterious circumstances in 964.

Subordination of the papacy

John's case is significant because he granted power to Otto and his successors. This dynasty installed a number of popes without consulting the clergy and without any thought for the church, including Benedict VI (r. 973–74), John XIV (r. 983–84), John XV (r. 985–96), and Gregory V (r. 996–99).

The timing of this discreditation of the papacy is important, because it acted as a catalyst for renewal and reform in the West. These movements were often led by churchmen or secular rulers operating outside Rome.

Antiphonary of St Benigne

Probably written c.980, this manuscript records Gregorian plainsong and is one of our earliest surviving pieces of written music. Its obscure method of notation predates the invention of the musical stave in the eleventh century.

The Church of St Peter and St Paul forms part of Cluny Abbey in Burgundy, France. Other monasteries were quick to follow Cluny's moral and spiritual example.

Monastic reform

Corrupt popes, constant invasions, and the complacency that often accompanies material success had contributed to the disarray of many monastic houses in Western Europe. It was against this backdrop that William "the Pious", duke of Aquitaine (died 918), founded the monastery of Cluny in Burgundy in 909–10.

Cluny Abbey

Cluny grew in importance largely because of its strict observance of the Benedictine rule. The Cluniac model valued education and learning; it stressed cultivating a pure spiritual life in individuals; and it emphasized good administration and organization. Neighbouring monasteries quickly adopted the high standards set by the Cluniacs. Under its second abbot, Odo

70

(c.879–942), many of the houses of southern France allied themselves with Cluny, and its reforming influence also spread to the great Italian monasteries of Monte Cassino and Subiaco. Under the fifth abbot, Odilo (c.961–1049), the number of Cluniac monasteries doubled to 65. Valued by churchmen, kings, and emperors, Odilo's influence was felt across Western Christendom.

"Truce of God"

Abbot Odilo was instrumental in establishing the Truce of God between warring factions of southern France and Italy. The truce was a formal suspension of fighting during holy days or seasons. In 1027 fighting between Saturday night and Monday morning was forbidden. The medieval church would eventually extend the truce to cover Advent and Lent.

Glastonbury Abbey

Celtic Christian communities had been in existence in Glastonbury in England since the seventh century. By the early tenth century attacks by Danish invaders had reduced the monastery considerably, and indeed monasticism was waning throughout the country. Dunstan (c.909–88) was made abbot of Glastonbury around 943. A strict ascetic, Dunstan brought the monastery back under the Benedictine rule. A revival of learning, piety, and organizational excellence ensued. Glastonbury became the main religious centre in England, leading the restoration of regular monasticism.

Later medieval legends would connect the abbey to Joseph of Arimathaea, Saint Patrick, and King Arthur, instituting Glastonbury as a major site of pilgrimage.

Codes of conduct

Dunstan was a royal counsellor to Prince Edgar (c.943–75). When Edgar became king of all England in 959 he appointed Dunstan archbishop of Canterbury. Together the two undertook a programme of major reform in church and state. A key product of this reformation was the *Monastic Agreement* (c.973). As well as regulating Benedictine observance across the country, this code also detailed the role of the sovereign as the patron of monastic life.

East

Mount Athos

A rocky peninsula jutting into the Aegean Sea off the coast of Macedonia, the "holy mountain" was already home to some monks before Athanasius (c.920–1003) founded the Lavra community in 961. With the strong backing of Emperor Nicephorus Phocas (r. 963–69), Athanasius instituted a monastic system following the ascetic, coenobite rule of Basil the Great (see chapter 3, **Eastern monks**).

When the emperor died, Athanasius was forced into exile on the grounds that his reform project was too closely aligned with imperial power. However, the new emperor, John Tzimisces (r. 969–76), also lent his support and Athanasius returned

to become abbot-general of the entire mountain. Under his influence, Athos would grow to eclipse Studios as the most important monastic centre of the Byzantine church. The mountain, which admitted (and still admits) no women, was home to fifty-eight (now twenty) semi-independent communities and 900 places of worship, serving, at the height of its popularity, up to 40,000 monks.

Roussanou Monastery on a cliff, Mount Athos, Meteora, Greece.

Bulgarians

Simeon I was the first Bulgarian ruler to adopt the title tsar in 917. Simeon's reign was marked by constant wars with the Byzantine empire, the Serbs, and the Magyars. But under his rule Bulgaria grew to be a major power in the region. It was also during his time that Constantinople was compelled to recognize the Bulgarian Orthodox Church as an independent entity, c.924.

Instead of using Greek, the autocephalous Bulgarian Orthodox Church adopted Slavic as its official language. Christian books translated from Greek into Slavic soon spread from Bulgaria to neighbouring nations. In this way the Bulgarians played a key role in the spread of both Orthodoxy and the Cyrillic alphabet (see chapter 8) to the Serbs and other Eastern Slavic peoples.

Bogomils

The vigorous Orthodox Bulgarian Church also produced an equally vigorous heresy. The Manichaean movement (see chapter 2) seems to have taken root in the Balkans through the Paulicians (see chapter 8), who had settled in Thrace. The Bogomils, who demonized created matter and did not recognize the authority of church or state, earned a reputation for immorality and licentiousness.

Bogomilism spread quickly, prompting the Bulgarian tsar Peter (r. 927–69) to request help from Patriarch Theophylact of Constantinople (915–56) in 950. Their efforts were ultimately unsuccessful, and in 972 the Bogomils were still attracting condemnation from the Bulgarian priest Cosmos. Eventually the sect would grow to dominate religion in the Balkans and Asia Minor, extinguished only by Islam in the fifteenth century. Bogomil ideas in Italy and France also influenced the Cathars and Albigensians (see chapter 12), heretical movements that would have a significant impact on church and state in medieval Europe.

Wenceslas (born c.907, ruled c.922–29)

This Bohemian duke was known for his Christian piety and learning. He favoured relationships with the West, and forged ties with the German princes, a move that was not welcomed by some of his pagan subjects. After Wenceslas was murdered by his brother Boleslav he soon became revered as a martyr and Czech national hero. An English Christmas carol by J. M. Neale (1818–66) celebrates "Good King Wenceslas", although the events it describes are imaginary.

Russians

Christianity had been introduced to the people of Russia before, but the impact had been negligible. Princess Olga of Kiev (c.879–969) was baptized c.955 after a visit to Constantinople. Neither her subjects nor her son Sviatoslav (died 972) accepted the faith, and the period following the end of Olga's reign in 964 was marked by a strong pagan revival. The Christianization of the country would not begin in earnest until the conversion and regency of Sviatoslav's son Vladimir (born c.955, ruled c.980–1015).

Prince Vladimir

According to tradition, the pagan Vladimir investigated various other faiths and Christian traditions before adopting Eastern Christianity c.988. He then married Anna, the sister of the Byzantine emperor Basil II (r. 976–1025) and began his campaign promoting Christianity. The success of the religion in Russia can be attributed in part to Vladimir's extensive church-building projects; however, he also practised forced baptisms. The upper classes and nobility accepted Christianity, but the countryside would remain largely pagan for another 500 years.

Monument to Princess Olga, in Pskov, Russia. She was one of the first to sow the seeds of Christianity in her nation, although she saw little success in her lifetime.

Royal conversions

The tenth century saw the conversion of a number of rulers leading to significant Christianization of the cultures concerned. Danish king Harald Bluetooth (c.940 – c.985) converted c.965, renewing an interest in Christianity that had lain dormant for a century. In 966 Prince Mieszko I of Poland (born c.930, ruled 960–92) adopted Christianity, probably under the influence of Western missionaries from Moravia. Stephen, the first king of Hungary (r. 997–1038), was baptized in 985 by the Czech missionary and Prussian martyr Adalbert (956–97).

The Eleventh Century

The first century of the new millennium saw Christianity spread further afield thanks in part to a revitalized Roman Church. The reformed papacy exerted its authority, leading to conflicts with secular rulers and a final breach with Constantinople. Advances in Christian architecture, philosophy, and music made in this era remain into the present age.

Military conquests by the Normans in the north and the continuing Iberian Christian reconquest in the south would form the contours of European Christendom and prepare the ground for Christian expansion into the New World. Conflict with Muslims in the east also leads to the first of many Crusades.

Iceland

Iceland had known sporadic Celtic, Viking, and Saxon Christian missionary activity since the early ninth century. The first concerted effort to institute Christianity as the official religion in Iceland came by way of the Norwegian king Olaf Tryggvason (ruled c.995–1000) in 1000. Isleifur Gizurarson (1006–80) became Iceland's first bishop in 1056, and his son and successor Gissur (1042–1118) presided

Detail from a medieval Icelandic manuscript held at the Thjodarbokhladan Library Museum. The strong tradition of sagas and stories sheds valuable light on the development of Christianity in Iceland.

as the second bishop from 1082 until his death. While the influence of Christianity on the culture and morals of the Icelandic people can be known from stories and sagas of the time, the official church itself was relatively weak, often subservient to the civil powers of the day. In addition the country was politically unstable and often under the sway of other Scandinavian powers. As a result the monastic and intellectual pursuits that sustained much of Christianity in early medieval Europe were bypassed in Iceland. It would not be until the Reformation in the sixteenth century that a stronger Icelandic church came into its own.

King of tides

The Danish warlord Canute (c.994–1035) conquered England in 1016. After his conversion to Christianity, Canute earned a reputation as a wise and humble ruler. Legend has it that some of his subjects once attempted to praise Canute by claiming that he could command even the sea and it would obey him. To quiet their flattery, Canute placed his throne in the water and ordered the tide to turn back. When it did not, he forced his followers to admit that there was a limit to his authority: "Let all men know how empty and worthless is the power of kings. For there is none worthy of the name but God, whom heaven, earth and sea obey."

since 997) with the blessing of Pope Sylvester II (r. 999–1003). Stephen's programme of Christianization was opposed by pagan factions, and he quashed an anti-Christian revolt in Transylvania in 1002. Nevertheless, Stephen laid down a constitution, creating ten new bishoprics and instituting Gran as the site of the archbishop's seat.

Pope Sylvester II

Sylvester was the first Frenchman to become pope. An avid reformer, Sylvester assumed responsibility for a papacy that had been plagued by years of corruption. Sylvester encouraged the spread of Christianity in Poland and Hungary, and he led the revival of philosophical, scientific, and mathematical studies in Europe. He is credited with the introduction of Arabic numerals to the West, and with the invention of the pendulum clock.

Hungary

Stephen was made the first king of Hungary in 1001 (having been duke of Hungary

Restoration of the papacy

By 1046 the papacy had once again fallen into disrepute. Three men, backed by

The first French pope, Sylvester II did much to restore the damaged reputation of the papacy and to aid learning throughout Europe.

different factions and noble families, vied for the position of pope. Seeking a legitimate pope who could crown him Holy Roman Emperor, the German king Henry III (r. 1039–56) convened a synod in the Italian town of Sutri to settle the dispute between Benedict IX (r. 1032–45), Sylvester III (r. 1045), and Gregory VI (r. 1045–46).

The claims of all three were quickly dismissed, and Suidger, a bishop from the German town of Bamberg, reluctantly accepted the position. Suidger, who took the name Clement II (r. 1046–47), marks the first in a long line of subsequent German popes who brought a Cluniac reforming influence to the Roman church.

Further reforms

Clement II's first major council met in Rome in 1047. Strict measures were put in place, including strong decrees supporting clerical celibacy and condemning simony, a practice that was widespread in the West at the time.

Building on Clement's work, Leo IX (r. 1049–54) is seen as the man who provided a new ideal for the office of pope. He travelled extensively, promoting the reform programme instituted by his predecessor and working closely with a host of rigorous-minded clergy. Two of these men (Stephen IX and Gregory VII) would go on to become reforming popes themselves on the pattern of Leo.

A modern day **cardinal** at the Vatican. Since the medieval era, cardinals meeting together in a process called the Conclave have been responsible for electing the new pope.

The College of Cardinals

Many of the problems plaguing the papacy arose from the way that new popes were appointed. In the face of growing popular and clerical demand, 113 bishops met in 1059 at the Lateran Synod to work out a new system for papal elections. The synod set out laws governing the election of a new pope by a congregation of bishops and other clergy known as the College of Cardinals.

This important development saw the appointment of the pope arising primarily from inside the church. This departed from the old system, which relied heavily on sponsorship from noble families or selection by the Holy Roman Emperor.

One of the central architects of the Lateran Synod was the papal adviser Hildebrand. The decisions made here prepared the groundwork for Hildebrand's major push for reordering the church. He continued the policy of organization and consolidation of power when he himself became pope in 1073.

Hildebrandian discipline

Hildebrand became pope by popular consensus, taking the name Gregory VII (r. 1073–85). Hildebrand had earned his reputation as a bishop and chief administrator, working for Pope Leo IX from 1049. Even before assuming the role of pope himself, he exerted great influence over the papacy and the programme of structural reform that followed in his wake is known as Hildebrandian.

Hildebrandian reforms were driven by the belief that the papacy functioned as a governmental institution, and thus legal and clerical structures were of utmost importance. To enforce discipline in the hierarchy, Gregory managed the higher clergy by strengthening decrees against simony and clerical marriage in 1074. Also central to the reforms was a ban on **lay investiture** – the appointment of bishops by authorities outside the church. The reforms served to lessen the ties a bishop might have to the local ruler and to increase his allegiance to Rome.

The measures were opposed, sometimes violently. King William I of England (r. 1066–87) baulked at the extent of Gregory's attempts to focus power in Rome. Philip I of France (r. 1060–1108) and Henry IV of Germany (r. 1056–1106) also proved especially resistant to the Hildebrandian regime.

The investiture struggle

In 1075 the German king Henry IV objected to Pope Gregory's ban on investiture since it meant that Henry had no control over powerful official appointments in his empire.

In 1076 Henry sponsored two synods, at Worms and Piacenza, at which Gregory's papacy was declared invalid. However, Gregory enjoyed more support and his position remained secure. In the same year he responded by excommunicating the king. Not only did this remove Henry from the church and deny him Christian communion, the pope emphasized that it also had the effect of releasing German nobles from their oaths of allegiance.

Henry the penitent

The threat to Henry's throne was severe and, in the face of rebellion, Henry travelled to Italy to subject himself to a programme of public penance in 1077 at Canossa. The event was historically significant in that it indicated to the other rulers of Western Europe the superior authority of the church, as well as the political consequences of excommunication.

Gregory restored Henry into the church, but the reconciliation was short-lived. Henry set up Clement III (r. 1080–1100) as a rival pope and in 1084 forced Gregory into exile (where he died in 1085). Henry's conflict with the pope was disastrous for the stability of his reign. The resulting unrest in church and state led to constant revolts and a looming civil war, averted only by Henry's death in 1106. The investiture struggle and its after effects contributed to the rise of feudalism and prince-fiefdoms in the medieval era.

The Great Schism of 1054 resulted in the division of Christian Europe.

> ### Norman expansion
>
> The Normans were a people largely from Viking and Frankish stock. Their outward expansion from the regions of northern France to occupy southern Italy (1054), England (1066), and Sicily (1091) would have a comprehensive effect on the culture and Christian traditions of Western Europe.

Road to schism

With the improved fortunes of Rome came an increase, once again, in tensions with Constantinople. The Western and Eastern traditions of the Christian church had long been at odds politically, linguistically, and theologically. Occasionally these differences had resulted in temporary schisms, but until now the conflicts had eventually been resolved.

The power of Constantinople

The Eastern emperor Constantine IX Monomachos (r. 1042–55) was seeking allies to defend against Norman expansion in southern Italy. In negotiations with Pope Leo IX, Monomachos agreed to hand over jurisdiction over the Italian churches of the region to the pope.

Patriarch Michael Cerularius (died c.1059) objected to the agreement and feared the dominance of papal influence. In defiance of his emperor's perceived sympathy with Rome, Cerularius enacted

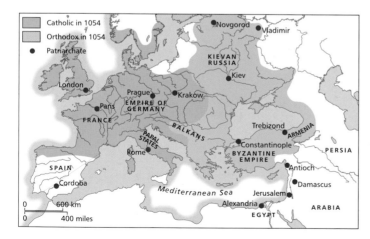

Catholic in 1054
Orthodox in 1054
● Patriarchate

Novgorod
Vladimir
KIEVAN RUSSIA
Kiev
London
Prague
Kraków
EMPIRE OF GERMANY
Paris
FRANCE
BALKANS
Trebizond
ARMENIA
PAPAL STATES
Constantinople
PERSIA
Rome
BYZANTINE EMPIRE
Antioch
SPAIN
Cordoba
Mediterranean Sea
Jerusalem
Damascus
Alexandria
ARABIA
EGYPT

0   600 km
0   400 miles

strict anti-Western measures. He forced all churches in the East to use Greek, and attacked Latin liturgical practices such as the use of *Filioque* (see chapter 5). The churches that refused to comply were shut down in 1052.

The primacy of Rome

The papacy responded by sending a legation led by Cardinal Humbert (died 1061). Humbert was a key Hildebrandian reformer and a champion of centralized Roman church authority. He objected to Cerularius's use of the title "ecumenical patriarch" and he demanded that Constantinople recognize the primacy of Rome. Cerularius refused. The failure of Humbert's legation resulted in formal declarations of excommunication from both sides, thus establishing the permanent breach between East and West in 1054 and formalizing the division of the church into the traditions now known as Orthodoxy and **Roman Catholicism**.

Anselm (c.1033–1109)

Anselm was archbishop of Canterbury in England from 1093. He was an influential church reformer and educator. As a philosopher, Anselm built on the Platonic tradition received through Augustine. He is a key figure in the school of "realism", and is also the source of the ontological argument for the existence of God.

The reconquest of Iberia

The Iberian Peninsula (modern-day Spain and Portugal) had been under Muslim control since the beginning of the eighth century. Known as Al-Andalus by its Moorish rulers, the region was, by the eleventh century, largely controlled by caliphs from the Umayyad dynasty based in the southern city of Cordoba.

The *Reconquista* refers to the long period from the eighth century onwards when Christians (mostly from small northern kingdoms) attempted to retake Al-Andalus. Owing to constant pressure from these assaults, the Arab caliphs recruited the Berbers – North African Muslim mercenaries – to aid in the defence of the territory. As the Berbers grew in numbers and strength, they too began to compete with the Arab rulers. Under these pressures the Umayyad caliphate collapsed in 1031 and the disparate armies of the *Reconquista* (often fighting with each other as much as with the Moors) began their advance southwards.

Iberian Christian advances

By 1034 the Christian Portuguese frontier was established at the river of Mondego. This in turn contributed to the creation of the kingdom of Galicia and Portugal in 1065.

The year 1034 also marked the height of the power of the king of Navarre, Sancho III "the Great" (r. 1000–35). As well as uniting various Iberian regions, Sancho did much to revive the church in Spain, including re-establishing the See of Pamplona, which was governed along Cluniac principles.

The Castilian military commander El Cid is depicted engaging in hand-to-hand combat. Detail from the 1344 manuscript *Chronicle of Spain*.

By 1077 the Castilian king Alfonso VI (r. 1072–1109) had proclaimed himself "emperor of all Spain". In 1085 Alfonso took the city of Toledo from the Moors. There he reinstated the influential diocese of Toledo under Archbishop Bernard de Sedirac (c.1050 – c.1125). Bernard, a Frenchman, was a Cluniac monk who also supported the reforming programme of Pope Gregory VII and did much to draw the Spanish church closer to Rome.

Iberian Muslim challenge

Alfonso's success and the Christian advance southwards were halted by the reinvigorated Berber armies of the Almoravid dynasty, which had come to power after the collapse of the Umayyad caliphate, and which practised a more vigorous form of Islam than their predecessors. Eventually the combined armies of the Spanish kingdoms were soundly defeated by the Berbers under the command of Yusuf ibn Tashfin in 1086.

The mercenary chief

It was only under the influence of the mercenary Rodrigo Diaz (c.1040–99) that Christian fortunes were revived. Diaz had earned his reputation as a soldier of fortune leading both Muslim and Christian armies and he was popularly known as El Cid (the chief). In 1094 a major victory was won for the Christians when El Cid conquered the Moorish city of Valencia after a two-year siege. El Cid ruled the city as his own principality, employing both Christians and

Muslims in his army and city administration, until his death in 1099.

Great buildings

A number of significant religious buildings and sites were either founded or destroyed in the eleventh century.

1009

Systematic destruction of the Church of the Holy Sepulchre in Jerusalem by the caliph Hakim. Rebuilding would not begin until the following century.

1037

Building of the Cathedral of Holy Wisdom in Kiev.

c.1050

Pecherska Lava (Monastery of the Caves) founded in Kiev.

1065

King Edward the Confessor rebuilds Westminster Abbey in England.

1070

The construction of the cathedral at the pilgrimage city Santiago de Compostela begins in Spain.

Canute the Holy (1080–86)

Canute IV became king of Denmark in 1080. He was a fervent supporter of Christianity and passed laws for the care of the poor and sick. His abortive 1085 invasion of England marked one of the last times in history that a Viking army was assembled to invade another European country. Canute was killed by pagan rebels in 1086 and is considered a martyr and the patron saint of Denmark by the Roman Catholic Church.

Road to Crusade

In 1028 the Eastern emperor Romanus III (r. 1028–34) allowed the patriarchate to persecute Monophysite Christians living in Syria. The subsequent flood of Monophysite refugees relocating to the surrounding Muslim territories sparked unrest in the regions that contributed to the eventual rise of the Seljuk dynasty. The Seljuks grew powerful, battling other Muslims for control of Jerusalem in 1070 before going on to defeat the forces of Constantinople at the Battle of Manzikert in 1071.

The First Crusade

This significant victory paved the way for Seljuk forces to control Asia Minor and Syria, regions that had previously served as recruiting grounds for the Byzantine army. Starved of resources and facing the increasing threat of Muslim forces, Emperor Alexius Comnenus (r. 1081–1118) requested help from the West. In spite of the breach that existed between Constantinople and Rome, Pope Urban II (r. 1088–99) answered the appeal. His proclamation of the First Crusade in 1095 called for Christian soldiers to liberate Jerusalem and protect Christendom against the Muslim invaders.

The Byzantine emperor Alexius Comnenus is depicted paying homage to Jesus Christ, who is seated on a throne.

The People's Crusade

The crusade was immediately popular, and sparked a religious revival especially among the poor. The promotion of war against non-Christians led to violent outbreaks against European Jews, who were also plundered to help pay for the armed pilgrimage to the Holy Land.

Many fighting groups were organized. One zealous preacher, Peter the Hermit (c.1050–1115), gained a massive following and in 1096 headed an excursion to the Middle East. Composed of over 20,000 untrained and ill-disciplined peasants, his "People's Crusade" proved to be a threat and a burden to the very regions it was supposed to protect. Despite the Turks' comprehensive defeat of the ragged army at Civetot in 1096, Peter escaped and was present at the crusaders' capture of Jerusalem.

Capturing the Holy Land

The official fighting force that Pope Urban assembled was composed of several armies from France and southern Italy. They fared better than Peter's untrained mob, and the city of Antioch was recaptured in 1098, with Jerusalem taken a year later. Victory was accompanied by a mass slaughter of the Jews and Muslims living in the city.

The First Crusade had achieved its main aims, yet the European occupation of the Holy Land was not complete and the Muslim presence remained a force in the region. Christian city-states, known as the Latin states, were set up at Antioch, Tripoli, Edessa, and Jerusalem. Duke Godfrey of Bouillon (1058–1100) was made the first Latin ruler of the Holy City in 1099, although he declined to assume a royal title. When Godfrey died, his brother Baldwin was not as reluctant and he was crowned king of Jerusalem on Christmas Day in the year 1100.

View of the city of Jerusalem from the Mount of Olives.

The Twelfth Century

War appears to overshadow Christendom's concerns in the twelfth century. As Western crusaders attempted to re-conquer the Holy Lands, they exacerbated tensions with the East. Christians challenged the Moors in Spain just as Islam continued to threaten Constantinople. Pagan Slavs and Christian heretics were violently suppressed in the East, while successive European kings attempted to dominate the Western church. Yet this fierce era also enjoyed the fruits of peace. Monasteries embraced simplicity, learning, and radical service to the poor. Mystics advised princes how to pray. Hospitals and universities came to prominence. Literacy, art, and law reached a level of sophistication not yet seen in Christendom.

The Latin states

The crusaders imposed a brutal rule over their newly captured city-states (see chapter 10), with many Muslim and Jewish inhabitants massacred. Control over the Latin states proved difficult to maintain, and Muslim armies led by Zangi (died 1146) captured Edessa in 1144. Fear that Jerusalem would also soon fall provoked Pope Eugenius III (r. 1145–53) to proclaim a Second Crusade in 1147.

Crusades against Christians

The crusaders' ostensible aim had been to defend the Byzantine empire against the Muslim threat, yet conflicts between Western and Eastern Christendom continued in the Middle East. After a successful crusading campaign, the Norman prince Bohemond (c.1052–1111) took control of Antioch rather than returning it to the possession of Emperor Alexius I in Constantinople. Alexius and Bohemond fought over the territory between 1105 and 1107, with Bohemond even gaining papal blessing for his "crusade" against the Christian emperor.

The power and wealth of the Church was displayed through its art and architecture. Here, gold-leaf mosaics adorn the Byzantine Basilica of San Marco, Venice, Italy.

Below: The Grand Master's Palace for the Knights of Malta, in La Valletta, Malta. Built 1570–80 by Girolmu Cassar.

Right: Nineteenth-century artist's representation of the Knights Templar, who are wearing their distinctive tabard with the cross of St George.

Temples and hospitals

The Knights Templar were a military religious order founded c.1118 with the original purpose of protecting crusaders and pilgrims as they travelled to the Holy Land. The Templars soon became powerful throughout the Holy Land and Europe, which contributed to political tensions, and to their eventual suppression in the fourteenth century.

The Knights Hospitaller were founded not later than c.1108 with the intention of caring for sick, poor, and wounded pilgrims. Under the leadership of Raymond du Puy (1083–1160) the influence of the order (made up of both men and women) soon spread throughout the Holy Land and Western Europe. The Knights of the Order of the Hospital of St John continue to exist today as the Knights of Malta. The order lies behind the foundation of many hospitals and the creation of the St John's Ambulance service in modern Britain.

Templer.

The Second Crusade

The influential Abbot Bernard of Clairvaux (1090–1153) was commissioned to organize and popularize the Second Crusade. The army – a combination of French and German troops led by the Roman king Conrad III (r. 1138–52) and the French king Louis VII (r. 1137–80) – ransacked Byzantine territory as it marched through on its way to Jerusalem, which led to deeper mistrust between East and West. They did not meet with success. Conrad was defeated in 1147 by Seljuk Turks; Louis was defeated the following year; and the crusaders were forced to withdraw from Damascus. Edessa was totally lost in 1145. In October 1187 the celebrated Muslim leader Saladin (1138–93) captured Jerusalem, and subsequently routed the crusaders from many of their fortified cities.

Maronite Church

This Syrian Christian church is predominantly based in Lebanon (where it currently constitutes the largest single religious group), with members found throughout the Middle East, as well as in North and South America. The Maronites trace their origins to the fifth-century teaching of Maron (died c.410). In the seventh and eighth centuries, the Maronites rejected the Third Council of Constantinople (the Sixth General Council; see chapter 6, **Two natures**) and were estranged from the wider church. Following their assistance to the crusaders in Syria, the Maronites were brought back into communion with Rome in 1182.

Bernard of Clairvaux

This French Cistercian monk stands as a towering figure in the twelfth century, and he was involved in most of the significant issues of the day. As a theologian Bernard is known primarily for developing the concept of the church as the "bride of Christ", and for being a pioneer of the Devotion to the Blessed Virgin Mary. Unlike most of his contemporaries Bernard opposed the persecution of the Jews.

The sultan Saladin. He led his armies against the Crusaders, taking many cities including Jerusalem.

Northern Crusades

The Crusades against Islam were accompanied by military adventures against the pagans of northern Europe and the Baltic states. The missionary Vicelin (c.1090–1154) had already been preaching peacefully among the tribes of northern Germany, but his small successes were swept away by Saxon and Danish crusades against the Wends in 1147. King Erik IX of Sweden (ruled c.1156–60) is reputed to have led a crusade against the Finns in the 1150s. King Canute VI of Denmark (r. 1182–1202), with the strong support of his archbishop Absalon (1128–1201), conquered the Pomeranian Slavs in 1184. The Baltic regions (present-day Latvia, Lithuania, and Estonia) were also subjected to forced conversions and military conquest following the crusade in 1193 sponsored by Pope Celestine III (r. 1191–98).

Iberian crusade

The 1147 crusade was also waged against Moorish Spain and Portugal as part of the *Reconquista*. That year, English crusaders aided Alfonso, since 1139 first king of Portugal (died 1185), in the siege and conquest of Lisbon. Some crusaders continued their journey to the Holy Land, but most stayed and fought the Moors throughout the region. Also starting in 1147 as part of the crusade, with the help of the French, the count of Barcelona, Ramón Berenguer IV (born c.1114, ruled 1131–62), invaded Moorish Valencia and reconquered Catalonia by 1148.

The Third Crusade

The rise of Saladin led to panic in Christendom. Faced with the prospect of losing all Christian presence in the Holy Land, Pope Gregory VIII (r. 1187) strove to unite the warring European kingdoms in a renewed effort to take Jerusalem. Gregory's efforts led to European truces and the organization of the Third Crusade under his successor Pope Clement III (r. 1187–91). Taking place between 1189 and 1192, this venture became known as the "Crusade of Kings" because of the involvement of Emperor Frederick I "Barbarossa" (r. 1152–90), Philip II of France (r. 1180–1223), and the "Lionheart", Richard I of England (r. 1189–99).

Even though much lost territory was regained, the crusade is not considered a success. When the German army collapsed after the death by drowning of Barbarossa in 1190, the French and English quarrelled, leaving Richard in sole command. Acre was retaken after a long and costly siege, but Jerusalem remained under the control of the Muslims, with Richard and Saladin coming to a three-year truce during which unarmed Christian pilgrims were allowed to enter the city. The failures and unrest following the Third Crusade would lead to the initiation of the Fourth Crusade and the Western sack of Constantinople in 1204.

East

Largely because of the effect of the Crusades on an already fractious Eastern Europe, both the Byzantine empire and the Byzantine church encountered considerable challenges in the twelfth century. Faced with wars of aggression from the Muslims in the south, as well as the ever-present threat of crusader invasion from the West, Constantinople looked to exert its dominance over its frontier territories.

Emperor Manuel Comnenus (r. 1143–80) led successful campaigns against Serbia (1150–52) and Hungary (1168), doing much to revive the fortunes of Constantinople. However, his reign represents the last high point for the empire; after his death a succession of poor leaders would contribute to the permanent decline of Byzantium and the dissipation of all that had been gained.

Byzantine rebellions

The heretical Bogomil movement (see chapter 9) had spread rapidly throughout the Balkans and Asia Minor. Among the Bulgarians, Bosnians, and Serbs, the Bogomil faith was closely connected to patriotic ideas of independence from Constantinople. These rebellious feelings were exacerbated by the imprisonment and execution of Bogomil leaders in Constantinople in 1110, and by violent repression in Serbia in 1180.

In that same year, unpopular and badly administered tax increases led to major revolts in Bulgaria and the loss of Byzantine control over the region. Years of rebellions followed, until the Byzantine empire recognized the independence of Bulgaria and Serbia in 1186.

Lalibela

In 1189 the ruling member of the Ethiopian Zagwe dynasty, Emperor Gebre Mesqel Lalibela (1172–1212), ordered the construction of the monolithic stone churches at Roha (now known as Lalibela). The thirteen churches were hewn from the rock, with their construction probably not completed for the next two centuries.

The sunken, rock-hewn church of Bet Giyorgis (St George), Lalibela, northern Ethiopia.

Opposite: South aisle of Canterbury Cathedral. Archbishop Thomas Becket's martyrdom here in 1170 sent shockwaves throughout European Christendom.

West

In the West, as in the East, the historical relationship between church and state had been filled with both mutual dependence and mutual antagonism. Kings and emperors needed the church to legitimize their claims to rule, and valued the vast material resources and moral authority that came with an alliance with the papacy. Yet at the same time secular rulers often resented the power of the church, which claimed, in principle, to be serving a master higher than any earthly ruler. Likewise, the church often looked to kings' coffers when it needed money and to the emperor's troops when it needed protection, although popes and bishops were loath to cede their authority to the state.

The investiture struggle of Henry IV (see chapter 10) did not end with his death in 1106. Various European kings found themselves embroiled in conflict with bishops who refused to pay homage or to accept priests who had been placed in their position by state rulers rather than the church.

Bishops against kings

In England, Archbishop Anselm of Canterbury excommunicated any layperson who installed priests, and any priest who accepted such a commission. Against the feudal system that demanded fealty in return for land, in 1100 Anselm refused to pay homage to the English king Henry I (r. 1100–35) in return for his landholdings, an act which seriously undermined the king's position. A compromise was reached with Henry in 1107 when the king agreed to give up his claim to lay investiture and in return priests would pay homage to him before being consecrated. The papacy had similar conflicts with Philip I in France and, most significantly, Emperor Henry V (r. 1106–25) in Germany.

The Concordat of Worms

In the first year of his papacy Pope Callistus II (r. 1119–24) excommunicated Henry V and opposed Gregory VIII (1118), the antipope (a person set up as pope in opposition to the person currently elected to the see or held to be in lawful possession of the office) endorsed by the emperor. With the aid of German princes, Henry and Callistus eventually came to a peaceful agreement, and the investiture struggle was formally resolved at a meeting in the German city of Worms in 1122. As a result of the Concordat of Worms, the emperor renounced his right to investiture and granted free elections of bishops to the church. The pope agreed to allow the emperor's presence at the consecration, and formalized the extent to which the emperor could adjudicate in the selection process of church officials.

The English pope

Nicholas Breakspear (c. 1100–59) became Pope Hadrian IV in 1154, the only Englishman ever to hold that office. Before becoming pope, Hadrian had spent time as a papal legate in Scandinavia. There he organized and reformed the churches of Norway and Sweden.

Emperor Barbarossa

As German king and emperor, Frederick Barbarossa reignited the tensions between church and state that had persisted after the Concordat of Worms. He was crowned emperor in 1155 by Hadrian, but soon came to resent the pope's assertion that the crown was a gift of the church. In 1157 Barbarossa distinguished between the *sacrum imperium* (holy empire) and the spiritual jurisdiction of the holy church or *sancta ecclesia*. In 1160, after an internal church debate over who should become the next pope, Barbarossa supported Victor IV (r. 1159–64) against the more popular candidate Alexander III (1159–81). The resulting church schism lasted seventeen years, and politically served to isolate Germany from the Lombards, French, and Normans. Finally, Barbarossa was forced to submit to Pope Alexander with the Treaty of Venice in 1177.

The troublesome priest

Archbishop of Canterbury from 1162, Thomas Becket (c.1118–70) opposed the attempts of King Henry II (r. 1154–89) to exert authority over the English church. In 1170 he was murdered in Canterbury Cathedral by four zealous knights, probably acting on an intemperate pronouncement from Henry. Thomas's martyrdom sparked outrage throughout Europe, and Henry was forced to do public penance in 1174. Becket's shrine remained a principal pilgrimage destination until it was demolished by Henry VIII in 1538.

The simple life

As the church grew richer and more powerful, reform movements also grew, led by churchmen who wanted to restore the original purity and simplicity of Christianity. Some of these movements were sanctioned by the church, while others attracted opposition and sometimes violent persecution.

Cistercians

Known as the White Monks, the Cistercian Order was founded in 1098, and came to prominence under the influence of Bernard of Clairvaux. By Bernard's death in 1153 there were 345 monasteries and nunneries established throughout Europe and the Eastern regions loyal to Rome. Cistercians promoted a strict rule and forbade ostentatious displays of wealth or power. They encouraged instead the practice of simplicity and manual labour; they became known for their agricultural expertise. The Cistercian way of life and the organization of Cistercian monasteries profoundly influenced other monastic movements in the Middle Ages.

Waldenses

The exact origins of the Waldense (or Valdense) movement is uncertain, and the term describes a number of similar groups operating throughout Europe. The most prominent of these centred around Peter Waldo (or Valdes, died c. 1218), a rich merchant from Lyons who gave away all his money to the poor and taught a life of simplicity. In 1179 Pope Alexander III gave Waldo his approval, provided that he preach only with the permission of the clergy. When Waldo and his followers broke this ban on unofficial preaching they were excommunicated and expelled in 1184. The Waldenses were considered to be schismatics and heretics, and they themselves soon splintered into different factions after the death of their leader. In later centuries many of the groups connected to the Protestant Reformation would claim affinity with the Waldensian movement.

Rise of the university

Alongside Christian warfare and conflict in this era must also be placed the flowering of Christian philosophy, debate, and reason. Great universities, such as those in Paris and Oxford, had their beginnings in the twelfth century. Originally founded as centres for theological study and the education of clergy, the universities soon became focal points for academic controversy, with some lecturers attaining fame or notoriety beyond the walls of the lecture hall.

Yes and No

Peter Abelard was lecturing in Paris about 1115. He attracted large audiences for his dialectical style of teaching and the daring theological conclusions that he reached. In 1121 the Council of Soissons condemned his views on the Trinity without Abelard being present to defend himself, but he continued to work. His most influential theological training manual, *Yes and No*, was produced in 1122. The book collected apparently contradictory statements from the Bible and from early Church Fathers, and required students to reconcile them while recognizing different expressions of authority.

Héloïse (1101–64)

While teaching in Paris, Abelard met and secretly married Héloïse, the niece of Fulbert, canon of Notre-Dame. The affair sparked an outcry; Héloïse was sent off to a convent and, notoriously, Abelard was castrated by a gang of men hired by Fulbert before retreating to a monastery himself in 1117.

The laws of the church

The monk and papal adviser Gratian (died c.1160) is considered to be the father of canon law. Like Abelard, Gratian collected together the occasionally contradictory thoughts of disparate authorities throughout the ages. However, where Abelard was interested in theological debate, Gratian focused on issues of church discipline. His *Treatise on Laws* (not earlier than 1139) is a collection of almost 4,000 texts and pronouncements from Church Fathers, popes, and councils, presented in a structured and harmonious form. Gratian's contribution was to make canon law (the regulations of the Christian church) a subject separate from theological doctrine and to provide a legal framework for the church's organization. The *Treatise on Laws* was taught in Oxford and Paris, and was a principal text for the University of Bologna, which became the European centre for canon and civil law.

Hildegard of Bingen (1098–1179)

A German Benedictine abbess, Hildegard was famous for her mystical theology, writing, and wide learning, which included natural history, musical composition, and medicine. From 1141, Hildegard experienced a number of visions, or "showings", which she wrote down in her principal work *Scivias* (*Know the Ways*). The mystical homilies were closely scrutinized (and approved) by the archbishop of Mainz around 1150 and by Pope Eugenius III and Bernard of Clairvaux in 1147.

This medieval illustration depicts Hildegard of Bingen receiving and recording one of her visions of the Divine.

Master of the sentences

The "master of the sentences", Peter Lombard (c.1095–1169), trained at Bologna before moving to Paris, where he was elected bishop in 1159. His *Book of Sentences* (completed c.1158) compiled the thoughts of Christian writers from the Church Fathers all the way up to near contemporaries including Abelard and Gratian. *Sentences* also introduced Western readers to the thoughts of Greek Fathers such as John of Damascus. By applying objective organizational principles and avoiding extremes, *Sentences* produced a clear summary of Christian thought and doctrine that became the standard textbook for university education throughout Europe well into the seventeenth century.

The Latin Qur'an

The abbot of Cluny, Peter the Venerable (c.1092–1156), was a friend of Peter Abelard and Bernard of Clairvaux, and was celebrated as an educational reformer. Peter wrote theological arguments against Judaism and Islam, and was responsible for the first translation of the Qur'an into Latin, a work completed in 1143.

Left: Details from an illuminated manuscript edition of Peter Lombard's *Sentences*. The book remained a standard university text for 500 years. This particular manuscript dates from the fourteenth century.

The Thirteenth Century

The thirteenth century saw the reign of the great medieval popes and the birth of major religious orders. It brought the development of technologies, philosophies, and theologies that continue to affect Christianity today. Despite attempts at reconciliation following the aftermath of the failed Fourth Crusade, the gap between East and West proved too great to close. Christians in large swathes of the East and south adapted to life outside of Christendom. Paradoxically, the Russian Orthodox Church enjoyed favour under the pagan Mongolian Empire, while the Roman church struggled at the hands of its Christian kings.

West

Vicar of Christ

Historians consider the time in office of Pope Innocent III (r. 1198–1216) a high point of the papacy of the Middle Ages. As the leader of Christendom, Innocent saw himself as occupying a space below God but above other men, and he was the first pope to make regular use of the title "Vicar of Christ". Innocent oversaw the reform and reorganization of church hierarchy and administration. He supported Francis

Pope Innocent III approves the new Franciscan order at the Lateran Council.

of Assisi (1181–1226), aided Dominic (c.1170–1221) in establishing his new order, and convened the influential Fourth Lateran Council in 1215.

Lateran Council

The council which met at the Lateran Palace in Rome marks the summation of much Christian thought and practice of the era. It established policies that would shape the church's agenda for centuries to come. The council confirmed the official doctrine of the eucharist, using the term **"transubstantiation"** for the first time. Yearly confession and Communion were made mandatory. Rebuttals of the Albigensian, Cathar (see below), and Waldensian (see chapter 11) heresies were formulated. Clerical abuse of **indulgences** (see chapter 15) was curbed, and the church's participation in trial by ordeal was forbidden. The new Franciscan Order was confirmed, provision was made for the Rule of the Dominicans, and the creation of future orders was curtailed in an effort to encourage church discipline and unity.

Political intervention

Politically, Innocent III asserted the right of the Roman church to oversee the affairs of kings, princes, and governors. He intervened in the coronation of the Holy Roman Emperor, supporting first Otto IV (r. 1198–1218) and then Frederick II (r. 1212–50) according to the strength of their fealty to the church. In English affairs, Innocent excommunicated King John (r. 1199–1216) in 1207 when the king refused to accept Stephen Langton (died 1228) as archbishop of Canterbury. John was forced to submit, and Langton was duly installed in 1213. Innocent's considerable influence was also known in France, Denmark, Spain, Portugal, Italy, the German and Baltic states, Cyprus, and Armenia. However, it was the unintended consequences of Innocent's earliest intervention that proved to have the greatest impact on Christendom.

Elizabeth of Hungary (1207–31)

The daughter of King Andrew II of Hungary (r. 1205–35), from an early age Elizabeth gained a reputation as an extreme ascetic and a holy woman. When her husband, Louis IV of Thuringia, died on crusade in 1227 Elizabeth became a Franciscan nun, serving the poor in Marburg. She was responsible for building one of Europe's first orphanages. The Gothic cathedral Elisabethkirche was built in her honour and her remains were interred there in 1236.

Major orders

The thirteenth century saw the creation of three major religious orders that remain active to this day.

Dominicans: Dominic had been active in preaching against the Albigensians since 1203. In 1206, with the support of the bishop of Toulouse, he founded a teaching convent for women. In 1216 Dominic established the Order of Preachers (also known as Black Friars in England). Dominican men and women became known for their great learning, and many universities were founded under their auspices. Dominicans were at the forefront of missionary activities in the New World and the East.

Franciscans: Francis of Assisi renounced worldly possessions after a pilgrimage to Rome in 1205, founding a society for preaching, poverty, and penance in 1209. From 1245 onwards adherents to the original ideal of poverty clashed with moderates who allowed corporate ownership of property. Today the Franciscans are composed of three orders – the Conventuals, the Observants, and the Capuchins.

Poor Clares: Francis founded a second order in partnership with Clare of Assisi (c.1193–1253). Established c.1213, the Poor Clare communities spread rapidly through Italy, France, and Spain. The Poor Clares' strict rule included perpetual fasting, sleeping on boards, and complete silence. Adherents to a milder version of the rule instituted by Pope Urban IV (r. 1261–64) in 1263 became known as Urbanists. A reform in the fifteenth century led by Abbess Collete (1381–1447) resulted in the Colletines, and another reform in the sixteenth century produced the Capuchinesses. All three branches still exist today. Devoted to prayer, fasting, penance, and manual labour, together they constitute the most austere order for women in the Roman Catholic Church.

Francis of Assisi (left) worked closely with Clare of Assisi (right) to found monastic orders for men and women.

The Fourth Crusade

The previous crusades had failed to secure Jerusalem or halt the advance of Islam. In 1202 Innocent launched the Fourth Crusade in yet another attempt to recover Egypt, North Africa, and the Holy Land. Europe's nobility were drained and weary from previous campaigns, and relatively few knights joined the crusade. In addition, the burden placed on the territories through which the crusaders had to march on their way to Jerusalem was great, leading once again to friction and instability within Christendom's borders. As a result, the army mustered by the pope was soon deflected from its original purpose.

The expense of transporting large numbers of troops was one of the main reasons the Fourth Crusade failed. *Departure of a Boat for the Crusades*, detail from a Galacian vellum manuscript, mid-thirteenth century.

Sack of Constantinople

The journey to the Holy Land required the assistance of Venetian ships. When the crusaders could not afford to pay the charges demanded of them, their leader Boniface of Montferrat (c. 1150–1207) and the Doge of Venice, Enrico Dandolo (c. 1107–1205), agreed instead to join forces and invade Constantinople. In 1204, against the express commands of the pope and some of the commanders present, the armies of the Christian West sacked and conquered the principal city of the Christian East. The Greek patriarch was removed from power and the Venetian Thomas Morosini installed in his place.

With the creation of the Latin empire of Constantinople, the advance of the Fourth Crusade on the Holy Land was abandoned and a union of sorts between the Eastern and Western churches was established under Pope Innocent III. However, the situation was unpopular, unstable, and temporary, with the Byzantines repeatedly attempting to regain control. The events of the Latin empire cast a long shadow over the future development of church and state in the West and in the East, entrenching bitterness between the two cultures and undermining Byzantium's ability to defend itself against future threats to its territory.

The final crusades

The abortive Fourth Crusade gave rise to further popular movements, not all of them welcomed or sanctioned by the church. The spontaneous Children's Crusade of 1212 involved thousands of poor children and peasants marching to Jerusalem. The ragged group dissolved at Genoa, with many participants returning home at the urging of the pope. From 1219 three more military crusades were raised in the attempt to win Egypt, retake Jerusalem, and defend Christian territories in Syria. The decisive loss of the last Christian stronghold in Acre in 1291 brought an end to the era of official crusades. However, crusading ideals continued to influence Christian military and missionary endeavours well into the sixteenth century and beyond.

How Constantinople was Attacked and Taken, by Loyset Liefet (1420–79).

Cathars and Albigensians

Since the time of the early Church Fathers, several heretical sects have been known as *Cathari*, a term that derives from the Greek for "pure". By the medieval era, the label was exclusively applied to those who followed a Manichaean dualistic religion that demonized the body and denied the incarnation of Christ (see chapter 2). The Cathars of the twelfth century were heavily influenced by the Bogomils from the East (see chapter 9) and they shared the politically subversive aspects of that Bulgarian sect. The movement was widespread throughout Germany, Italy, and France, and the term "heretic" is synonymous with "Cathar" in medieval church documents.

Many of the findings of the Fourth Lateran Council of 1215, the formation of the Dominican preaching order in 1216, and the institution of the Inquisition from 1233 were developed as responses to the Cathar heresy. In France the Cathars were known as Albigensians because they were based around the town of Albi in the Languedoc region. In 1208 Pope Innocent III sent Peter of Castelnau on a preaching mission. When Peter was murdered a long and bloody war followed. By 1229 the Languedoc culture had been decimated and the region incorporated under the rule of northern France. Further action by the Inquisition ensured that the Albigensian faith all but disappeared by 1300.

Inquisition

The growing threat of heretical groups gave rise to the formation of the dedicated tribunal known as the Inquisition, formalized by Pope Gregory IX (r. 1227–41) between 1231 and 1235. Suspects were invited to confess voluntarily. Those that did not were subject to examination, with the testimony of two witnesses considered sufficient for conviction. The use of torture was permitted by Pope Innocent IV (r. 1243–54) in 1252. The church oversaw mild penalties, but obstinate heretics were occasionally handed over to the state authorities for execution.

East

Orthodoxy and union

In 1261, Michael VIII Palaeologus (r. 1259–82) regained control of Constantinople, finally bringing an end to the Latin empire of the East. In order to protect against further threats, especially from Charles of Anjou (king of Naples and Sicily, r. 1266–85), Emperor Michael sought an expedient alliance with Rome. In return for the allegiance of the Orthodox Church, Pope Gregory X (r. 1271–76) agreed to provide financial support and check the ambitions of Latin warlords with designs on Constantinople.

Official union

In 1274 Pope Gregory convened the Second Council of Lyons, attended by some 1,600 churchmen, including 500 bishops. Legates from the emperor and representatives of the Orthodox Church were also present, providing assurances that they were ready to submit to the authority of the Roman church. The Orthodox churchmen accepted the Roman doctrines of **purgatory**, the sacraments, and the primacy of the pope. At a special High Mass celebrated by Pope Gregory on 29 June, the Greek clergy recited the Nicene Creed and sang the *Filioque* clause three times.

Popular opposition

The Byzantine emperor and the Roman pope had achieved their aim of closing the schism between East and West. Yet the politically motivated union was not popular with wider Orthodoxy, and the submission to Rome was soon repudiated by Greek clergy in defiance of their emperor's wishes.

The patriarch of Constantinople, Joseph I Galesiotes (died 1282), abdicated in 1275, and was replaced by John Bekkos (c.1230–97), a patriarch loyal to the union. Bekkos defended the Council of Lyons on intellectual and theological grounds, while the emperor used military might to enforce his will. Ultimately this combination of argument and compulsion was unsuccessful in converting the majority of the Orthodox to the cause. After Michael's death in 1282, Bekkos was considered by many to be a traitor to the Orthodox faith. He was forced into exile, where he died in 1297.

Serbia

The consequences of Latin influence in Constantinople were being felt elsewhere in the realms of Eastern Orthodoxy.

Sava (or Sabas, c.1175–1235) was the son of Stephen Nemanja, a strong Serbian prince (ruling 1168–96) responsible for uniting much of Serbia as a nation against Byzantine rule. Sava became a monk in 1191, and he and his father founded the Hilandar monastery on Mount Athos c.1197. The monastery would go on to become a major centre for Serbian culture. Sometime between 1206 and 1208 Sava left the monastery to return to his native Serbia. The country was in disarray, in part because of power struggles prompted by the Western presence. As king of Serbia, Sava's brother Stephen Nemanjich (died 1227) enjoyed close ties with Rome (having been crowned by the pope in 1217), but the political situation proved unstable and the nation was on the verge of civil war. Sava countered the Latin influence by forging strong links with the patriarch of Nicea and organizing an independent Serbian Church hierarchy loyal to Eastern Orthodoxy. The autocephalous Serbian Church was established in 1219, with the Orthodox Church in Bosnia and Herzegovina also tracing its roots back to this event.

Christianity and the Mongol empire

Nestorian (see chapter 4) Christianity had been present in Mongolian culture since the seventh century, but it was the rapid expansion of the Mongol empire under Genghis Khan (c.1165–1227) and his successors that brought the most significant opportunities for Christian contact.

A Nestorian wall painting of Palm Sunday found in Chotscho, Chinese Turkestan.

1240

Pope Gregory IX sends a missionary group of Dominicans to the Georgian city of Tiflis, where they encounter the Mongolian court.

1245

Pope Innocent IV sends four Franciscan missions, one of which is led by Giovanni da Plano Carpini (c.1180–1252). Carpini became an early and important Western chronicler of Central Asia, although the mission was not a success.

1253

The Franciscan William of Rubruck (c.1200 – after 1256) travels to the

Mongolian capital Karakorum. He finds a religiously tolerant culture with evidence of Nestorian, Cathar, and Muslim believers.

1271

Kublai Khan (r. 1260–94) sends a letter to Pope Gregory X (1271–76) requesting Christian teachers to be sent to aid the Nestorian church already present in the Chinese Mongolian empire.

1275

Marco Polo (r. 1245–1324) journeys to the home of Kublai Khan (near modern-day Beijing).

1289

Pope Nicholas IV (1288–92) sends the Franciscan Giovanni of Monte Corvino (1246–1328) to China. En route, Giovanni sees some missionary success in India in 1291. Despite Nestorian resistance, he builds a Catholic church in Beijing in 1299 and translates the Psalms and the New Testament into Mongolian. By the time of his death, Giovanni is reported to have overseen the conversion of 6,000 people. With the Chinese overthrow of the Mongolians and the establishment of the Ming dynasty in 1368, Christianity is once again driven underground.

1295

Ghazan Khan (r. 1295–1304) declares Islam the official religion of the Middle Eastern (Ilkhanid) division of the Mongolian empire.

Russia

In Russia, two main military–political factors shaped the development of the Orthodox Church. One was Mongolian

The armies of Genghis Khan fight European soldiers in this detail from the early fifteenth-century manuscript *The Travels of Marco Polo*.

advance and rule under Batu Khan (ruling the Golden Horde 1227–55); the other was the actions of Prince Alexander Nevsky (c. 1220–63) against the Latin armies of the West.

The Golden Horde

By 1223 Mongol invaders had begun raids on Russian territory, and by 1237 the invasion was fully underway. In 1238 the invaders sacked and burned Moscow. In 1240 the principal city of Kiev was conquered and Russia came under the rule of the Mongolian Golden Horde, led by Batu, grandson of Genghis Khan.

Initially, the sweep of the Mongolian army across Russia wreaked havoc on the church. Monasteries and church buildings were burned and looted, while monks and priests were killed or captured. Yet the social

instability brought by the raiders eventually led to the consolidation of the church as the sole remaining national, cultural, and political centre of Russian life. This was recognized by the new Mongolian rulers, who granted the church special privileges. A charter of immunity (*iarlyk*) was granted to the church in 1267. The decree meant that the clergy were free from being pressed into labour or military service, and it exempted the church from taxation by Mongol or Russian authorities.

Eastern Rite Catholic Church

The division between Eastern and Western Christianity has not always been clear. Some churches retained Orthodox structures and liturgy while remaining under the authority of Rome. These groups are sometimes called Uniate churches. The early development of the Eastern Rite Catholic Church arose from the 1246 agreement reached between Pope Innocent III and Daniel Romanovich (c.1201–64), ruler of the territory comprising much of modern-day Ukraine and Poland. Romanovich sought to be protected from the Mongolian invaders, and accepted the sovereignty of the pope in return for assistance. This development would come to fruition in the Union of Brest-Litovsk in 1596.

Mongolian alliance

At the same time as the Mongols were consolidating their rule over Russian territories, Prince Alexander Nevsky governed the principalities of Novgorod (1236–52), Kiev (1246–52), and Vladimir (1252–63). He allied himself with Batu Khan, suppressing rebellions and collecting taxes for the new rulers of Russia. Through his alliance with the Mongolians, Nevsky is credited with preserving and uniting a Russian culture that would otherwise have been destroyed. He was especially supported by the Russian Orthodox Church, which considers him a national saint.

The Battle on the Ice

Nevsky's contribution to Orthodoxy arises primarily from his defeat of Western invaders, which prevented Rome from dominating the Russian church. In 1240 Nevsky's army prevented Swedish forces from crossing the River Neva. At the same time, Pope Gregory IX sent German soldiers on a crusade to the Baltic, with the intent of Christianizing the pagans and exerting Roman control over the region. The Teutonic Knights continued their campaign into Russia. In 1242 Nevsky decisively defeated the mounted soldiers as they struggled on frozen ground near Lake Peipus in an engagement known as the "Battle on the Ice".

Alexander Nevsky is celebrated for stopping the Teutonic Knights from invading Russia. Fresco from the Archangel Cathedral, Moscow, Russia.

As a result, Orthodoxy affirmed its position as the predominant church tradition in Russia.

Teutonic Knights

This German religious and military order was initially founded as a hospital order, confirmed by Pope Clement III in 1199. The knights were active in Hungary (1211–25) and Prussia (from 1231), becoming powerful rulers in their own right. The character and importance of the order were decisively altered by the Reformation in the sixteenth century and the French Napoleonic advance in the nineteenth.

From Kiev to Vladimir

The greatest churchman from this era, Kirill III (or Cyril, died c. 1282), was consecrated **metropolitan** c. 1245. Under Kirill, the centre of the Orthodox Church migrated from the city of Kiev, devastated by the Mongols in 1240, to Vladimir, setting in motion a series of relocations that would only end when Moscow became the home of the Russian church in the 1320s (see chapter 13).

Kirill was convinced that the Mongolian occupation was a punishment from God on a Russian church that had grown lax and immoral. During his long service, Kirill worked to reorganize the church, taking advantage of its favoured status and forging close relationships with the khan in order to bring about restoration.

Council of Vladimir

Opposite: Nave of the medieval Sainte Marie-Madeleine basilica in Vezelay, France. The Church in France struggled bitterly against King Philip IV.

Sometime around 1270 Kirill obtained a copy of the Canon Law from the Bulgarian church. This valuable Greek document collected Orthodox doctrines, decrees, and interpretations dating from the twelfth century. With the Canon Law as a template,

in 1274 the Council of Vladimir issued a strict code rectifying errors in the liturgy and practice of the church in Russia. Under Kirill, Orthodox Christianity enjoyed a time of resurgence, and the institution of the church grew in wealth and power.

West

At the same time, in the West, the fortunes of the Roman church were not faring as well. In 1277 Giovanni Gaetani Orsini became Pope Nicholas III (r. 1277–80). As pope, Nicholas fought to protect Rome's independence from ambitious rulers such as Charles of Anjou and King Rudolf I of Germany (r. 1273–91). He was the first pope to make the Vatican his main residence, and expanded the papacy's territories, granting governorship to members of his own family. Nicholas earned a reputation for nepotism and was portrayed in Dante's *Inferno* (see chapter 13) as the chief example of simony.

Thomas Aquinas (1224–74)

The influence of this Doctor of the Church on Western philosophy, theology, and ethics continues to be felt. Born in Italy, Thomas Aquinas spent most of his working life teaching in Paris. His *Summa contra Gentiles* (1261–64) is a compendium of Christian apologetics and his *Summa Theologia* (1265–73) systematizes Christian thought following the philosophy of Aristotle.

Boniface supreme

The continuing power struggle between the church and various European kingdoms came to a crisis point during the papacy of Boniface VIII (r. 1294–1303). When he became pope, Boniface inherited a situation already unstable owing to internal and external conflicts. Boniface sought to uphold the tradition of supreme papal power associated with predecessors such as Gregory VII and Innocent III, but the political mood toward the church had shifted and he was unable to do so.

Boniface humiliated

In 1296 Boniface issued the **bull** *Clericis laicos.* The document was directed primarily against the kingdoms of England and France. It forbade any secular power from exacting taxes from the clergy without prior papal consent. Furthermore, any layman who accepted this money was threatened with excommunication.

Edward I "Longshanks" (r. 1272–1307) and Philip IV "the Fair" (r. 1285–1314) refused to comply. Edward effectively outlawed all clergy by withdrawing royal protection from the church in England. Philip halted the export of gold and valuables from France, thus depriving the church of its revenues from the realm. In the face of this challenge, Boniface was forced to concede in a humiliating, and public, climb-down.

Decline of the papacy

Boniface persisted in making claims for the papacy that were resisted by secular rulers. The struggle with Philip of France continued when Boniface issued the bull *Unam sanctam* in 1302, proclaiming that "it is altogether necessary to salvation for every human creature to be subject to the Roman pontiff". Philip responded by sending a force to arrest the pope. Boniface was briefly taken prisoner in 1303 and died a few weeks later. His passing marks the last in the line of medieval popes who could expect to enjoy absolute authority, and his failure is seen as a turning point in the history of Christianity in the West, leading Christians to think about their relation to the world in new ways.

The Fourteenth Century

Christians of this era continued to wrestle with the internal tensions that arise when a religion of humility, peace and powerlessness assumes responsibility for wealth, law, and command. At the same time as the Western church became more associated with rulers and kings, Christian groups emphasizing reform, poverty, and study flourished. The Great Catholic Schism was brought about as much by nationalism as by theology. In the East, the last of the Slavs converted to Christianity, Constantinople faced the prospect of life under Muslim rule, and the Russian Church enjoyed a mystical revival as it prepared to throw off the Mongol yoke.

West

Philip and Boniface

The beginning of the new century was not auspicious for the Roman church. The 1302 papal bull *Unam sanctam* failed to exert power over the secular states of Europe, instead resulting in a humiliating climb-down for the papacy. In 1303 further conflicts with Philip IV of France led to Pope Boniface VIII's capture by Guillaume de Nogaret (died 1313) and Sciarra Colonna (died 1329). Boniface died shortly thereafter and his successor, Benedict XI (1303–1304), only held the office of pope for a year. Following Benedict, the cardinals of the church were divided and the papacy was left in a precarious position. Further challenges to the integrity of the church came with the election of Pope Clement V (r. 1305–14).

Cupola of the Church of San Lorenzo, Florence, Italy.

Captivity of the church

Clement founded the universities at Orléans (1306) and Perugia (1308) to support the study of medicine and oriental languages. His Council of Vienne (1311–12) provided also for the study of Arabic, Chaldean, Hebrew, and Greek at the Universities of Paris, Oxford, Salamanca, Bologna, and Rome. However, Clement is best known not as a scholar but as the pope who was responsible for making the church subservient to French interests. In 1309 the centre of the church was moved from Rome to Avignon – a region adjoining the kingdom of France that had only relatively recently been cleared of Albigensians (see chapter 12). Avignon would become the home for the papacy until 1377, inaugurating a seventy-year period that is often referred to as the "Babylonian captivity of the church".

Templars suppressed

The riches amassed by the Knights Templar (see chapter 11) proved too much of a temptation for Philip IV. Besides furthering the work of universities, the Council of Vienne met primarily to settle the future of this military and religious order. At first, the council held that charges of immorality and heresy levelled against the Templars by Philip were baseless. But when Philip and his army arrived at Vienne in 1312, Pope Clement issued a decree suppressing the order and allowing Philip to appropriate much of their property.

Babylonian captivity

This phrase alludes to the capture and deportation of the Hebrew people as told in 2 Kings 24:25. It was first used by the poet Francisco Petrarch (1304–74) with reference to the situation of the church in Avignon. During the Protestant Reformation in 1520 Martin Luther (see chapter 15) would use the phrase to denounce various doctrines that he thought held the church in bondage. The life of the Orthodox Church under Ottoman rule in the sixteenth century is also sometimes referred to along similar lines.

Pope Boniface VIII died after being held in captivity by men acting for Philip IV of France.

Poverty or wealth?

Struggles over property would also become the flashpoint for Clement's successor, although in the case of Pope John XXII (r. 1316–34) the proprietor in question was not a warlord or a king, but Jesus Christ.

When Jacques Duèse became Pope John he continued to bind the church closer to the kingdom of France. He strengthened the papal presence in Avignon, following the policy that, when it came to the heart of the church, "Rome" was where the pope lived. Under John, Avignon became a centre for wealth, learning, and culture. It was home to many of the artists and scholars who would later be considered the founders of the humanist movement known as the Renaissance. Yet its celebration of the wealth and culture of Christian civilization led once again to a clash with those who sought to maintain the original Christian ideals of poverty and humility.

Francesco Petrarch, Italian poet, was the first to describe the early medieval era as "the Dark Ages".

Renaissance and humanism

The European Renaissance began in the fourteenth century. Culture experienced a renewal of interest in the classical world and Greek history, poetry, and philosophy. This emphasis on the classical "humanities" is also known as humanism. Humanist writers of this period were not necessarily setting themselves against religion. Indeed, the leading figures of Renaissance humanism were often clergy or closely allied with Christian movements and ideas. Nevertheless, humanists tended to treat the church as a secular institution, and their interest in pagan culture led them into tension with other Christian schools of thought.

Francesco Petrarch

Francesco Petrarch is considered the father of humanism. As well as describing the "Babylonian captivity" of the church, he is also credited with being the first to call the early medieval period the "Dark Ages" because of its lack of classical culture.

Spiritual Franciscans

Debates between Franciscans over the exact rule and purpose of the order had been in progress since the middle of the previous century (see chapter 12). The main split was between the Conventuals, who supported a moderate rule, and the Spirituals, who wanted to retain Francis's original idea of simplicity and complete poverty. In 1317 Pope John XXII dissolved the Spiritual party and denounced their teaching. Closely related to their ideals

Dante Alighieri (1265–1321)

Dante was an Italian poet, exiled from Florence when he opposed the political ambitions of Pope Boniface VIII. His *Divine Comedy* (possibly 1305) is a magisterial work imaginatively describing the circles of hell, purgatory, and heaven in three volumes: *Inferno*, *Purgatory*, and *Paradise*.

was the question of whether Christ and his apostles owned property, and whether the complete renunciation of possessions was required to live a life in imitation of Christ. In 1322 and 1323 Pope John issued further decrees allowing for the ownership of property, and declaring it heretical to claim that Christ lived in absolute poverty.

Bavarian challenge

The decision did not quell the debate. In 1328 a group of Spiritual Franciscans fled to Bavaria, accepting the protection of the German king Louis IV (r. 1314–47), whom Pope John had excommunicated in 1324. The same year Louis invaded Rome and had himself crowned Holy Roman Emperor. Louis set up a Spiritual Franciscan, Pietro Rainalducci (died 1333), as pope under the title Nicholas V (r. 1328–30), claiming that, since John resided in Avignon, he had abandoned any claim to head the Roman church. Louis eventually returned to Bavaria after he was unable to gain the support of the city's population, and Nicholas submitted to the authority of Pope John in 1330. Nicholas is regarded as an antipope and the name was used again in the fifteenth century.

The supremacy of the state

In addition to these military actions, a fierce theological debate arose over the issue, with major theologians including John of Jandun (c.1286–1328) and William of Ockham (c.1280 – c.1349) taking sides. The war of ideas culminated in *Defender of the Peace* in 1324, by Marsiglio of Padua (c.1275 – c.1342). This influential book took a strongly anti-papal line, maintaining that it is the state, and not the church,

The Palais des Papes and Pont Saint Benezet, Avignon.

which forms the unifying element of any society. Marsiglio argued that the pope only had spiritual power – any earthly power he enjoyed was a gift from kings, princes, and emperors. The book was condemned by the pope in 1327, but won the favour of King Louis, who made Marsiglio his chief vicar in Rome when he seized control of the city. When Louis' attempt to establish imperial authority in Italy failed, Marsiglio returned to Bavaria and relative obscurity. However, his *Defender* was carefully studied by later Reformers in the sixteenth century.

Brethren of the Common Life

Elsewhere in Europe, dissatisfaction with the opulence and power of the church led to the growth of movements emphasizing the Christian values of simplicity, charity, and learning. In 1374 the Dutch theologian Geert de Groote (1340–84) was converted under the influence of a Carthusian monk who preached strict contemplation. Geert never became a priest, but he began to call for repentance, speaking against corruption and clerical self-indulgence. Hostile factions within the church managed to have him banned from preaching in 1383, and he died from the plague the following year before he could appeal. People drawn to Geert's message later became known as the Brethren of the Common Life. The Brethren demanded no vows, and their clerical and lay members remained in their original vocations. Nevertheless, they became an influential presence, paying for their acts of charity by copying manuscripts and founding schools. Later the Brethren influenced such significant figures as Thomas à Kempis (see chapter 14), Nicholas of Cusa (see chapter 14), and Desiderius Erasmus (see chapter 15).

Black Death

This was the name given to the bubonic plague that swept through China, India, and Europe between 1347 and 1351. The Black Death gave rise to some extreme religious responses, including the practice of flagellation, in which groups of men publicly scourged themselves in penance for the sins of the population. In 1349 Pope Clement VI (r. 1342–52) called on church and state authorities to suppress this movement. The Black Death had a cataclysmic effect on the populations it touched, with some urban centres in Europe losing up to 40 per cent of their people. The church was directly involved in care for the sick and dying, and a large number of educated priests and scholars were lost to the plague. As a result, the quality of Christian teaching and practice for the following generations was affected as the church was forced to take on a large number of incompetent or illiterate clergy to fill their ranks.

John Wycliffe

Marsiglio, based in Bavaria, had challenged the authority of the church by appealing to the state. Fifty years later, in England, similar ideas were promoted by the priest

and theologian John Wycliffe (c.1329–84).

In 1375 Wycliffe published *On Civil Dominion*, which distinguished between the "invisible", eternal, and true aspects of the church and the "material" reality of the daily life of its members. When the material church went wrong, Wycliffe argued it was the duty of the civil government to put it right by punishing immoral clerics. Wycliffe's ideas were condemned in 1377 by Pope Gregory XI (r. 1370–78). Wycliffe carried his attack further, arguing in 1378 that the Bible, and not the pope, was the sole authority on Christian doctrine, and calling in 1382 for the king to disband religious institutions and reform the church in England. Wycliffe and his followers also translated the Bible from Latin into English and attacked the doctrine of transubstantiation.

Julian of Norwich (c.1342 – after 1413)

A mystic and anchorite, Julian lived in a cell built into the wall of her church. In 1373 she experienced a series of "showings" or mystical visions which were then written up as *Revelations of Divine Love*. In 1393 Julian produced a major theological reflection on her experiences, drawing parallels between divine action in the world and human motherhood.

The massive scale of the Black Death affected every facet of European life for generations to come. Here, Death is depicted reaping his victims in a French illuminated manuscript from the early sixteenth century.

The Great Schism

In an effort to restore order among the populace in Italy, Pope Gregory returned the papacy to Rome in 1377. His death a year later and the events surrounding the appointment of his successor led to considerable division within the Western church: a time known as the Great (or Western) Schism.

Urban VI

Under popular pressure from the people of Rome, the Italian Bartolomeo Prignano was appointed Pope Urban VI (r. 1378–89). Yet four months into his pontificate suspicions arose that Urban was not mentally stable; he displayed frequent outbursts and extravagant rages as he attempted to carry through his desired church reforms. The French members of the Sacred College of Cardinals questioned the validity of Urban's election and claimed that they had been forced to vote for an Italian.

Clement VII

The cardinals returned to France, where they installed Robert of Geneva as Pope Clement VII (r. 1378–94). The University of Paris recognized his election as legitimate, the king of France welcomed the decision, and Clement established Avignon once again as the centre for the church. Clement is now considered to be an antipope by the Roman Catholic Church, but at the time he divided the loyalties of Western Christendom, commanding the support of France, Naples, Scotland, Spain, and Sicily. For his part, Pope Urban in Rome was recognized by the Germans, English, Hungarians, Scandinavians, and Italians.

Three popes

The Great Schism lasted for decades, with successions of popes and antipopes along both lines claiming legitimacy. In 1409 attempts to resolve the conflict led to the creation of a third line of popes based in the city of Pisa, beginning with Alexander V (r. 1409–10). The schism would not be healed until the Council of Constance in 1417 and the unanimous election of Pope Martin V (r. 1417–31; see chapter 14). By this time a generation or more of European laity, clergy, and theologians had known only a divided Christendom of competing claims underpinned by nationalistic allegiances. This prepared the political, spiritual, and intellectual ground for the events of the Reformation.

East

The Crusades and the Latin rule of Constantinople during previous centuries had taken their toll on the resources and confidence of the Byzantine empire and its Orthodox Church. The relationship with Western Christendom was marked by continued mistrust and hostility. In the north, Constantinople struggled with the growing power of the Slavic kingdoms and their drive for political and religious autonomy. In the south, pressure from the armies of Islam was ever present, with the advance of Ottoman Turks threatening the very existence of Eastern Christendom.

Ottoman advance on Constantinople

1321

Ottoman Turk armies reach the Sea of Marmara, threatening Byzantium.

1331

Ottomans control Nicea.

1352

Serb army defeated by Ottomans at Maritza River.

1363

The Byzantine emperor John V Palaeologus (r. 1341–91) formally recognizes Ottoman rule of its conquered European territories.

1389

Overthrow of the Serbian empire. Prince Lazar (r. 1371–89) was defeated in Kosovo by the Turkish forces of Murad I (r. 1359–89).

1396

First Ottoman siege of Constantinople is lifted when the Ottoman army is diverted to fight the battle of Nicopolis instead.

Outer turmoil, inner peace

In the face of this outward military, ecclesial, and political instability, at this time more than ever before Orthodoxy began to focus on the inward, mystical aspects of Christianity. The tradition of meditation and mystical experience had always been present in the East, especially in the prayer practices of the monks of Mount Athos. The monks drew on the writings of Gregory of Nyssa (died c.394), John Climacus and Maximus the Confessor (c.580–662) among others.

Hesychasm

The practice known as "hesychasm" (from the Greek for "quietness") primarily involved the constant repetition of the "Jesus Prayer" and strict discipline of body posture and breathing. The aim was to align the thoughts of the head with the movements of the heart in order to attain a material vision of the Divine Light – the mystics believed that they were witnesses to the light of the transfiguration of Christ as described in Matthew 17. In the fourteenth century the development of this mystical tradition reached its height under the influence of Gregory of Sinai (c.1265 – c.1346), Nicephorus of Mount Athos (fourteenth century) and especially Gregory Palamas (see overleaf).

The Jesus Prayer

"Lord Jesus Christ, Son of the Living God, have mercy upon me, a sinner." The prayer has its roots in Greek mystical writers of the sixth and seventh centuries, but came to full flowering in the fourteenth century in the practice of hesychasm. The method of prayer continues to be important within Orthodoxy, and is also widely practised in the West.

Criticism of superstition

The Hesychasts came under intense criticism in 1337, led by a prominent monk in Constantinople. Barlaam (c. 1290–1348) was born into an Orthodox family from Calabria in southern Italy. He had earlier been involved in the movement to reunite the Orthodox and Catholic Churches. Upon his return to Constantinople, Barlaam accused the Mount Athos monks of encouraging superstition. He and his followers were particularly dismissive of the Hesychasts' physical practices and their claims to experience the divine directly through their meditations. When the Council of Constantinople sided with the Hesychasts in 1341, Barlaam returned to the West, where he served as a Catholic bishop until his death.

The energies of God

Barlaam's main opponent in this debate was the monk and archbishop of Thessalonica Gregory Palamas (c. 1296–1359). In response to Barlaam's claim that God was completely unknowable, Gregory wrote *Triads in Defence of the Holy Hesychasts*

(1338). Here he differentiated between the *energies* of God, which could be experienced, and the *essence* of God, which could not. The monks of Mount Athos accepted the teaching in 1340. Constantinople followed in 1341. Further councils in 1347 and 1351 served to confirm the Hesychast practice as an essential part of Orthodox Christianity.

Pagan Lithuania

The last officially pagan nation in Europe at this time was Lithuania. Christianity had been present among the people for a number of generations but had not made significant inroads. King Mindaugas (died 1263), an uncertain Catholic convert himself, had attempted to Christianize his people as Roman Catholics, but the exercise was short-lived. Even before his assassination, paganism had quickly reasserted itself. In addition, various Slavic aristocratic families had close ties with the Orthodox Church. Through them Byzantium exercised some influence over the Russian territories of Lithuania, leading to a period of vacillation between East and West. The prevarications came to a climax with the crusade of the Teutonic Knights from 1336. A succession of pagan Lithuanian rulers resisted the Christian invaders, but the pressure was too great. In 1384 Grand Duke Jogaila (Jagiello in Polish, c. 1351–1434) sought an alliance with Polish nobility, who, although Catholic, were also hostile to the German knights. Jogaila was baptized into the Catholic Church in 1386 and, in return for ceding Lithuanian lands to the Polish empire, became the royal consort of Poland. Although the conversion was instigated for political reasons, under Polish Franciscan influence Lithuanian Christian culture flourished, leading to the foundation of schools and hospitals, as well as closer integration with Western Europe. However, tensions with the East – especially Russia – remained.

Mother Moscow

Although Russia was under Mongol rule, the Orthodox Church enjoyed a favoured position and was allowed to operate relatively freely. In 1325 Metropolitan Peter (in office 1308–26) moved from Kiev to Moscow. In 1326 construction began on the Cathedral of the Assumption (or Dormition Cathedral) in Moscow and by 1328 the transfer of power was complete. Moscow became the official seat of Russian Orthodoxy, and the cathedral became known as its mother church.

Sergius

Born in Rostov, Bartholomew (c.1314–92) adopted the name Sergius when he became a monk in 1336. In the 1350s he founded a community in the forest of Radonezh which would later become the great Monastery of the Holy Trinity. The community reintroduced the practices of monastic life that had been disrupted by Mongol rule and it established Sergius as a leading church authority and reformer. Sergius intervened in Russian politics and averted four civil wars through his relationship with Muscovite princes. As a result, Russia was more able to resist the Mongol invaders.

Battle of Kulikovo

In 1380 Sergius gave aid to Prince Dmitri (c.1350–89) in fending off the Mongol army massing at Kulikovo, south of Moscow. Following Sergius's encouragement and counsel, Dmitri was victorious over the Golden Horde and its Lithuanian allies. The battle led to the liberation of the Russian people and church from Mongolian rule, an event that would have lasting significance for Europe and for the future of the Orthodox Church. For this reason, after his death Sergius came to be considered one of the greatest patron saints of Russia.

The domes of St Basil's Cathedral, Moscow.

The Fifteenth Century

In the fifteenth-century West, the universal authority of the pope was increasingly challenged by the rise of nation-states and independent Christian groups. The reformation movements of the following century had their roots in these developments. Rapid exploration, too, would give rise to new expressions of Christianity as Christendom spread to the New World at the end of the century.

In the East, Byzantine Orthodoxy entered a time of "Great Captivity" under the Ottoman Empire. At the same time, Moscow came into its own as Russia emerged from Mongolian rule.

East

Second siege of Constantinople

In 1422 Turks led by Sultan Murad II (r. 1421–51) resumed their siege of the city of Constantinople. The siege was unsuccessful, but it served to entrench the Ottoman invaders even further in Byzantine territory.

Temporary unity

In the face of the Ottoman threat, unity within Christendom was the best policy for halting further expansion. The Council of Florence met between 1438

After a siege lasting for seven weeks, the city of Constantinople fell to Ottoman Turks in 1453.

and 1445 with the primary aim of once again seeking rapprochement between the Western and Eastern churches. The East was represented by Emperor John VIII Palaeologus (r. 1425–48) and Patriarch Joseph of Constantinople (1360–1439), among others, the West by Pope Eugenius IV (r. 1431–47) and Cardinal Julian Cesarini (1398–1444). After long discussions and disagreements, a union of sorts was established in 1439, although it never enjoyed popular approval in Constantinople and many Orthodox bishops refused their support.

Collapse of Eastern Christendom

As part of his project of unification, in 1442 Cardinal Cesarini travelled to Hungary to preach a crusade against the Ottomans. In 1444 he convinced the king of Hungary and Poland, Władysław III (or Vladislav, r. 1434/40–44), to break the "Peace of Szeged", the uneasy truce that existed between the Christians and the Turks.

   Instead of the intended aim of reinvigorating Eastern and Western Christian opposition to the invaders, the renewed war led to a rout of the would-be crusaders. The Christian army was defeated and Cesarini and Władysław were killed at the battle of Varna in Bulgaria in 1444. The collapse of this force paved the way for a string of Ottoman victories, including a success in Kosovo in 1448 which ensured Turkish rule over the Balkans. In 1453 Ottoman soldiers led by Sultan Mohammed II (r. 1451–81) conquered Constantinople. Turkish rule continued to be consolidated

further into the Balkans, including Moldavia (1455), southern Greece (1456–60), southern Serbia (1459), and Wallachia (1474). Successful Turkish wars against the Poles (1497–99) and the Venetians (1499–1503) threatened Western Christendom while decisively demonstrating the collapse of Byzantium and the end of the Eastern Roman empire.

Mohammed II, Sultan of Turkey. His rule over Constantinople marked the end of the Eastern Roman Empire.

Fall of Constantinople

The Turks invaded the city of Constantinople by land and sea in 1453. Although significantly outnumbered, the Byzantine forces held off the invaders for seven weeks before the city was captured. Even though the Church of the Holy Wisdom was turned into a mosque, the Ottomans treated the Christians with a fair degree of tolerance. Agreements between the patriarch and the sultan allowed the Orthodox Church to continue, although Christians were heavily taxed, forbidden to serve in the army, and banned from missionary work or proselytizing.

The Great Captivity

For the Eastern church, the period under Muslim rule is sometimes known as the Great Captivity. In return for political obedience, the church was allowed to continue exercising its spiritual and civil authority. The **concordat** reached between the Ottoman rulers and the Orthodox Church would govern relations until 1923.

Patriarchate under Islam

The first patriarch of Constantinople under this new arrangement was George Scholarius (c. 1405 – c. 1472). Sultan Mohammed II himself invested Scholarius as Patriarch Gennadius II in 1454. Gennadius had supported Cesarini's scheme for church union at the Council of Florence (1439) but by this stage he was a bitter opponent of Rome – a position attractive to Constantinople's new Ottoman ruler. Gennadius resigned, or attempted to resign, the patriarchate a number of times, but was ordered to occupy

Opposite: Ivan III, Grand Duke of Russia, did much to make the Russian Church assume the mantle of Byzantine Orthodoxy.

the office by the sultan. Gennadius wrote a number of theological and philosophical works – including a translation of Thomas Aquinas from Latin into Greek.

The rise of Russia

As the Byzantine Greeks adapted to their new life under non-Christian rule, the Russians – already used to living with Mongolian rulers – assumed greater prominence within Orthodox Christianity. The Russians had wholly refused the 1439 union compromises of the Council of Florence. As a result, they considered themselves to be more authentic preservers of the Orthodox faith than the Greeks. In 1448 Russian bishops elected Jonas (died c. 1461) as metropolitan of Kiev without making any reference to the hierarchy in Constantinople. The action effectively created an autocephalous Russian church, although this was not formally recognized by Constantinople until 1589.

Ivan the Great

Ivan III "the Great" (r. 1462–1505) married Sophia (1455–1503), niece of the last Byzantine emperor, helping to strengthen Russia's claim to be the natural successor to Byzantine Orthodoxy. When the Russians, under the leadership of Ivan, defeated their Mongolian rulers in 1480 these claims were further enhanced, laying the foundation for the idea of Moscow as "third Rome", which would rise to prominence in the following century.

Ethiopian church

Although the Abyssinian church operated largely independently of the mainstream Catholic and Orthodox traditions, a small group of Ethiopian monks are recorded as attending the Council of Florence in 1441. The Ethiopian church at this time was experiencing cultural revival and reform, especially under the influence of the Christian emperor Zar'a Ya'qob (Zara Jacob, 1434–68). The emperor wrote hymns and theological reflections on the creed of the Ethiopian church. In addition, many Arabic and Western European texts were translated into Ge'ez (Ethiopic) in this period, and most of the copies of the ancient Ethiopic Bible date from the fourteenth and fifteenth centuries.

West

Closing of the schism

The Great Schism had divided Europe since 1378, with allegiance to the different popes falling along nationalist and political lines. The situation was untenable for the church and in 1409 the cardinals convened the Council of Pisa to resolve the matter. The council declared the papacies of both Gregory XII (r. 1406–15) and Benedict XIII (r. 1394–1417) invalid and unanimously elected a third pope, Alexander V, who died before he could fulfil his promises to unite the Catholic Church. He was succeeded by John XXIII (1410–15). Despite the validity of his election being contested, John commanded more support than the other popes. The Roman Catholic Church now considers John, Benedict and Alexander to be antipopes and re-used the name John XXIII in the twentieth century.

Conciliar movement

By creating three papal lines, Pisa had made the schism worse. Yet its attempts to heal the breach led to the calling of the 1414–18 Council of Constance and the eventual end of the Great Schism. Two French theologians figured prominently at Constance. Pierre D'Ailly (1350–1420) and Jean Gerson (1363–1429) helped to formulate a radical cure for the problems by arguing that the office of pope only existed as the "head" of the "body" of the church. If the head was failing the body, the faithful church had the right to call it to account. The family of doctrines that maintain that the supreme authority of the church lies with the General Council of Bishops, rather than the one pope, is known as Conciliar Theory. The failure of the conciliar movement to flourish much past the fifteenth century is a contributing factor to the Protestant Reformation of the following century.

Council of Constance

At the instigation of the Holy Roman Emperor Sigismund (r. 1410–37), John XXIII agreed to call the Council of Constance in 1414. The council, which was well attended, fully embraced conciliarism by decreeing: "This Council holds its power direct from Christ; everyone, no matter his rank or office, even if it be papal, is bound to obey it in whatever pertains to faith…"

John was the first pope to be persuaded to abdicate, in 1415. Gregory XII followed within a few months, and Benedict XIII was deposed in 1417. Finally, Pope Martin V (r. 1417– 31) was elected, bringing an end to the Great Schism. Martin returned the seat of the papacy to Rome, re-established control over the Italian Papal States, and resumed authority over the Western church.

Thomas à Kempis (c.1380–1471)

A German priest and mystic, Thomas spent his life in the Augustinian monastery at Zwolle, where he was a celebrated author and spiritual adviser. Thomas is most known for *The Imitation of Christ* (although a minority of scholars question his authorship). The *Imitation* is a manual of spiritual devotion which is popular with many different Christian traditions and has never gone out of print since it first began to be circulated in 1418.

Jan Hus

As well as uniting a schismatic church, the Council of Constance also met to deal with an anti-papal Christian movement that had taken root among the Czechs of Bohemia.

Jan Hus had been teaching at the University of Prague for five years before he encountered the radical theology of the English reformer John Wycliffe (see chapter 13) in 1401. Wycliffe's ideas inspired a Czech reforming party which encouraged a more rigorous obedience to Scripture and was opposed to German political and religious dominance in their country. In 1409 the Czechs sided with the election of Pope Alexander V against the German favourite Pope Gregory XII. Further conflict arose when Hus opposed Pope John XXIII's sale of indulgences (see chapter 15) and was exiled from Prague in 1412. The conflict reached its climax when Hus was called to attend the Council of Constance in 1414.

grievances against the dominating Catholic Church and the German influence in Bohemia. Part of the Hussite programme was laid out in *Four Articles of Prague* (1420), which anticipated later Protestant Reformation developments in some key ways. The Hussites argued for a more disciplined clergy, access to **Communion of both kinds** – bread and wine – for all people, the liturgy in the local language, and a mutual independence of church and state. Their religious concerns thus had a political dimension. With the Hussites reacting violently against Catholic Europe, Holy Roman Emperor Sigismund launched a number of "crusades" against the Czechs from 1420 to 1434.

Far left: Ponte St Angelo and St Peter's Basilica in Rome at dusk.

Left: Christian reformer and national hero, Jan Hus was betrayed and executed in 1415.

Betrayal

Jan Hus travelled under assurances of safe conduct from Emperor Sigismund, with the belief that he would be given an opportunity to defend his views. Despite the emperor's efforts, shortly after his arrival at Constance Hus was imprisoned and charged with heresy. After a public hearing in which he was not permitted to present or defend his own views, he was denounced as a heretic, charged with being a "Wycliffite", and handed over to the secular government for execution in 1415.

The Hussites

Following these events, Hus became a national hero in Bohemia, with the University of Prague declaring him a martyr. Hus became a focal point for Czech

The anti-papal Council of Basle

The agitation of the Hussite Wars coincided with the growing conciliar movements within the church. The controversial Council of Basle was convened in 1431 and was presided over by Cardinal Cesarini. When the newly elected Pope Eugenius IV (r. 1431–47) tried to dissolve the meeting, Cesarini and the other bishops disregarded the order, reaffirming the idea that the General Council was superior to the pope. The cardinals were widely supported in their action.

Basle enforced a number of anti-papal decrees and placed strict limitations on the office of the pope while enhancing the authority of bishops and lower orders of clergy. In 1437 the council found in favour of some Hussite demands, allowing a degree of independence to the Bohemian church that the papal party tried to oppose. In the face of these tensions, in 1438 Eugenius transferred the council from Basle, first to Ferrara and then to Florence, where a short-lived union between the Eastern and Western churches was achieved (see above).

Nicholas of Cusa (1401–64)

This German priest and theologian was also a celebrated humanist and philosopher. His *On Catholic Reconciliation* (1433) argued for the superiority of the General Council over the pope, although he later retreated from this view. Nicholas worked for reconciliation with the Hussites and he supported union between East and West – travelling to Constantinople from 1437 to 1438. A scholar of mathematics, astronomy, and history, Nicholas was also responsible for creating the first geographical map of central Europe. In 1459, together with his father and sister, he founded a hospital in his native town of Cusa.

Joan of Arc (1412–31)

This peasant "maid of Orléans" was born into a period of conflict, during the Hundred Years War with England and continuing civil strife between the great houses of France. In 1425 she had the first of many visions, claiming from these experiences a supernatural mission to fight for France. In 1429 she convinced King Charles VII and his court theologians of her mission and was allowed to lead a successful military campaign to liberate the city of Orléans. Captured in 1430 by her enemies, Joan was eventually executed for witchcraft in 1431. Pope Callistus III (r. 1455–58) reviewed her case in 1456 and declared her to have been wrongly condemned. She is considered a national hero and is the second patron saint of France.

France

The papacy's relations with France were especially strained because of the French church's increasing assertions of autonomy from Rome, a tendency known as Gallicanism. In 1438, while Eugenius was preparing to relocate the council from Basle, the French clergy issued *Pragmatic Sanction of Bourges*. The declaration upheld the right of the French church to administer its own affairs and not to pay taxes to Rome, and denied the pope a say in the appointment of French bishops. The French king, Charles VII (r. 1422–61), endorsed the anti-papal decrees of Basle and supported the *Sanction*, which halted the flow of money from France to Rome.

England

The victory over the French at Agincourt in 1415 contributed significantly to the growing national self-awareness of the English. The protracted Hundred Years War with France, physical distance from Rome, and the controversies surrounding the "Babylonian captivity" and the Great Schism all meant that the English church in the fifteenth century operated largely independently of the mainland Catholic hierarchy. The result was a stronger relation between the English monarchy and the English church, at the expense of allegiance to the papacy.

The Lollards

The English church faced opposition of its own from the Lollards, followers of John Wycliffe. The name "Lollards" is probably a derogatory term meaning "mumblers". The Lollards supported the translation of the Bible into the local vernacular rather than Latin, and believed that church practices should be drawn only from Scripture. For this reason they disapproved of church hierarchical systems, clerical celibacy, transubstantiation, praying for the dead, and Christian participation in war. In 1401 the first Lollard martyr was burned at the stake. But Lollardy continued to grow and became associated with disaffection from the English government, culminating in a march on London that was dispersed by the soldiers of King Henry V (r. 1413–22) in 1414. There is evidence of Lollard activity in 1431, 1455, and later, with some historians linking the movement to the regions where the sixteenth-century Anglican Reformation was most enthusiastically received.

Reading and learning

Books and their study flourished in Western Christendom.

c.1448

Johannes Gutenberg (c.1398–1468) develops his printing press using movable type.

1448

Pope Nicholas V (r. 1447–55) establishes the Vatican Library. By 1481 it has the largest collection of manuscripts in the West.

1456

Appearance of the Gutenberg Bible, the first printed book in Europe.

c.1475

Foundation of Copenhagen University.

1494

Bishop Elphinstone (1431–1514) founds King's College, Aberdeen.

The radical English theologian John Wycliffe insisted that the Bible should be translated into local languages. He influenced later generations of Reformers across Europe.

Portugal

Under the influence of leaders such as Prince Henry "the Navigator" (1394–1460), the Portuguese undertook many voyages of discovery during the fifteenth century, establishing their empire's reach in India, Africa, and East Asia, with the Americas soon to follow. In 1452 Pope Nicholas V issued the papal bull *Dum diversas*, granting the Portuguese crown rights over all the people and property they discovered on their overseas explorations.

Witchcraft

Classical, early medieval, and Orthodox Christianity were generally cautious about encouraging belief in the power of witches. However, Western European interest in witchcraft steadily increased in the fifteenth century, largely as a result of the 1486 publication of *Hammer of Witches*. Written by German Dominicans, the book singled out women as the main culprits and would go on to have popular influence in later years. Its content and style were controversial even in its own time, and it was never fully accepted by the church.

The Spanish Inquisition

An Inquisition in Spain was instituted through papal bulls issued by Pope Sixtus IV (1471–84) in 1478 and 1483. Its inception was largely due to the encouragement of Ferdinand V of Aragon (1479–1516) and Isabella I of Castile (1474–1504), styled the "Catholic King and Queen" for their enthusiastic political protection of the church. In contrast to previous Inquisitions (see chapter 12) the Spanish Inquisition was characterized by its subservience to the secular authorities, who appointed the examiners and conducted trials.

Inquisitor Torquemada

The Inquisitor General was nominally under the authority of the pope, although in reality he served the policy of the Spanish crown. Tomás de Torquemada (1420–98) took charge of the Inquisition in 1483, establishing by his *Ordinances* (1484) an organizational system that would remain in place for the best part of three centuries. The earliest phase of the Spanish Inquisition was the bloodiest, with the principal targets comprising Catholic

The Spanish Inquisition reached all corners of Spain's empire, including Mexico as depicted here.

heretics (deemed enemies of the state), Moors, Moriscos (converts from Islam whose Christianity was suspect), and Marranos (converts from Judaism). Under his authority thousands were interrogated and some 2,000 executed, earning Torquemada a reputation for cruelty throughout the wider church. Successive appeals to the pope to curb Torquemada's excesses were often unfruitful, as the papacy had limited influence over this Inquisition.

The new Spanish empire

In 1492 the reconquest of Granada was complete, marking the union of the Spanish kingdoms of Aragon and Castile and the final defeat of the Moors by the Catholic monarchs. As part of the reconquest, the Inquisition oversaw the expulsion of all unconverted Jews from Spain. Also in 1492, the explorer Christopher Columbus (c.1451–1506) claimed the Americas in the name of Ferdinand, Isabella, and Catholic Spain. The explosion of Spanish exploration prompted Pope Alexander VI (1492–1503) to issue *Inter caetera eximiae devotionis* in 1493, the papal bull granting the Spanish crown the responsibility for spreading Christianity in all its territories. The 1494 Treaty of Tordesillas divided the newly "discovered" territories in South America between Spain and Portugal, giving the conquistadores free rein over their expansion. That same year a service was held at the settlement of La Isabella on the island of Santo Domingo (modern-day Haiti and the Dominican Republic) – the first Mass to be celebrated in the New World.

Florence's skyline in the fifteenth century was dominated by the newly erected cathedral dome. Designed by Brunelleschi, "The Duomo" remains one of the largest in the world. Construction of the cathedral was not completed until the nineteenth century.

The Sixteenth Century

The sixteenth century was, for Christianity, a time of revival and expansion in the New World, a time of massive reform in Europe, and a time of consolidation in Russia as power shifted from Constantinople to Moscow.

Orthodox consolidation

Third Rome

Following the Turkish captivity of Constantinople in 1453, the Russian church had become the largest and most influential church of the Orthodox communion.

In 1503 the Orthodox Church held a council to settle a dispute between the followers of Joseph of Volokolamsk (c.1440–1515) and those of Nil Sorsky (c.1433–1508). The council sided with Volokolamsk's advocacy of a strong national church, and Sorsky's suggestion that the church should avoid political engagement and ownership of property was condemned in 1504. The result was a stronger relationship than ever before between the church and the Russian state. By 1510 the monk Philotheus (c.1465–1542) could write of Basil (Vasili) III (r. 1505–33), grand prince of Moscow: "[You are] on earth the sole emperor of the Christians, the leader of the Apostolic church which no longer stands in Rome or in Constantinople, but in the blessed city of Moscow... Two Romes have fallen, but the third stands and a fourth there will not be."

Orthodox Church, Kazan, Tatarstan Republic, Russia. In the sixteenth century Russia became a powerful Christian centre rivalling Rome and Constantinople.

Tsar of All Russia

With the new settlement, the state began to exert more influence over the church. In 1521 Basil deposed Metropolitan Varlaam (in office 1511–21) when the churchman refused to allow Basil a divorce. Varlaam's successor Daniel (in office 1521–33) proved more pliant, and Basil remarried in 1525. This new union produced the desired heir, Ivan IV (r. 1533–84). "Ivan the Terrible" would be the first ruler to adopt the title Tsar of All Russia in 1547.

Seeing himself as "God's appointed" ruler, Ivan cultivated a close relationship with the Orthodox Church. In 1551, Ivan convened the Council of Moscow (also known as the Council of the 100 Chapters) alongside Metropolitan Macarius (c.1482–1564). The council gave jurisdiction to church courts and strengthened church discipline. It also affirmed the tsar as the champion of the true faith, and in turn gave the church a role in conducting domestic and foreign policy.

Constantinople

Although under foreign rule, Constantinople traditionally retained its primacy in Orthodox Christianity. The most significant figure at this time was Patriarch Jeremias II (c.1530–95). Between 1573 and 1581 Jeremias entered into serious correspondence with German Reformers from Tübingen when he was sent a copy of the *Augsburg Confession*. His reply, known as *The Three Answers*, made clear the points of agreement and difference between the two traditions, and the work remains influential in the Orthodox Church.

In 1582 Jeremias condemned the new papal calendar decreed by Pope Gregory XIII (r. 1572–85). It was also under Jeremias's rule that the growing autonomy of the Russian church was formally recognized and the autocephalous patriarchate of Moscow was created in 1589. The death of the patriarch in 1595 led to a time of more chaos in the church than during its Ottoman captivity. In the next 100 years there would be sixty-one changes to the patriarchal throne, with many men being deposed and reinstated multiple times.

Calendars

The original calendar was mandated by Julius Caesar around 45 BC. The Julian calendar introduced an error of one day every 128 years. Owing to various innovations and additions, it had grown unwieldy, and it proved difficult to calculate accurate dates for Easter. Pope Gregory XIII decreed a reformed calendar in 1582. The Gregorian calendar shifts approximately one day every 3,300 years. It simplified the leap-year process and attempted to provide uniformity for the calculation of Easter. Many Protestant and Orthodox countries resisted the new calendar as a Catholic imposition; however, it has since been adopted as the civil calendar in most parts of the world. The national Orthodox churches continue to use a revised form of the Julian calendar for religious purposes.

Ottoman empire

1517

Ottomans control Mecca and Jerusalem. (The Ottomans will rule in Jerusalem until defeated by the British in 1917.)

1529

Vienna successfully repels the first Ottoman siege.

1541

Suleiman "the Magnificent" (r. 1520–66) conquers most of Hungary.

1551

Ottomans victorious in Tripoli against the Knights of Malta.

1571

Major Christian victory against the Ottoman navy at Lepanto.

Protestant reform

At the same time that Christianity was consolidating in Russia the mood in Europe was for reform.

The authority of the papacy and the standing of the church in Rome had been weakened by the Great Schism and the conciliar movements of the previous century. Inside and outside Rome there was popular feeling that the Western church was financially worldly and politically corrupt. Monastic communities were banding together, instituting rules for holy living. Throughout Europe, movements for clerical reform and a return to early Christian standards were coming to the fore.

Pre-Reformation

In 1508 Michelangelo (1475–1564) was contributing to the church's earthly standing with his painting on the Sistine Chapel ceiling. In the same year, the celebrated author Desiderius Erasmus (c.1466–1536)

was attacking the church for losing its spiritual way in *The Praise of Folly*. By 1511 the Congregation of Windesheim, a group of Dutch monasteries and convents dedicated to reforming principles, had grown to ninety-seven member houses. Acknowledging the need for reform, the Fifth Lateran Council met in 1512. It called for improved clerical training and discipline, and criticized the papacy for its over-involvement in temporal matters.

The highly decorated walls and ceiling of the Sistine Chapel.

Desiderius Erasmus

Europe's best-selling author, Erasmus held teaching posts in Oxford, Cambridge, and Basle. His satires, biblical translations, philosophical works, and theological writings were enormously influential. Although highly critical of the clergy and Roman church of his day, Erasmus also distanced himself from the Protestants and he wrote books critical of Martin Luther (see below).

The first Polyglot Bible

In Alcalá, Spain, in 1514 a team of compilers published the first full Bible to have parallel texts in Hebrew, Greek, and Latin. The work paved the way for serious textual study of the Old and New Testament Scriptures.

Indulgences

The Lateran Council's calls for reform were ineffective. By its end in 1517 the situation of the church seemed hardly to have changed.

Years earlier, in conjunction with Albrecht von Hohenzollern, archbishop of Mainz (1490–1545), Pope Julius II had instituted a special indulgence in order to pay for the building of St Peter's Church in Rome. After Julius died (in 1513) his successor Leo X (r. 1513–21) continued with the plan. Half the money was to pay off Albrecht's debts; the other half went to the lavish building project.

The German friar Johann Tetzel (c. 1465–1519) was employed to preach the indulgence. Tetzel promised that the indulgence would provide absolution for any crime, and that anyone who bought an indulgence would instantly free their loved ones from pain in the afterlife: "As soon as the coin in the coffer rings / The soul from Purgatory springs."

Philothei of Athens (1522-89)

During the Ottoman period in Greece, women were forced into Turkish harems. The nun Philothei offered sanctury to these women and was killed as a result. A "New Martyr", Philothei is considered a patron saint of Athens.

Wittenberg

Tetzel's success with the German peasants worried many reform-minded theologians. One of these was Martin Luther, a lecturer at the University of Wittenberg. Luther wrote his concerns up in 1517 and posted them in the usual way – by nailing them to the door of the main city church. Luther's *Ninety-five Theses against Indulgences* caused an outcry. Rome's efforts at discipline failed and in a public debate with the theologian Johann Eck (1486–1543) in

Portrait of Erasmus, by Hans Holbein the Younger.

1519, Luther formally denied the primacy of the pope. At the Diet of Worms in 1521 Luther was excommunicated by the church and outlawed by the emperor. All who followed his ideas were declared heretics.

Martin Luther

Luther was a German priest and theologian. Sometime between 1512 and 1515 his reading of Augustine and the apostle Paul led to his conviction that "faith alone justifies without works". The idea that God's salvation could be received independently of obedience to the demand of religious law and the church hierarchy would become central to the political and spiritual aspects of the Protestant Reformation.

Martin Luther nailing his Ninety-Five Theses on the door of Wittenberg Church. His action became symbolic for the new movement of "Protestants" opposed to the pope and some Roman Catholic practices.

Protest in Europe

Luther supported the close coalition of church and state, and he wrote to the German princes encouraging them to take reforms into their own hands. By the 1530s, the rulers of Saxony, Hesse, Brandenburg, and Brunswick, along with a number of German "free cities", had adopted Lutheran principles. The movement also found European supporters keen on religious reform or political emancipation from Rome. By 1526 Sweden and Denmark were seeing disputes between Catholics and the new, reform-minded "evangelical" party, and Olaus (1493–1552) and Laurentius (1499–1573) Petri had translated the New Testament into Swedish. In 1527 the Swedish crown assumed control of Catholic property. In 1536 Christian III (r. 1534–59) established the Lutheran Church as the national church of Denmark.

A new name

The First Diet of Speyer in 1526 had determined that each prince should be allowed to order church affairs within his own sphere of influence, thus sanctioning the spread of Lutheranism. But this toleration of religious innovation was reversed at the Second Diet of Speyer in 1529, which was controlled by a council majority of Catholic leaders who agreed to end Lutheran toleration. Six princes and representatives from fourteen German cities issued a formal letter of protest against the ruling, giving the new movement the name "Protestant".

Anabaptists

The general designation for those reform movements which refused to allow infant baptism and insisted on the rebaptism of adult believers. Main groups include the followers of Thomas Müntzer (c.1490–1525), the Swiss Brethren of Zurich (active 1525), the Moravian communities founded by Jacob Hutter (died 1536), and the followers of the Dutch priest Menno Simons (1496–1561). Most **Anabaptist** groups tended toward pacifism. They practised the communal sharing of property and they encouraged non-participation in civic life, including the withholding of taxes. Both Roman Catholics and Protestants routinely persecuted Anabaptists; however, their ideas continue in the **Mennonite** Church, and in the exclusive Hutterite and Amish communities of North America.

Swiss Reformation

In 1520, writing under the influence of Erasmus (and probably also of Luther), Huldrych Zwingli (1484–1531) developed his own evangelical teaching. After a series of public disputations in Zurich in 1523 and 1524, the civic authorities adopted his reforms for their city. The movement quickly spread to other Swiss cantons. In 1527 divisions between the Reformers were revealed when Zwingli and Luther clashed over the doctrine of the eucharist.

In 1536 the leadership of the Swiss Reformation passed to John Calvin (1509–64), a former priest fleeing persecution in his native France. From 1541 Calvin's *Ecclesiastical Ordinances* established a highly organized theocracy in Geneva according to which the town council assumed the authority for religious and moral discipline in the population. Calvinist reforms soon became the model for church and civic governance throughout Europe, especially in western Germany, Scotland, Holland, and France.

Huldrych Zwingli, theologian and leader of the Reformation in Switzerland.

Huguenots

These were French Calvinists. The Huguenot Church was formalized at the Synod of Paris in 1559. The support offered to the Huguenots by some foreign Protestant territories against the Catholic majority resulted in a protracted civil war in France between 1562 and 1594.

St Bartholomew's Day Massacre

The events of 23–26 August 1572 represent the height of antagonism between Huguenots and Catholics in France. Following an assassination attempt on the Protestant leader Gaspard de Coligny (1519–72), Queen Catherine de' Medici allowed Catholic troops to attack the Huguenots. This in turn spurred further mob riots, leading to the deaths of over 5,000 Parisian Protestants. The violence shocked all Europe, Protestants and Catholics alike.

Detail showing St Bartholomew's Day, by François Dubois (1529–1584).

Witch trials

Fear of sorcery was a constant feature of both Catholicism and Protestantism during this era. Prosecutions often involved multiple accusations and indictments. The vast majority of those tried and executed were women.

1532

Holy Roman Empire requires death for practitioners of black magic.

1541

Luther approves of the burning of four witches in Wittenberg.

1550 – c.1560

Courts in Geneva try ninety witches.

1563

Johann Weyer's *On the Delusions of Demons* argues that witches are not demonic, merely deluded and of unsound mind, and should not be prosecuted.

1580s

England, France, Germany, and Sweden experience a surge in witch trials.

1588

Michel de Montaigne's *On Lameness* is critical of those who believe in witchcraft and diabolic forces.

1590–91

North Berwick witch trial. King James VI of Scotland (later James I of England; r. 1567/1603–1625) prosecutes women he thinks were using witchcraft to try to kill him.

The Anglican Reformation

The influence of the Reformation and national separation from Rome followed a different course in England from the rest of Europe and led to the foundation of the Anglican Church.

1521

Pope Leo X awards King Henry VIII (r. 1509–47) the title "Defender of the Faith" for Henry's published theological refutation of Luther.

1525

William Tyndale (c.1494–1536) publishes his English translation of the New Testament.

1533

Without Rome's permission, the archbishop of Canterbury, Thomas Cranmer (1489–1556), annuls Henry VIII's marriage to Catherine of Aragon.

1534

The Act of Supremacy establishes Henry VIII as supreme head of the church in England.

1535

Execution of the statesman Thomas More (1478–1535) and Bishop John Fisher (1459–1535) for refusing to swear loyalty to the crown.

1536–40

Dissolution of the monasteries in England.

1547

Death of Henry VIII. German Reformers arrive in London.

1552

The revised *Book of Common Prayer* abolishes the Mass, prayers for the dead, and Latin liturgy.

1553

The Catholic Mary I (r. 1553–58) assumes the English throne. English Reformers deported or imprisoned.

1555

Execution of John Hooper (c.1498–1555), Nicholas Ridley (c.1502–55), and Hugh Latimer (c.1485–1555) among 300 other English Protestants. Cranmer burned a year later.

1558

Death of Mary I and accession of Queen Elizabeth I (1558–1603). Restoration of English Protestant reforms and persecution of English Catholics.

Catholic revival

It was not only the Protestants who wished to reform the church. The revival of European Catholicism during this era is often referred to as the "Counter-Reformation"; however, many of the movements occurred independently of reaction to the Protestant schism.

New monastic orders such as the Theatines (1524) and the Capuchins (1529) (see chapter 12, **Franciscans**) were keen to restore original Christian practice. These orders were soon eclipsed by the "Society of Jesus", formally endorsed by Pope Paul III (r. 1534–49) in 1540. Called Jesuits, they had two aims: to reform the church while guarding against Protestant innovations and to engage in missionary activity. Governed by the *Constitutions* of Ignatius of Loyola the Jesuits flourished, seeing particular success in Poland, southern Germany, East Asia, and the New World.

Ignatius of Loyola (c.1491–1556)

A nobleman, Ignatius made a vow of poverty, chastity, and mission, along with six companions in 1534. He became the first Jesuit General in 1540. Loyola's *Spiritual Exercises* contain rules for Christian meditation designed to aid prayer and self-discipline. Still influential, the *Exercises* have been in constant circulation since they were written c.1522–23.

Teresa of Avila (1515–82)

A Spanish Carmelite nun, Teresa was the author of *The Way of Perfection* (c. 1562) and *Foundations* (1572) among other works. Her accounts of ecstatic "spiritual marriage" combined with practical discipline ushered in a new era of Christian **mysticism**.

John of the Cross (1542–91)

A Spanish mystic and Doctor of the Church, John worked closely with Teresa of Avila in reforming the Carmelite Order. He wrote on the self's transformation in the presence of the divine. John's idea of the "dark night of the soul" has subsequently influenced much Christian life and thought.

Ignatius of Loyola helped found the Jesuits. His main writings remain influential and have never been out of print.

Opposite: Palm trees sway over Vagator Beach in Goa, India. Goa was the main staging ground for missions to India, China, and Japan.

Tridentine reforms

Jesuit influence was strong during the three sessions of the Council of Trent of 1545–63. Summoned by Pope Paul III and his successors, the council marked the high-point of the Counter-Reformation and ensured the impossibility of reconciliation with the Protestants. Trent renewed Catholic spiritual life by affirming that the church had the sole authority to interpret the Bible. It opposed Reformer doctrines of the eucharist by upholding transubstantiation and affirming the Mass.

Trent also revised the Latin Vulgate Bible and paved the way for reform and simplification of the Breviary, the liturgical book of prayers, lessons, and Psalms to be used in Catholic worship. In 1568 the Hail Mary was introduced to the Breviary. In 1577 the publication of *Incomparable Virgin Mary* by Peter Canisius (1521–97) further emphasized the difference between Protestant and Catholic spirituality. Protestantism was increasingly sceptical of devotion to the Virgin Mary.

New World expansion

The revival of Catholic Christianity was not confined to the Old World. The sixteenth century saw great missionary projects to the New World, as well as to India, Japan, and China.

By 1500 Franciscan missions had been established in the Caribbean. The first bishoprics appeared in Santo Domingo shortly thereafter. In 1508 the papal decree *Universalis ecclesiae* granted the Spanish the right to appoint bishops and collect tithes across the New World.

Imperial expansion in the name of God brought the enslavement and abuse of native populations. At the same time, many missionaries intervened on behalf of natives during the 1520s and 1530s, including the priests of newly created bishoprics in Mexico, Lima, Colombia, and Cuba. The bishops saw some small success and encouraged restraint, but there was little immediate change to Spanish and Portuguese colonial excesses.

Bartolomé de las Casas (1474–1566)

The "Apostle to the Indians", las Casas devoted himself to opposing the cruel exploitation of natives living under Spanish imperial rule. From 1543 to 1551 he was the Dominican bishop of Chiapa in Mexico. His *Destruction of the Indies* (1552) gave detailed accounts of settler abuses.

The Americas

In 1531, ten years after Hernán Cortés (1485–1547) conquered the Aztec empire, recent Aztec Christian converts reported seeing visions of the Virgin Mary. The shrine of Our Lady of Guadalupe became a focal point for Mexican national identity, as well as for the emerging movement of Marian devotion. An early supporter of Guadalupe, Mexico's first bishop, Juan de Zumárraga (1468–1548), led campaigns to destroy pagan sites of worship, and in 1539 set up the Americas' first printing press.

Cuba had its first bishop in 1518, Nicaragua in 1531, and Bolivia in 1552. In Brazil, the 1549 Jesuit mission of Manuel de Nóbrega (1517–70) led to the installation of a bishop, also in 1552. Bogotá became Colombia's first diocese in 1564. Most missionary work with the native inhabitants of the Americas was now undertaken by Jesuits and they established the first parish in Florida in 1566, although the mission did not flourish.

First American martyr

A Spanish military chaplain, Juan de Padilla (c.1500–44) travelled with colonial explorers into what is now Kansas. The explorers turned back in 1542, but Father Padilla elected to remain among the Tíguez people. Slain by a neighbouring tribe in 1544, he is considered to be the first Catholic martyr in North America.

India

In 1510 Alfonso Albuquerque began the Portuguese invasion of Goa. Expansion continued through Muslim and Hindu territories for the next two decades, establishing Goa as a trading and religious centre of the Portuguese empire. In 1542 Francis Xavier (1506–52) made Goa the headquarters for his Jesuit mission.

Xavier saw much success in gaining Roman Catholic converts in south India.

Christianity had existed in India since at least the fourth century. However, until imperial influence began to make itself felt the native Syrian and Thomas churches had been left alone (see chapter 3, **India**). A Catholic bishopric was established at Cohin in 1577, and at the Synod of Diamper in 1599 the Portuguese archbishop of Goa, Alexis Menezes (1559–1617), ordered the Indian churches to swear an oath of loyalty to the pope. He faced stiff resistance from the patriarchs and thus under Portuguese patronage Christianity in India was divided into three groups: the Latin Catholics, the Syrians (who kept Syrian liturgy but obeyed Rome), and the Independent Thomas Christians.

Japan and South-East Asia

In 1545 Xavier travelled to Malaya, the Spice Islands, and Sri Lanka. In 1549 he arrived in Japan and enjoyed early success. The Jesuits were followed by Franciscans, Dominicans, and Augustinians; and Christianity became accepted in the islands of Kyūshū and Honshū. By 1580 the Japanese Christian population was estimated to be around 150,000 and in 1587 the ruling warlord Hideyoshi (1537–98) attempted to expel all Christian missionaries with their foreign ideas. He was not successful, and the next year a bishopric was created at Funai. Official hostility toward Christianity persisted. Six missionaries and twenty-six converts were crucified at Nagasaki in 1597, the persecution driving Christianity largely underground.

Ōmura Sumitada (1533–87)

Sumitada was the first Japanese warlord to convert to Christianity, in 1563. Taking the Christian name "Bartholomew", he forged close links with the Jesuits, opened the port of Nagasaki to foreign trade, and waged an unpopular campaign against Buddhism and the Shinto religion.

China

Francis Xavier died in 1552 while awaiting permission to enter China. A parish had been created in Macao in 1576, but it was not until the missionary journey of the Jesuits Michele Ruggieri (1543–1607) and Matteo Ricci (1552–1610) in 1582 that Christianity made an impact. Ricci gained the esteem of his hosts through his method of adapting Christian concepts to Chinese systems and beliefs. He allowed the use of *t'ien* for God, and found a way to incorporate traditional Chinese ancestor worship into Christian forms. A Christian community flourished, but the Jesuit method of accommodation would eventually draw censure from Rome, contributing to the overall suppression of the Jesuits and the collapse of Christianity in China until the Protestant missions of the nineteenth century.

Ruins of Sao Paulo Church, Macau, China. The church was built by the Jesuits between 1582 and 1602.

The Seventeenth Century

The story of Christianity in this era can be told in three main strands. The revival and expansion of Catholicism continued, leading to a church stronger and more united in some key ways than before the Reformation. Protestantism too continued its course set in the previous century by creating multiple, vibrant reforming groups in Europe and beyond. As Orthodoxy confirmed its central statements of faith, the Russian church grew from strength to strength, dealing with schismatic movements of its own in the process.

Holy Trinity Chuch in Bavaria, Germany. It is a small pilgrimage church, built in 1689 by Georg Dietzenhofer.

Wars of religion?

In the seventeenth century the emergence of nationalism and the sectarian strife between autonomous states would have profound (and bloody) consequences. The series of wars that racked Europe during this time are sometimes referred to as the "wars of religion". Conflicting religious feelings were obviously exploited during these wars; however, the rifts tended to follow national allegiances rather than simply religious differences.

Thirty Years War

The Thirty Years War (1618–48) was a protracted series of conflicts dominated by the two great Catholic houses of Europe.

The war began in Prague in 1618 when Protestant Bohemians rebelled against the Holy Roman Emperor's attempt to enforce uniformity on his territories. Fighting soon spread to include Holland, Denmark, and Sweden, with the actions of Ferdinand II (r. 1619–37) alienating both Protestants and Catholics. In 1630 the conflict incorporated the ongoing struggle between Bourbon France and the Hapsburg houses of Spain and Germany. The Bourbons and their Protestant allies represented the interests of the emerging independent nation-states; the Hapsburgs and the Catholic League defended the old imperial order. Without interference from Pope Urban VIII (r. 1623–44), the French cardinal Richelieu provided material support to the Protestant Swedish king, Gustavus II Adolphus (r. 1611–32), who entered the war in 1630. In 1635 Catholic France directly entered the war on the side of the Protestant groups opposed to imperial power.

Cardinal Richelieu (1585–1642) effectively ruled France and exerted enormous influence throughout Europe. A major patron of the arts, he built the Palais Royal and founded the French Academy in 1635.

Francis de Sales (1567–1622)

A Counter-Reformation missionary to the Swiss Calvinists in 1599, Francis is reported as saying "Love alone will shake the walls of Geneva." In 1610, along with the nun Jane Frances de Chantal (1572–1641), he founded the charitable Order of the Visitation. He was declared a Doctor of the Church in 1877.

The Treaties of Westphalia

The two Treaties of Westphalia brought a decisive end to the Thirty Years War in 1648. Westphalia ushered in a new age of ideological nationalism by recognizing the sovereignty of individual countries, and by superseding the medieval notion that Christendom was united under the highest authority of the church. Westphalia endorsed the formula *cuius regio eius religio*: the subjects of each nation should follow the religion of their ruler. Protection was given to religious minorities and the political legitimacy of the Calvinists was recognized along with that of the Lutherans and Catholics. Church land, too, was "secularized" (a term first used at Westphalia) and distributed among the several nations who participated in the war, to the chagrin of Pope Innocent X (r. 1644–55), whose protest was ignored.

Catholicism

Catholic Christianity did not lose out entirely after the Thirty Years War, despite ceding some ground to the Reformers. The Hussites and other Protestants were

outlawed in Bohemia and the region was declared Catholic. The opening of the century also saw gains for Catholicism in Poland, which, as of 1569, also included the kingdom of Lithuania (extending into modern Belarus and Ukraine).

Ruthenian Catholics

Since the 1596 Union of Brest-Litovsk, many significant Ukrainian Orthodox churches had placed themselves under the authority of Rome, with more bishoprics following in 1694 (Przemysl) and 1700 (Lvov). Thus the majority of Ukrainian (also called Ruthenian) and Polish nobility in this era were Eastern Rite Catholics (see chapter 13).

Transylvanian Catholics

The principality of Transylvania had long been the target of Hungarian Catholic, then German Lutheran, missionary efforts. Though the majority of the population adhered to Orthodoxy, by the opening of the century a minority of the nobility were Calvinists. When Romania was unified in 1600–1601 under the Greek Orthodox hierarchy, these Transylvanian Protestants forced the church to accept many points of reformed doctrine. When the region came under Hapsburg control in 1691 Catholicism was once again added to Calvinism, Lutheranism, and Unitarianism as a "received", officially sanctioned, religion. Under Metropolitan Atanasie Anghel (died 1713), the Transylvanian Greek Catholic Church was born in 1698. In return for accepting the *Filioque* (see chapter 5) and the authority of the pope, the new church was able to keep its liturgy intact, and its clergy were also considered to be "received". The Eastern Rite Transylvanian Church was not initially accepted by the majority of the population, but it would go on to become the centre of Romanian national identity in the eighteenth and nineteenth centuries.

The Jansenist movement

France remained a bastion of Catholic Counter-Reformation ideas and movements, some of which went further than even Rome was willing to follow. One enthusiastic theologian was the bishop of Ypres, Cornelius Otto Jansen

The Black Madonna of Czestochowa. The painting, housed in the Jasna Góra monastery, has long been a focus for Catholic pilgrimage and is a symbol of Polish national pride. Its ancient origins are obscure.

(1585–1638). Jansen's vision was to attack Protestantism with its own weapons and reshape Catholic Christianity through a radical appeal to the writings of Augustine. In 1627 Jansen's project brought him into conflict with the Jesuits. Although Jansen was declared heretical by the University of Paris in 1649 and by Pope Innocent X in 1653, the Jansenist movement retained its popularity and included among its number the scientist and philosopher Blaise Pascal (1623–62).

Sacred Heart

Devotion to the heart of Jesus has its roots in the mystical and meditative tradition of the Middle Ages. John Eudes (1601–80) and Margaret Mary Alacoque (1647–90) gave theological shape to the practice, linking it closely with devotion to the Sacred Heart of Mary. It would become one of the most popular Catholic devotional practices.

Catholic missions

Catholicism rapidly expanded around the world, usually by way of Spanish and Portuguese Jesuit missionaries and often on the back of colonial expansion, leading to occasional tensions between natives, churchmen, and profiteering explorers.

Japan

c.1600

Japanese Christian population estimated to be around 210,000.

1613

The Tokugawa Shogun banishes all Europeans and issues decrees against Christianity.

1640

An estimated 150,000 secret Christians remained in the country.

China

1601

Matteo Ricci (see chapter 15) arrives in Peking.

1615

The Chinese Christian population is estimated at around 5,000.

India

1600

The first Portuguese bishopric established at Angamale.

1606

Diocese of Mailapur established.

1623

Pope Gregory XV (r. 1621–23) intervenes in the controversy over Indian Christians who retain Hindu social customs and cultural practices.

1637

Matheus de Castro of Divar (c.1594–1677), a native of Goa and member of the Brahmin caste, is appointed bishop over the regions not covered by the Portuguese mandate.

South America

c.1600

Jesuits active in Paraguay.

1610

Establishment of the Inquisition in Colombia, Venezuela, and the Spanish Caribbean.

1617

Creation of the Diocese of Buenos Aires. Pedro Carranza (1567–1632) appointed first bishop in 1620.

c.1638

Jesuits active in the Amazon region.

North America

1603

First activity of French Catholicism in Nova Scotia and Quebec.

1609

Missions established in Santa Fé (modern-day New Mexico).

1680

Indian rebellion against colonial rule results in the destruction of the Santa Fé missions. They are restored in 1692.

1687

Eusebio Francisco Kino (1645–1711) establishes early missions in Arizona.

1697

Permanent mission outpost founded in Baja California.

Robert de Nobili (1577–1656)

A Jesuit missionary, Robert arrived in India in 1605. He adopted local customs and became one of the first Europeans to have knowledge of Sanskrit and the primary sacred documents of the Hindu religion. Robert faced opposition, but by the time he retired in 1654 his unorthodox methods had resulted in several thousand converts from all social castes.

Slavery

A small band of churchmen stood against the exploitation and slavery that came with European colonial expansion. The Portuguese Jesuit missionary Antonio Vieira (1608–97) attracted controversy for his **apocalyptic** sermons and for his persistent defence of the Indians of Brazil against colonial exploitation. In 1622 the Caribbean Catholic Synod produced elaborate regulations for the right treatment of the native populations in the West Indies. From 1616, Pedro Claver (1580–1654), a Spanish missionary in Colombia, did much to alleviate the suffering of African slaves brought to the region. The success of his mission among the slave ships led to the condemnation of slavery in a bull issued by Pope Urban VIII in 1639.

Protestantism

Since the previous century, Protestantism had been embraced across Europe both as a vehicle for political freedom and as a vibrant expression of Christianity. Yet the hallmarks of Reformation theology (including the belief in the priesthood of all believers, the high value placed on individual interpretation of Scripture, and the rejection of many hierarchical systems) opened the way to a myriad of different expressions.

Calvinism

John Calvin died in 1564, leaving behind a sophisticated theological system and a wealth of literature such as *Institutes of the Christian Religion* (1536–59). In the seventeenth century, the majority of European Protestants who were not Lutherans were Calvinists of some description, and the movement thrived in France, parts of Germany, Transylvania, Hungary, Scotland, and the North American colonies. The English Puritans were greatly influenced by Calvinist thought. The Netherlands adopted Calvinism as the state religion in 1622.

Predestination

The doctrine that God's eternal plan requires that only the "elect" will be saved while others are predestined to damnation was not originally a central feature of Calvin's thought. Yet under the influence of the theologian Theodore Beza (1519–1605) "predestination" assumed greater importance. This picture of the divine nature prompted opposition from some of Beza's former students. Jacobus Arminius (1560–1609) sparked controversy in his native Holland when he argued against Calvinist determinism in the university and before the legal courts.

Arminianism

Shortly after Arminius's death his followers published *Remonstrance* in 1610, which detailed their major divergence from Calvinism, namely that Christ died for all people and thus it is possible for all to be saved if they freely choose to believe. Theologically the debate struck at the heart of doctrines of God and salvation. Politically, the situation threatened the stability of the Netherlands, which was engaged in ongoing hostilities with Spain.

Synod of Dort

Prince Maurice of Orange (1567–1625) convened the Synod of Dort in 1618–19, welcoming delegates from England, Scotland, Switzerland, and Germany. Originally intended to settle the Arminian problem, Dort had the effect of crystallizing the key doctrines of Calvinism and the theology of the Dutch Reformed Church. By finding *Remonstrance* to be unorthodox, the synod ousted over 200 Arminian leaders from the country. However, Arminianism would go on to exert considerable influence on Christian thought, including that of John Wesley and the Methodists of the following century.

Lutheranism

Martin Luther died in 1546. By the seventeenth century the confessional movement that bore his name was flourishing in most of Germany, Scandinavia, Hungary, and Poland. The number of Lutheran churches and groups produced a variety of expressions, but they all took as their doctrinal guide the 1580 *Book of Concord*, a collection of Luther's *Small* and *Large Catechisms*, the *Augsburg Confession*, the *Smalcald Articles* and other key texts of the German Reformation.

Pious Longings

In reaction to the confessional strife of the Thirty Years War and the potentially stifling effect of Lutheran dogmatism on church and state, the German Lutheran pastor Philip Jakob Spener (1635–1705) wrote *Pious Longings* in 1675. This tract expressed a Reformed Christianity emphasizing personal Bible study, the avoidance of religious arguments, fervent devotion, and faith expressed as love for neighbour rather than knowledge. It counselled against engaging in political power struggles.

Pietism

The movement that arose from Spener's community and writings became known as Pietism. Spener had not invented Pietism, but was drawing on earlier theologians such as Johann Arndt (1555–1621). Nevertheless, Spener became seen as the leader of the new subversive movement and was expelled from Leipzig by his mainstream Lutheran opponents in 1690. Pietism would reach its height under the leadership of Count Zinzendorf (1700–60), and the Pietist influence would be felt in the Protestant revivals of the nineteenth and twentieth centuries.

Opposite: The Protestant Reformer John Calvin died in 1564. It was not long before Calvinist Christianity prevailed in continental Europe, the British Isles and North America.

Below: The interior of a Lutheran German church in Motis, Romania.

Anglicanism

Anglicanism, while not generally as abrupt a departure from Roman Catholic beliefs and practices as the Protestant movements of the European continent, nevertheless existed as a distinct alternative to Roman Catholicism. The English church experienced some of its most formative events in the seventeenth century.

Puritans

The Puritan movement aimed to implement a full Calvinist Reformation within the Anglican church. Puritans considered that a literalist interpretation of the Bible was the only authority in matters of doctrine, ethics, and church structure. Personal conversion and strict morality were emphasized, as was a heightened awareness of the **"end times"**. Puritanism was a driving force behind the English Civil War and a foundational element in the creation of the new American colonies.

Presbyterians

The name derives from the biblical term *presbyter* (elder), and refers to congregations that elect their own governor rather than submit to a system of bishops and priests. Under the leadership of John Knox (c.1514–72) and his successors the national church (or kirk) of Scotland was strongly Presbyterian, often engaging in a struggle against the imposition of Anglicanism. The Presbyterian Scottish Kirk was finally established in 1692.

King James

King James VI of Scotland assumed the English throne after the death of Elizabeth I in 1603. During his reign, James opposed the Presbyterian movement in Scotland and sought compromise with the Puritans of England. In 1605 the discovery of the "Gunpowder Plot" to destroy the Houses of Parliament led to stricter laws against English Roman Catholics and exacerbated the continuing tensions with Catholic nations, especially Spain. James was keenly interested in church affairs and his endorsement of a new English translation of the Bible led to the "King James" Authorized Version in 1611.

The English Civil War

James's successor, King Charles I (r. 1625–49), tended to adopt policies favourable to Catholicism and to move the church away from the Calvinist influence of his predecessors. A series of disastrous military expeditions abroad, coupled with an authoritarian rule at home, led to Charles's extreme unpopularity. In 1640 his powers were severely curtailed by Parliament. The ensuing English Civil War (1642–48) saw the execution of the Anglican monarch and the imposition of a Puritan republic under the rule of Oliver Cromwell (1599–1658).

Republic and Restoration

Cromwell's dissolution of the old Church of England and his attempt to impose a new, Puritan style of church and government ultimately proved unpopular with the people. In 1660 the exiled Charles II (r. 1660–85), a Catholic sympathizer and eventual convert, was welcomed back as king, with the country and church forging a new settlement known as the Restoration.

Uniformity and nonconformity

The 1662 Act of Uniformity restored the Establishment by commanding universal adoption of the *Book of Common Prayer* and Anglican ordination. The result for those churchmen who refused to comply was the creation of the **nonconformists,** a category including the English Presbyterians, Quakers, Congregationalists, Baptists and, later, Methodists. It was largely nonconformism that brought about the energizing influence of Protestant Christianity in the New World.

Opposite: James I of England (by John de Critz the Elder). His Authorized Version of the Bible is one of the most widely read books in the world.

John Bunyan (1628–88)

As a young Puritan, Bunyan fought in the Civil War. Following the Restoration, between 1660 and 1672 Bunyan was imprisoned for his Dissenting preaching. While incarcerated he wrote *The Pilgrim's Progress* (published in two parts, 1678 and 1684), an allegory of the Christian life that would go on to become one of the most widely read books in the history of Christianity.

Quakers

Also known as the Religious Society of Friends, the Quakers were originally a Puritan sect founded in 1647, who earned their name for the way in which they trembled before the word of God. Their founder, George Fox (1624–91), preached that Christians should seek the Holy Spirit rather than the words of men as a guide to Christian worship. As a result Quakers became known for their silent meetings. Women share equal responsibility with men in leadership and Quakers refuse to participate in violence. They were instrumental in the abolition of slavery in the eighteenth century.

Congregationalists

These Puritans contended that the church should consist only of those who have made the conscious decision to follow Christ, opposing on principle the idea of a national church and emphasizing the independence of local congregations. The Pilgrim Fathers set off from a Congregationalist church in 1620 and, since then, the movement has been integral to the organization of Christianity in North America.

Baptists

In 1609 the separatist Puritan John Smyth (c.1560–1612) led his congregation into the practice of believer's baptism – establishing a church around freely converted adults – rather than infant baptism. By 1660 there were around 300 Baptist churches in England and Wales. With their strong missionary focus, Baptist denominations have been hugely influential in the spread of Christianity throughout the world.

Protestant Americans

1607

Anglican church established at first permanent North American settlement in Jamestown, Virginia.

1620

Puritan pilgrims sail from England and Holland to America in the *Mayflower*.

1630

John Winthrop (1587–1649) founds a Congregationalist settlement in Massachusetts.

1639

Roger Williams (c.1603–83) founds the first American Baptist church in Providence, Rhode Island.

1643

Roman Catholicism is outlawed in Virginia.

1663

John Eliot (1604–90) publishes the first Bible to be printed in North America, in the language of the Algonquian people.

1664

The Dutch colony New Amsterdam is taken over and renamed New York by the English. The Dutch Reformed Presbyterian Church (present since 1628) continues to flourish under English rule.

1682

William Penn (1644–1718) leads an emigration of over 2,000 Welsh Quakers to the newly created state of Pennsylvania.

1692

Witch trials in Salem, Massachusetts.

1690s

English Protestants are joined by French Huguenots (see chapter 15), German Mennonites, and Dutch Calvinists in the American colonies.

Orthodoxy

The influence of the Protestantism of Western Europe was also felt in the East, which was still living largely under Ottoman Muslim rule.

The Calvinist patriarch

Cyril Lucar (1572–1638) became ecumenical patriarch of Constantinople in 1620. Lucar was familiar with the controversies of the Reformation, having used some Protestant writings during his conflict with Rome at the 1596 Synod of Brest-Litovsk. He forged close ties with European Protestants, especially in England. In 1628 he presented the

Codex Alexandrinus to the English king – a fifth-century copy of the Bible, and the earliest surviving example of Byzantine text. As a result of Ottoman opposition, Lucar was deposed numerous times during the course of his patriarchate, but was restored to the position partly with the aid of Dutch and English ambassadors to Constantinople.

In 1629 Lucar published the thoroughly Calvinist *Confession of Faith* which laid out his vision for an Orthodox Church following Reformed doctrine. In 1638 he sponsored a translation of the Bible into modern Greek, the same year that he was put to death by Sultan Murad IV (r. 1623–40) for treason against the Ottoman Turks.

Orthodox reaction

Lucar's Calvinist leanings were more positively received in Western Europe than they were at home. Shortly after his death a series of councils repudiated his attempted reforms. As a result, these councils helped to clarify Orthodox theology, leading to the establishment of key statements of Orthodox faith.

Synod of Jassy

Lesser synods at Constantinople in 1638 and 1642 began the process, but it was the Synod of Jassy (also in 1642, in what is now Romania) that did much to consolidate Orthodox tradition. Jassy condemned the Calvinist teaching of Lucar, and at the same time positively endorsed the *Orthodox Confession* of Peter Mogila (c.1596–1646).

Peter Mogila

The metropolitan of Kiev from 1633, Mogila is credited with doing much to educate the clergy and laity of the Orthodox Church. His *Confession* was first composed in 1638 and is regarded as a primary document of Orthodoxy, providing a comprehensive survey of the faith. Originally Mogila's text was criticized for its debt to Roman Catholic Thomist theology, but after revision it was accepted by Jassy and published in 1645. Mogila was able to outline further the Orthodox objection to both Catholic and Protestant claims, with the *Confession* eventually earning the endorsement of the great Synod of Jerusalem in 1672.

Synod of Jerusalem

Along with Jassy, the Synod of Jerusalem is the most important council in the history of the Orthodox Church. Seven metropolitans and sixty-eight Orthodox bishops convened at the Church of the Nativity in Bethlehem. The main acts of the synod fell into two categories. The "Six Chapters" put a conclusive end to the Protestant influence of Lucar's *Confessions*, while the "Eighteen Articles" provided a detailed catechism of Orthodox faith.

Russian Orthodox church, Copenhagen, Denmark.

Russian troubles

In Russia, the period between 1598 and 1613 is sometimes known as the "Time of Troubles" on account of the chaos following the death of Ivan IV "the Terrible" and the institution of the new Romanov dynasty. The patriarchs of the Russian church played an important part in leading the people through this time, including especially Germogen (c.1530–1612) and Filaret (c.1550–1633). Filaret was the father of the Romanov tsar Michael (1613–45), and he dominated national politics. Under Filaret and his successors, state and church became indistinguishable, leading to much material corruption and abuse of power.

Zealous reform

The situation in the Russian church prompted a groundswell of desire among the clergy to return the faithful to a life of sincere devotion. One such zealous monk was Nikon (1605–81), who in 1652 was appointed patriarch of Moscow by the new, reform-minded Tsar Alexis (1645–76). Alexis and Nikon revised the Russian liturgy and corrected various corruptions that they felt had crept into the service.

Old Believers

The deep reforms were enforced throughout the land, prompting much resentment. At times, Alexis and Nikon were even identified with the antichrist and accused of bringing the church into further error. When the new liturgical practice was finally endorsed in 1666, a section of the church under the leadership of Archpriest Avvakum (c.1620–82) refused to comply. Avvakum (whose *Autobiography* is considered a landmark in Russian literature) was imprisoned and martyred in 1682. His movement, called the Old Believers or *Raskolniki* (schismatics), included thousands of peasants, townsfolk, and priests and they experienced fierce persecution. Old Believers fled to Serbia and Karelia, and many committed mass suicide rather than face execution at the hands of the tsar's soldiers. Despite sporadic persecution, especially under Peter the Great (1682–1725), the Old Believers persisted in various factions and remain a feature of the Russian religious landscape.

Dositheus (1641–1707)

Dositheus was patriarch of Jerusalem from 1669 and, under his considerable influence, Orthodoxy combated Protestant innovations and continued to resist Roman Catholic inroads. He established printed presses to encourage Orthodox literature, limited Franciscan access to the holy places in Jerusalem, opposed the development of the Eastern Rite (see chapter 13) churches and sought to extend the Greek influence over the Russian church.

The Western Wall and Dome of the Rock mosque at dusk, Jerusalem.

The Eighteenth Century

In the eighteenth century, key features of Greek Orthodoxy were developed under Muslim rule, while in Russia a series of visionary leaders drew the Church closer to the seat of government. For Protestantism, the philosophical Enlightenment had far-reaching effects on Christian thought and practice.

At the same time, Evangelical revivals swept England and America with a new form of personal and practical faith. Meanwhile Roman Catholicism thrived in India, China and Korea, while the success of the Jesuit network led to concerted efforts to dismantle its power. In France, the Revolution offered a bloody rebellion against the old order that would have reverberations throughout the world.

Orthodoxy

Russia

Nikon, the patriarch of Moscow between 1652 and 1658, had brought in controversial reforms striking at the heart of the old Russian way of religious life (see chapter 16). In the process, he had also claimed that the patriarch, and not the tsar, should be the *Veliki Gosudar* (Great Sovereign) of the state. Unsurprisingly, this claim was not welcomed by the

The Preobrazhenskaya Church of Transfiguration on Kizhi Island, Russia, was built in 1714 and features twenty-two shingled domes.

imperial power, and Nikon was exiled
and imprisoned in a remote monastery
for fourteen years, to be succeeded by
a number of ineffectual patriarchs. The
assertion of the power of the tsar over the
church reached its height in the reign of
Peter "the Great" (1682–1725).

Peter the Great

A secularist and admirer of Western
innovations, Peter saw the church as an
obstacle to his plans. At the same time, he
used the church to extend the ideology
of complete obedience to the ruler and
strengthened the practice of serfdom.
When Patriarch Adrian (1627–1700)
died, Peter let the post remain vacant for
twenty-one years. As a way of enforcing
the cultural influence of Orthodoxy,
compulsory confession was introduced in
1716, and church attendance on Sundays
and holidays was made a legal requirement
throughout the land in 1718. In 1721,
the same year that Peter proclaimed
himself Emperor of All the Russias, he also
concentrated all the power of the church
under the tsar.

College of Spiritual Affairs

In 1721, along with Bishop Prokopovich
(1681–1736), Peter abolished the Russian
patriarchate, instituting the College of
Spiritual Affairs in its place, with himself at
its head. The college was soon renamed the
"Holy Synod" to make it more palatable to
reluctant bishops; nevertheless the church
effectively became a wing of the Russian

government. In 1722 Peter nullified
the traditional practice of confidential
confessions, ordering instead that priests
report any insults or conspiracies against
the tsar, handing over their parishioners
to the state police. This system by which
the Holy Synod was closely bound to the
interests of the state would remain in
Russia for the next two centuries, leading
to divisions between the ruling elite of the
church and the common clergy serving the
majority of the population.

Tikhon of Zadonsk (1724–83)

Tikhon was a writer and bishop who retired to the Zadonsk monastery in 1769. His humility and care for the poor inspired later Russian writers, including Dostoevsky, who used Tikhon as the model for the character of Father Zosima in *The Brothers Karamazov* (1880).

Empress Catherine II. Catherine "the Great" brought a measure of religious toleration to Russia.

Catherine the Great

One beneficiary of the Holy Synod settlement was Catherine the Great, who reigned from 1762 until her death in 1796. Catherine, a German princess, continued to exert a Western, Enlightenment influence on the Russian church. In 1764 Catherine confiscated much church and monastic land, thus depriving Russian Orthodoxy of over three-quarters of its annual income. In 1767 she issued an *Instruction* which called for the "prudent toleration of other religions", and in 1771 Old Believers were allowed to set up limited communities in Moscow. Keen to maintain educational standards, Catherine also briefly welcomed back the Jesuits, allowing for the creation of a Roman Catholic bishopric in Mogilëv in 1773.

Moscow's reach extends

The Russo–Turkish War of 1768–74 ended with the Treaty of Kuchuk Kainarji (signed in Bulgaria), granting the victorious Catherine political and economic rights over vast swathes of the Ottoman empire. More far-reaching was the right granted to the Russian tsar to intervene in the affairs of Christians living under Ottoman rule. Thus, in the 1780s Catherine assumed control over the kingdom of Georgia, bringing its church under the influence of the Russian Holy Synod. Furthermore, Greek Orthodox citizens in Moldavia, Wallachia, the Aegean Islands, and elsewhere in the Ottoman empire began to look forward to the prospect of protection under the Third Rome of Moscow.

The New Martyrs

Although the Ottoman sultan's power was waning, the majority of Orthodox Christians in the eighteenth century still lived under Muslim rule. The era witnessed a number of martyrs, who in subsequent Orthodox tradition would be celebrated as "New Martyrs". In 1716 Anthimos, a Georgian monk and printer and the metropolitan of Wallachia, was executed by Turkish soldiers. Kosmas Aitolos (died 1779), a Greek monk and educator, was caught up in the 1770 Peloponnesian revolt against the Turks before being captured and executed as a Russian sympathizer in Albania. The following year monks at the Monastery of the Cross in Jerusalem were massacred. In 1788 the Bosnian Theodore Sladich and 150 of his followers were burnt at Moshtanica, a Serbian monastery. Sladich had agitated against Eastern Rite movements toward Catholicism, Serbian secularization, and Ottoman rule, and was thus considered a disturber of the peace by the Turkish authorities.

The Monastery of the Holy Cross stands alone on a plot of land outside the Old City of Jerusalem.

Greek decline

Despite sporadic persecution of Christians under the Ottoman empire, the ecumenical patriarch of Constantinople worked under Ottoman permission and remained the nominal leader of the Orthodox church. But the 1774 Russian victory that weakened Ottoman power also led to a decline in Greek leadership of the church. Although in the new reality of the Eastern church the Russians were becoming dominant, nevertheless the Greeks continued to assert their traditional authority within Orthodoxy.

Useless waters

Opposition to the Latin influence was a persistent theme in Orthodox life. Beginning in 1749, the ecumenical patriarch Cyril V (died 1775) sought to counteract the Protestant and French Catholic presence in Constantinople and in the Holy Land. In 1755 he published *Anathema of Those Who Accept Papal Sacraments*, a tract that was popularly received in the churches of the city. In the same year, together with the patriarchs of Jerusalem and Alexandria, Cyril released *Decree of the Holy Great Church of Christ*. The *Decree* was primarily concerned with the legitimacy of Catholic and Protestant baptism, declaring: "we reject and abhor baptisms belonging to heretics... They are useless waters."

Love of the beautiful

Cyril died in retirement on Mount Athos in 1775, the same year that the Greek monk Nicodemus (c.1749–1809) took up residence there. Nicodemus of the Holy Mountain produced a number of spiritual writings. He produced a Greek version of Ignatius of Loyola's *Spiritual Exercises*, keen to allow Western thought to illuminate the Eastern tradition where it could. In 1782, together with Macarius of Corinth (1731–1805), Nicodemus produced *Love of the Beautiful*, a collection of spiritual writings from the fourth to the fifteenth centuries which dealt primarily with the Jesus Prayer and the Hesychast tradition (see chapter 13). Through widespread distribution, with translations into Slavonic (1793) and Russian (1876), *Love of the Beautiful* became one of the most important texts for modern Orthodoxy, acting as a force for unification in a tradition that had seen much division.

PROTESTANTISM

Two often opposing intellectual and cultural forces affected the development of Protestant Christianity in the eighteenth century: Enlightenment and Evangelicalism.

Enlightenment

The intellectual developments and ideals known as "the Enlightenment" built on the mechanistic and rationalist philosophies of René Descartes (1596–1650), John Locke (1632–1704), and other seventeenth-century thinkers. The German philosopher Immanuel Kant (1724–1804) defined the movement in a famous essay, *What is Enlightenment?* (1784): "Enlightenment is man's emergence from his self-imposed immaturity... *Sapere Aude* [dare to know]! 'Have courage to use your own understanding!' – that is the motto of enlightenment."

Enlightenment thinkers were often opposed to orthodox Catholic and Protestant Christianity and some philosophers supported **deistic** or atheistic world-views. Leading figures include David Hume (1711–76), Adam Smith (1723–90) and Jean-Jacques Rousseau (1712–78). Enlightenment thinkers were not uniformly anti-Christian, however, and many (such as Kant) saw themselves as reforming traditional faith. The German theologian Friedrich Schleiermacher (1768–1834) appealed to Enlightenment principles while at the same time critiquing the excesses of intellectual rationalism. His 1799 *Religion: Speeches to its Cultured Despisers* has been enormously influential in the development of Protestant theology.

Evangelicals

The term "evangelical" (derived from the Greek *euaggelion* meaning "gospel" or "good news") had long been associated with the established Reformation churches of Germany and Switzerland. In the English-speaking world of the eighteenth century the term began to refer not to

Immanuel Kant, "Father of the Enlightenment" and Professor of Logic and Metaphysics of Konigsberg University, Germany.

a denomination but to those Christians who emphasized personal conversion and faith in the atoning death of Jesus Christ. Evangelical convictions were accompanied by a culture of mission and social activism, leading, among other things, to the institution of Sunday schools to promote literacy in England, social reform in India, and the abolition of slavery in the British empire in the nineteenth century. Formative influences on evangelicalism included John Newton (1725–1807), the former slave-trader who wrote the hymn "Amazing Grace". However, it was with the brothers Charles (1707–88) and John (1703–91) Wesley and their friend George Whitefield (1714–70) that evangelical sentiments became closely identified with a new movement known as Methodism.

Nikolaus Ludwig Graf von Zinzendorf, Moravian Count and pietist pastor.

Moravians

In 1722 the Moravian Count Zinzendorf established the Moravian Brotherhood when he welcomed a group of Czech Pietists (known as Bohemian Brethren) on to his estates at Herrnhut (in modern-day Saxony, Germany). The Moravian Brotherhood emphasized a pietistic "religion of the heart" rather than strict doctrine. Moravian missions were founded in the West Indies (1732), Greenland (1733), and South Africa (1736), and among the Inuit people of Labrador in 1752. The Moravian Church remains in existence, with a large proportion of members residing in Tanzania, where a mission was established in the nineteenth century.

A strange warming

Methodism had its roots among a group of serious-minded Oxford theology students, including the Wesley brothers, who gathered together to pray methodically and study the Bible. The group disappeared when John and Charles left Oxford for London in 1735, but was revived after contact with a Moravian group led by Peter Boehler (1712–75). It was after one such meeting in 1738 that John Wesley described in his *Journal* how his heart was "strangely warmed".

Methodists

Finding the traditional churches closed to their style of worship, Whitefield and the Wesleys took their message of "vital practical religion" to the masses, preaching to great effect in the open air from 1739. The successful movement soon brought a separate sense of identity to the adherents, formed in large part by Charles Wesley, who penned over 9,000 Methodist hymns in his lifetime. John Wesley – theologically an Arminian (see chapter 16) – broke with the Calvinist George Whitefield in 1741. By 1751 Wesley's organization of lay preachers spanned England and the movement had taken root in America. In 1784 Wesley appointed Thomas Coke (1747–1814) as superintendent, or bishop, of the American Methodist Church. After Wesley's death a number of secessions would lead to the formal divide between various Methodist groups and the Church of England in the first decades of the nineteenth century.

Protestant India

The first Protestant missionaries to India were sponsored by the Danish king Frederick IV (r. 1699–1730). Bartholomaeus Ziegenbalg (1682–1719) and Heinrich Plütschau (1677–1747) arrived at the Danish Indian settlement of Tranquebar in 1706. Despite facing severe opposition from Roman Catholics and Hindus, the Pietist (see above) missionaries managed to attract a Tamil congregation. Churches, schools, orphanages, and printing presses followed, with Ziegenbalg producing the first Tamil translation of the New Testament in 1714. Ziegenbalg and Plütschau's accounts of their exploits became popular in Britain, helping to stir up English enthusiasm for mission.

"English" missions

Concurrent with the evangelical revival at home, the English sponsored many missions abroad, often employing non-British missionaries, with a focus on south India. One of the most celebrated of these was Christian Friedrich Schwartz (1726–98), a Prussian Pietist who arrived in India in 1750 having already learned Tamil. Schwartz was active in Ceylon (1760), Trichinopoly (1767), and the kingdom of Tanjore (1772), where he was highly honoured by the rajah and given positions of political responsibility.

Luz Church at Mylapore in Chennai, Tamil Nadu, India.

Selina Hastings, Countess of Huntingdon (1707–1791)

Lady Huntingdon did much to introduce Methodism to the upper classes, using her influence to employ many Methodist chaplains as priests in the Anglican Church. When barred from establishing more chapels and making more appointments within the Church of England she registered her chapels as dissenting places of worship, thus founding the Countess of Huntingdon's Connexion in 1779.

Mission and social reform

Schwartz was a great influence on Charles Grant (1746–1823), a director of the British East India Company. Grant was a driving force behind the British and Foreign Bible Society, the Church Missionary Society, and the Society for the Propagation of the Gospel. A member of the influential Clapham Sect (see below), Grant opposed the British government's aggressive policy in India. His arguments brought him into opposition with the long-standing position of the East India Company, which opposed any Christian activity that would undermine their commercial dominance.

The father of modern mission

The cobbler William Carey (1761–1834) founded the Baptist Missionary Society in 1792. As the East India Trading Company had banned missionaries travelling in British ships, in 1793 he journeyed to Bengal in a Danish vessel.

A skilled linguist, Carey translated the Bible and other books into Bengali and other Indian languages. He also established a number of schools and hospitals, and waged a long campaign against infanticide and the traditional custom of *suttee* where widows were expected to die on their husband's funeral pyres. The practice was eventually abolished, with the order translated into Bengali by Carey's own hand in 1829.

American colonies

Under the influence of theologians and pastors such as Cotton Mather (1663–1728), whose *Christ's American Miracles* was published in 1702, North America began to develop a Christian identity distinct from that of Europe. Catholicism retained a hold in the French and Spanish areas; however, it was often suppressed or outlawed in the English colonies in favour of Puritan and evangelical Protestantism.

Great awakenings

Between 1725 and 1760 a series of "stirrings" among Dutch Reformed and Presbyterian congregations followed the fervent preaching of pastors such as Theodore Frelinghuysen (1691–1747) and Gilbert Tennent (1703–64), who emphasized personal conviction of sin and the need to be "born again". These evangelical movements became known as the "Great Awakening". Together the disparate spiritual revivals would have deep social implications and influence the 1776 American Revolutionary War and the Declaration of Independence, and later the Civil War and abolitionist movements of the next century.

Edwards and Whitefield

The foremost Puritan theologian of this time was Jonathan Edwards (1703–58). From 1735 the Great Awakening movement became closely identified with Edwards and his friend the English

African-American churches

The Great Awakening inspired white Christian missions and attracted increasing numbers of black slaves and freedmen to Christianity in the 1740s. Black-led churches were suppressed in the South, but after the revolution a handful of black Methodist, Baptist, and other congregations grew up in the North. A coalition of Quakers and freed slaves founded the Free African Society in 1787, eventually leading to the opening of the "Mother Bethel" African Methodist Episcopal (AME) Church in 1794. The driving force for the project was Richard Allen (1760–1831), who would go on to become the first Methodist bishop of a fully independent African-American denomination in 1816. The first American foreign missions were undertaken by black preachers such as the Baptist George Liele (c.1750–1820), working in Jamaica, and David George (c.1742–1810) in Sierra Leone.

Methodist George Whitefield, who was seeing enthusiastic responses during his preaching tour of the colonies. Both Edwards and Whitefield were conservative Calvinists, opposed to Arminianism (see chapter 16) and cautious about excessive emotionalism. In 1746 Edwards published the *Treatise Concerning Religious Affections,* an answer to criticisms that the revivals were merely products of emotional manipulation. At the same time as defending the evangelical movement as a work of the Holy Spirit, the study took seriously the negative effects of the awakening on Christian thought and practice, recognizing the marked tendency toward division among congregations affected by the revivals.

The choir of Greater St Stephen's Baptist Church, New Orleans, USA.

American Revolution

The feelings of individualism, religious voluntarism, and moral seriousness sweeping the North American colonies contributed to growing political and economic disaffection with England. In turn, the American Revolution of 1776–83 had a number of effects on Christianity in the United States. Congregationalists, Baptists, and Presbyterians were largely behind the revolution and thus enjoyed cultural prominence, while the pacifist Quakers and Mennonites suffered persecution for refusing to fight for either side. With clear connections to England, Anglicanism and Methodism were forced to adapt. Many Anglican loyalists fled to Canada, while the American Methodist Church was "set apart" from the Wesley connection under its new superintendent, Thomas Coke, in 1784. However, the most significant and enduring legacy for the liberty and diversity of American Christianity came in 1791 with the adoption of Article I of the Bill of Rights: "Congress shall make no law respecting an establishment of religion."

Canada

Canadian Christianity had originally been established under the aegis of French Jesuits in the seventeenth century. The first German Lutherans arrived in 1750. Baptists, Quakers, and Moravians followed in the 1760s. The extension of British control over the French Canadian territories in 1763 brought an influx of English-speaking Irish and Scottish Catholics, as well as Presbyterians and other Protestants. French Roman Catholics became no more than a significant minority. Methodist churches followed in 1775 and Loyalists swelled Anglican ranks after the American Revolution. The spread of the Anglican Church of Canada was further aided by the Constitutional Act of 1791, which divided Quebec into Upper and Lower Canada and reserved land, rent, and income for Anglicans. The act contributed greatly to feelings of resentment among Roman Catholic French nationalists.

Last of the witch hunts

In 1697 Judge Samuel Sewall (1652–1730) publicly repented of his involvement in the witch trials at Salem, Massachusetts. Prussia (1714), England and Scotland (1736), Germany (1755), and Poland (1776) all repealed capital laws against suspected witches during this time.

Catholicism

India

At the opening of the century Catholic Christianity was thriving in the southern Indian regions of Madura and Mysore under Portuguese colonial rule. Christian practice followed the pattern set by the Jesuit Robert de Nobili (see chapter 16), and was overseen by popular priests such as the Frenchman John Venantius Bouchet (1655–1732) and the Italian Costanzo Giuseppe Beschi (1680–1747), who wrote and taught in Tamil.

Malabar Rites

The Capuchins (also active in India) questioned the "accommodation" methods of the Jesuits, who adopted Hindu customs and allowed their converts to retain many of their cultural and religious practices. In 1703 Pope Clement XI (r. 1700–21) sent Cardinal de Tournon (1668–1710) to investigate. In sixteen articles Tournon condemned the so-called "Malabar Rites" as mixing idolatry with Christianity, and commanded the missionaries to serve all Indians regardless of caste distinctions. The Jesuits felt they had been misrepresented, and challenged the practical worth of Tournon's recommendations. As a result the decree was revised in 1734 and in 1744 Pope Benedict XIV (1740–58) issued *Omnium sollicitudinum*, a bull creating missionaries specifically to work among the pariah or untouchable castes so as not to offend Brahmin sensibilities.

China

Jesuit fortunes in China followed a similar path to that in India. Following the success of Matteo Ricci (see chapter 15), Chinese Christianity flourished alongside the honouring of Confucius and some forms of ancestor reverence. The Dominican missionaries present in China alleged that the Jesuit "Chinese Rites" constituted idolatry and superstition. In 1704, and again in 1715, Pope Clement XI issued bulls commanding the Jesuits to suppress all pagan practices. (Benedict XIV would confirm the ruling against the Jesuits in 1742.) The imposition of foreigners pronouncing on Chinese affairs drew the ire of Emperor K'ang Hsi (1661–1722), who banished all missionaries in 1717. This began a campaign against Christianity that would culminate in the Great Persecution in Shandong in 1784–85.

Korea

Unlike neighbouring countries for which Christianity was a foreign import, Korea saw Christianity take root primarily through the initiative of Koreans. In 1783 Lee Sung-hun (1756–1801) was sent to China to learn more about Catholicism. He was baptized and upon his return in 1784 set about founding a new Korean church. The congregation had no formal priests, although the ex-Jesuit missionary Peter Grammont did secretly enter the country in 1785

and in 1794 the Chinese Catholic priest Chu Munmo (1752–1801) began work baptizing and ordaining. By 1801 there were an estimated 10,000 Korean Catholics. Christianity's attack on ancestor worship was considered subversive, resulting in state opposition. The 1801 Shinyu persecutions claimed the lives of over 300 people, including Chu Munmo and Lee Sung-hun.

The old order

The opposition to Jesuit missionary tactics in India and China reflected a wider move against the Society of Jesus. Across Europe traditional institutions, with their economic, political, and religious ties, were being replaced by new settlements. Symbolically, in some ways the Jesuits represented the height of this old older. With their international networks, educational establishments, and pledge of ultimate allegiance to the pope, the Jesuits also posed a material obstacle to the emerging nation-states and their corresponding empires.

Jesuit suppression

In the eighteenth century a number of local suppressions occurred. Russia expelled the Jesuits in 1719 (although Catherine the Great permitted them to return in 1773; see above). In 1759 the Catholic king José (r. 1750–77) banished the society from Portugal and all Portuguese territories. In 1762 the French king Louis XV (r. 1715–74) confiscated Jesuit property and forbade Jesuits to teach or recruit. Two years later the Jesuits were totally

Left: A cross has been on the Royal Mount in Montreal, Quebec since first erected by French missionaries in 1643. Today, an illuminated cross dominates the skyline of the city.

expelled from the country. In 1767 Charles III (1759–88) ordered the deportation of 5,000 Jesuits from the Spanish empire. Finally, combined pressure from the great imperial and lesser state powers led Pope Clement XIV (1769–74) to issue the bull *Dominus ac redemptor*, dissolving the society in 1773.

Anti-Catholic Enlightenment

In Protestant Europe the Enlightenment was largely led by Christians keen to reformulate the religion along rationalist lines. Despite the cultural, scientific, and philosophical contributions arising from the Jesuit educational system, the Enlightenment of Catholic Europe tended to take a more explicitly anti-Christian turn. The appropriation of Enlightenment values as a way to attack the church was most evident in France. The French church of the eighteenth century had been racked by disputes over Protestantism, Gallicanism, the Counter-Reformation, and the rigour of Jansenism (see chapter 16). The conflict between Jesuits and Jansenists soon became a focal point for many of the bitter divisions present in French society.

The Jansenist revival

The Taking of the Louvre, Paris by Jean Louis Bezard (1799–1860) commemorates a scene from the French Revolution.

In 1713 Pope Clement XI, at the instigation of King Louis XIV of France (r. 1643–1715), vigorously condemned the Jansenists with the papal bull *Unigenitus*. However, their repression was unpopular, and unsuccessful, and from 1727 a Jansenist revival swept through Paris. In 1729 the *Parlement* supported the Jansenists against the king and the church, declaring liberty of conscience for all France.

The *philosophes*

These popular anti-papal sentiments soon developed into a more explicitly anti-Christian movement, led by intellectuals and political theorists known collectively as the *philosophes*. The *philosophes* held a variety of opinions, but all agreed that Christianity was an obstacle to the rational reorganization of society that they wished for. Some prominent figures such as the satirist Voltaire were deists, while others including Denis Diderot (1713–84), editor of the controversial *Encyclopaedia*, were militant atheists. In an effort to counter the amoral and nihilistic implications of a godless society, Jean-Jacques Rousseau devised a "civic religion". His *Social Contract* (1762) set out a vision for society based on the general will of the people, making the state, and not the church, the ultimate object of a person's allegiance. Rousseau's ideas were enormously influential on the modern relationship between Christianity and government, and he helped define the new politics of revolutionary North America and Europe.

French Revolution

France in the late eighteenth century faced financial ruin, in part following that country's support of the American War of Independence in 1776. With the aim of creating a national body capable of raising funds, King Louis XVI (r. 1774–92) revived the legislative institution of the States General in 1789, incorporating the aristocracy, the clergy, and a third group of wealthy commoners. Louis' plan did not work. In rebellion against the king, the "Third Estate" created a separate National Assembly and that year passed the "Declaration of the Rights of Man".

Oath of obedience

The Declaration announced a break from the old order of the *ancien régime*, effectively creating a national church answerable to the (male, land-owning) electorate. In 1791 all the clergy were required to swear an oath of obedience to the Civil Constitution. Pope Pius VI (r. 1775–99)

issued a formal condemnation of the oath and half of the clergy refused to comply, bringing their parishioners with them and splitting the country between revolution and church.

The Terror

From 1792 the state perpetrated mass executions and violence against the aristocracy and clergy within France, as well as declaring war on the Holy Roman Empire and the Catholic Church. In 1793 the king and queen of France were executed. A bloody de-Christianizing campaign was fully underway, which saw the drowning of priests, nuns, and monks, the destruction of churches, and the dismantling of all Christian institutions.

The revolution spreads

Instability within France affected the wider church. In retaliation against Pius VI's condemnation of the oath of obedience, the revolutionaries annexed the papal territories of Avignon and Venaissin in 1791. French troops, led by Napoleon Bonaparte (1769–1821), occupied the Papal States in 1798. That same year a French-sponsored revolution in Rome led to the capture of Pope Pius VI, marking the lowest point of prestige for the papacy.

Napoleonic restoration

Pius died in exile in 1799, the same year that Napoleon staged a coup. He recognized that the dismantling of Christianity had alienated France from much of Europe and had led to disillusion among the people, especially the poor and weak who benefited most from church institutions. Accordingly, in 1801 Napoleon sought peace by reaching an agreement with the new pope, Pius VII (r. 1800–23). The concordat of 1801 restored the Catholic Church in France and reinstated the public standing of the papal office, signalling a new direction for Western Christendom in the nineteenth century.

Revolutionary religion

In the place of Christianity, the French revolutionaries instituted secular pageantry and ceremonies. In Paris, the Church of St Geneviève, which had been rebuilt by Louis XV, was converted as a pantheon in honour of humanistic heroes, an opera singer representing the Goddess of Reason was installed in Notre-Dame Cathedral, and rationalist liturgy was produced to praise the revolution.

View of the facade of the Pantheon, Paris, France, built 1757–90.

The Nineteenth Century

The nineteenth century was a time of political revolution accompanied by cultural upheaval and intellectual unrest. Here, Catholicism tended toward conservatism, establishing as dogma some of its most distinctive articles of faith.

Protestantism faced change in different ways. Some groups embraced liberal, critical scepticism of established doctrine. Others bypassed academic debates in favour of practical religion and mission. Social reform thrived, with many Christians opposing slavery. The issue also featured in Orthodox debates over the treatment of Russian serfs and the merits of a peasant, national religion. Indeed, as autonomous churches emerged from under Ottoman rule, the entire Orthodox world was taken up with nationalistic ideas.

Catholicism

Napoleon

The 1801 concordat between Napoleon Bonaparte and Pope Pius VII had the immediate effect of restoring the Catholic Church in France. However, with the *Organic Articles* of 1802 its terms were soon altered to the extent that the government retained firm control over public worship and religious education. Napoleon had Pius crown him Emperor of the French in 1804. By 1808 Napoleon's troops occupied Rome and the Papal States, and

Napoleon Bonaparte, Emperor of the French. His military advance across Europe unsettled church and state and set the stage for future revolution.

he had abolished the Inquisition after assuming control over Spain and Italy. In 1813 he engaged Pius in intense negotiations, eventually forcing the pope to sign another concordat granting the emperor control over the bishops of France and Italy. The church resisted the clergy placed there by Napoleon, with the Belgians especially proving intransigent. In 1814, weakened by defeat in Russia and challenged on many military fronts throughout Europe, the emperor was forced to release the pope, restore the papal territories and repudiate the concordat. A coalition of British, Prussian, and other forces defeated Napoleon at the Battle of Waterloo and forced him to abdicate in 1815. Napoleon left behind a shell-shocked, fragmented Europe, a fresh legacy of unstable church–state relations, and a culture of revolutionary idealism.

Revolutionary Spain

The 1808 French occupation of Spain had brought revolutionary ideas of anti-clericalism and political liberalism to the country, sowing the seeds for the socialist, anarchist, republican, and regional nationalist movements that would define the cultural landscape for the following century and beyond. In these ideological and military conflicts, the Catholic Church in Spain was firmly associated with conservatism and support for royalty.

Anti-clericalism and its discontents

As a result, the church often suffered under revolutionary liberal governments, such as that of Prime Minister Juan Álvarez Mendizábal (1790–1853), who confiscated church lands in 1835 and 1836. This programme of confiscations was accompanied by a fierce anti-clerical movement: monks and priests were murdered, convents were dissolved and churches destroyed. In reaction to this popular rejection of the church, a wave of "Neo-Catholic" thinkers also thrived at this time, with political writers such as Juan Donoso Cortés (1809–53) and the philosopher Jaime Luciano Balmes (1810–48) writing spirited defences of conservative Catholicism in the face of liberal, secular, and Protestant challenges. With the restoration of the monarchy in 1874 and the constitution of 1876, Catholicism was once again recognized as the religion of Spain.

Kulturkampf

Under Otto von Bismarck (1815–98) Germany in the 1870s underwent an anti-Catholic movement known as the *Kulturkampf* ("culture struggle"). Bismarck suppressed many areas of public Catholic life and imprisoned leading bishops. A peace agreement was eventually reached with Pope Leo XIII (r. 1878–1903) and finalized in 1887.

Catholic South America

In the nineteenth century countries under Spanish and Portuguese colonial rule began to assert their independence, renegotiating their relationship with Rome at the same time.

1808–25

Many Spanish American countries struggle for independence. The Catholic Church sides with Spain during these conflicts.

1822

Brazil gains independence from Portugal.

1830

Death of Simón Bolívar (1783–1830), a Spanish American hero who fought against Spain for the liberation of Bolivia, Colombia, Ecuador, Peru, and Venezuela.

1859–75

Independent Ecuador is governed by the conservative and Catholic Gabriel García Moreno (1821–75). Shortly after being elected to a third term as president he is assassinated outside the Cathedral of Quito.

1889

Brazil is declared a Republic and the Catholic Church is disestablished.

Catholic North America

Catholics in the United States began the century as a persecuted minority but soon grew to significance largely as a result of mass immigration and militant US expansion.

1789

John Carroll (1735–1815) of Baltimore is the first and only Catholic bishop in the United States. The Catholic population is estimated at around 50,000.

1809

Educator, social reformer and peace campaigner Elizabeth Ann Bayley Seton (1774–1821) founds the Sisters of Charity, the first Catholic order for American women.

1845–50

The Great Blight devastates Ireland's potato crops. The resulting influx of Catholic immigrants to America prompts a rash of anti-Catholic "Nativist" riots.

Opposite: Prince Otto von Bismarck presided over a unified Germany as the "Iron Chancellor".

Left: Missions, such as this one founded by the Spanish Franciscan Junipero Serra in 1750, proliferated throughout the Americas, attracting loyal support and fierce opposition in equal measure.

1846–48

The US war with Mexico is fuelled by ideas of "manifest destiny" – the popular and largely Protestant belief that the US was divinely ordained to control all of North America. The war inflames anti-Catholic feelings, however, since as the USA expands its territories it also absorbs a large Catholic Mexican population.

c.1860

Roman Catholicism the largest single Christian denomination in the USA, with an estimated 3.5 million adherents.

1899

Pope Leo XIII condemns "Americanism", a liberal and individualistic movement propagated by some US Catholics.

Revolutionary Italy

Social instability also continued in Italy, and a revolution broke out in the Italian Papal States shortly after the election of Pope Gregory XVI (r. 1831–46). Gregory was twice forced to call in assistance from Austria in order to quell the rebellion, an action that brought unwelcome outside attention to the internal administration of the Papal States.

Throne and altar

South Korean Catholics attend a Mass for Pope John Paul II at the Myoung-dong Cathedral, 2005 in Seoul, South Korea.

Gregory was a proponent of the doctrine that would become papal infallibility (see below), and he favoured a strong church which could enter into an "alliance between Throne and Altar" while maintaining its

distinct authority. In 1839 Pope Gregory's papal brief *In supremo* denounced slavery and the trading of human beings as against the teachings of Christianity. He also supported the ordination of native clergy in South America and Asia and encouraged extensive mission work.

Korea

By the end of the eighteenth century there were several thousand native Korean Catholics, prompting the establishment of an apostolic vicariate (precursor of a permanent diocese) in 1831 and the arrival of Pierre Maubant (1803–39) from the Paris Missionary Society in 1835. Korean Christians suffered sporadic persecutions throughout the nineteenth century. The fiercest wave of violence (1863–76) was instigated by Prince Regent Taewongun (1821–98), leading to the deaths of more than 2,000 people.

The error of the new

In order to strengthen the church, Gregory XVI issued numerous encyclicals attempting to stem many of the new ideas animating European culture: ideas which,

Japan

Since 1638 foreigners had virtually been banned from Japan and Christianity had been suppressed. In 1859 treaties with the French allowed for the return of Christian missionaries. In 1865 thousands of Japanese Catholics were discovered living in small communities that had persisted through two centuries of persecution without contact with the wider church. An apostolic vicariate was established in 1866. Persecution of these Japanese Christians eased in 1873 and toleration was granted in 1890. The next year a Catholic hierarchy was established, although the church continued to be challenged by growing Japanese nationalist and self-reliance movements.

he argued, were based on religious error. Revolution and the secular drive to separate church and state were attacked. Movements within the church were also resisted, most notably with the 1834 *Singulari nos,* a document attacking the liberalism of the French political theologian Félicité Robert de Lammenais (1782–1854).

Liberal Catholicism

Early liberal Catholics included writers such as Georg Hermes (1775–1831) and H. D. Lacordaire (1802–61). The school of thought drew much from rationalists such as Kant and from the theories of Rousseau (see chapter 17, **The philosophes**), emphasizing progress in history and embracing the political ideals of freedom and humanist equality.

Church opposition

The church's official resistance to modernism was part of a larger trend within Catholicism at this time. The intellectual innovations and political agitation of the nineteenth century served as a crucible for key Roman Catholic doctrines. Negatively, for example, the church defined itself against socialism and communism (1849); liberalism, secular government, religious toleration and unrestricted press freedom (1864); and attempts at an Anglican–Catholic reunion (1866).

Positively, Catholicism embraced new articles of faith. In 1854 Pope Pius IX (r. 1846–78) issued *Ineffabilis Deus,* declaring that the long-standing general belief in the **Immaculate Conception of the Virgin Mary** was official church dogma. Pius also extended the devotion to the Sacred Heart (see chapter 16), which had originated in France, to the universal church in 1856. In 1858 the peasant girl Bernadette Soubirous (1844–79) reported visions of the Blessed Virgin at Lourdes, with the resultant site of pilgrimage receiving official recognition in 1862.

The heart of Jesus, illuminated by the flames of love and wounded by a crown of thorns, is the main symbol for the devotion of the Sacred Heart, a practice proliferate throughout the world.

PRESENTED BY MRS. M. JONES.

Lebanon

The Eastern Rite Maronite (see chapter 11) Christians of Lebanon had an association with the Roman Catholic Church and enjoyed close ties with France. When ethnic tensions between the Christians and the Druze (members of a sect derived from Islam) led to violent conflict in 1860, hundreds of churches and villages were destroyed and tens of thousands of Maronites were killed, as well as many Druze and Muslim people.

Pius IX (1792–1878)

The long-serving Pope Pius IX came to power with a reputation for sympathetic liberalism. The 1848 revolutions in Rome forced him to flee to Gaeta, south of Rome. After this his opposition to liberal politics hardened considerably. Pius became a force for conservatism, centralizing papal authority and consolidating many traditional devotional practices in the church. His declaration of papal infallibility in 1870 at the First Vatican Council led to much controversy.

Ultramontanism

In England, France, and Germany, disillusion with bloody revolutions, discredited clergy and anti-Catholic governments contributed greatly to a movement known as Ultramontanism. Ultramontanes favoured a strong pope and centralizing power in Rome, rather than distributing it among diverse regional churches. The movement reached its height under Pope Pius IX.

Papal infallibility

The question over the meaning and full implications of papal primacy had been debated since the Council of Constance in 1415. At Vatican I there was significant resistance to the idea of defining papal infallibility as a dogma, both from within the Catholic Church itself and from Protestant and Orthodox theologians. Eventually the council affirmed that the pope's decisions were infallible and independent of consent from the church, but it also made clear that papal infallibility was restricted to those times when the pontiff was acting in virtue of his apostolic authority to pronounce on matters of universal church doctrine. Shortly after this announcement of spiritual authority, Italian nationalists led by Victor Emmanuel (r. 1861–78) seized Rome, depriving Pius of all temporal power.

Protestantism

The Protestant world was undergoing similar revolutions to the Catholic world. These political upheavals provide one important backdrop to the development of Protestant Christianity. Also of importance are the ideological and intellectual movements of the nineteenth century.

Higher criticism

Protestant scholars such as Hermann Reimarus (1694–1768), Gotthold Lessing (1729–81), and Johann Eichhorn (1752–1827) had sown the seeds of the sceptical and liberal ideas that would hold sway in most of the theological academies of the nineteenth century. Now, "higher critical" research began in earnest to analyse the literary aspects and construction of the Scriptures. The critics disregarded many of the historical claims found in the Old and New Testaments, questioning the authorship and modes of production of the texts that had long been assumed among biblical scholars.

The Tübingen school

Closely related to this examination of biblical texts was the study of the groups who produced them. Led by the liberal theologian F. C. Baur (1762–1860), the school at the University of Tübingen adopted a non-supernatural approach to history and to the development of religious ideas. According to their theory of historical development (which had affinities with the thought of G. W. F. Hegel [1770–1831]) most of the New Testament texts were inauthentic, late documents of early Christianity.

The life of Jesus

One of Baur's students was David Friedrich Strauss (1808–74). His *Life of Jesus* appeared in 1835 to much controversy. By applying the theory of mythic development to the Gospels, Strauss denied the historical veracity of any of the supernatural aspects of the life of Jesus Christ. His conclusion, that the essence of Christianity was to be seen in the light of a Hegelian philosophy of human development and that there was an unbridgeable chasm between the "historical Jesus" and the "Christ of faith", was hugely influential for subsequent liberal Protestant thought and practice.

The nineteenth century saw a renewed interest in the historical details of stories about Jesus, as in this painting *Jesus Preaching on a Boat* by James Tissot (1836–1902).

Dutch Reformed Church

Although Napoleon's yoke had been thrown off, the Dutch king William I (r. 1813–40) continued the Napoleonic tradition of exercising considerable powers over the church in the Netherlands. Under his influence, liberalism thrived and the church took a broad approach to matters of dogma. In 1834 a conservative movement inspired in part by the heartfelt religion of Willem Bilderdijk (1756–1831) and Isaak Da Costa (1798–1860) separated from the state-sponsored Dutch Reformed Church, forming the Calvinist Christian Reformed Church. Further opposition to the modernist school led to another major secession in 1886. This was led by Abraham Kuyper (1837–1920), the Calvinist theologian, anti-revolutionary, and Christian Democrat who would go on to exert considerable influence when he became prime minister in 1901.

Oxford movement

One significant response to liberalism in the Church of England was the creation of Anglo-Catholicism. The movement, led by the Oxford clergymen John Keble (1792–1866), Edward Pusey (1800–82), and John Henry Newman (1801–90), published its first tract in 1833. The group resisted Reformation theology and encouraged closer relations with Rome. Newman himself converted to Catholicism in 1845 and was made a cardinal in 1879.

Danish People's Church

At this time the established Lutheran church in Denmark was largely under the influence of cultural elitists such as Bishop Jakob Pier Mynster (1775–1854) and relatively liberal Hegelians such as Hans Larsen Martensen (1808–84). In reaction to this a revival movement swept the church, led by the poet and preacher N. F. S. Grundtvig (1783–1872). A nationalist theologian, Grundtvig sought to awaken the "Danish spirit" of the people by connecting their Christian present with their pagan, Norse past. Following the bloodless revolution in 1848, the state church was recreated as the more populist Danish People's Church, and a number of *Folkehøjskoler* (People's High Schools) were established.

Søren Aabye Kierkegaard (1813–55)

Deeply opposed to both the Hegelianism of Martensen and the nationalism of Grundtvig, the Danish writer Kierkegaard sought to "reintroduce Christianity into Christendom" through his philosophical, theological, and polemical works. Relatively ignored in his lifetime, Kierkegaard would later be celebrated as one of the most profound thinkers of the nineteenth century, influencing **dialectical theology**, psychology, and modern existentialism.

Evangelical action

Scepticism in the universities and seminaries did nothing to undermine the convictions driving English-speaking Evangelical Christianity, which reached its highest points of social action and mission in the nineteenth century.

Africa

There had been a Christian presence in Africa since the sixteenth century, most of which centred around Catholic Portuguese outposts in Angola and Mozambique. However, it was not until the mass Protestant missions and the colonial "scramble for Africa" in the nineteenth century that Christianity firmly took root throughout the continent.

British missions

British pioneers such as Robert Moffat (1795–1883) worked among the Hottentot, Bechuana, and Sechwana peoples in the south, providing translation materials and services that laid the foundation for future missionary endeavours. In 1840 Moffat persuaded the Scottish Presbyterian David Livingstone (1813–73) to travel to South Africa. Livingstone saw more success as an explorer than as a missionary; nevertheless reports of his discoveries aroused much interest in England, inspiring many more missionary projects.

Mission and colonialism

While Christian mission and colonial interests often coincided, a number of missionaries spoke out against the exploitation and abuse of native Africans.

Catholic mission church, Pella, Northern Cape Province, South Africa.

South Africa

The Presbyterian Church of Scotland was especially effective in South Africa. Early African Christian leaders converted by the Scots include the hymn-writer Ntsikana (died 1821), the professor and politician Tengo Jabavu (1859–1921), and Tiyo Soga (died 1871), who translated the Bible and *Pilgrim's Progress* into Xhosa. A Wesleyan minister, Nehemiah Xoxo Tile (died 1891), founded the first independent tribal Tembu Church in 1884.

Nigeria

In the latter half of the century other African Christians began to organize themselves independently of the original European missions, aided in large part by the "native clergy" policies of the Clapham Sect secretary of the Church Missionary Society, Henry Venn (1796–1873). British missionaries were first invited to Nigeria in the 1840s at the request of former Yoruba slaves who had converted to Christianity while living in Sierra Leone. The most effective of these missionaries was Samuel Ajayi Crowther (c.1807–91), himself a Yoruba, who led an all-African Niger mission from 1857 and was the first African to be ordained an Anglican bishop, in 1864. Crowther's authority was undermined by white missionaries in 1889, leading to the creation of the Niger Delta Pastorate in 1891 and the United Native African Church in 1892.

Worldwide Protestantism

1801

Establishment of the Church Missionary Society (CMS).

1815

Chief Pomare II of Tahiti (died 1824) converts to Christianity.

1822

Wesleyan missionaries active among Maoris in New Zealand.

1825

Abdul Masih (1776–1827) becomes one of the first native Anglican clergymen to be ordained in India.

c.1830

Native Tahitian missionaries introduce Christianity to Fiji. Tongans introduce Christianity to Samoa.

1865

J. Hudson Taylor (1832–1905) founds the China Inland Mission.

1876

First Protestant missionaries arrive in Korea.

Clapham Sect

In England, an informal group of well-connected Anglican Evangelicals such as Charles Grant (see chapter 17, **Mission and social reform**), Henry Thornton (1760–1815) and Granville Sharp (1735–1813) had been meeting since the end of the previous century. Known as the Clapham Sect, the group was responsible for promoting foreign missions, bettering working conditions for the poor, and encouraging literacy through Sunday schools. However, by far the most pressing issue of the day was slavery.

Hannah More (1745–1833)

A celebrated English playwright, Hannah More was drawn into the Clapham Sect at the encouragement of the hymn-writer John Newton. She founded a number of countryside schools and used her writing talents to produce tracts of moral and religious edification for the poor.

Salvation Army

The Methodist William Booth (1829–1912) founded the Christian Mission to London's East End in 1865, which was renamed the Salvation Army in 1878. Booth campaigned tirelessly for the poor and marginalized in urban settings, establishing missions throughout the world.

Abolition of slavery

The most prominent Clapham Sect member was the parliamentarian William Wilberforce (1759–1833). Largely as a result of Wilberforce's political activity, and bolstered by a popular campaign appealing to Christian morality, the slave trade was made illegal in England in 1807. Shortly before his death in 1833 the Emancipation Act abolished slavery throughout the British empire.

Evangelical Alliance

Slavery was a crucial component of many national economies, and its abolition remained an issue. When the interdenominational Evangelical Alliance was founded in England in 1846, largely as a response to liberalism and Anglo-Catholicism, it was welcomed throughout Europe. However, conflicts over slavery at its first meeting meant that a branch of the alliance would not be opened in the United States until 1867.

Evolution

Charles Darwin (1809–82) published *On the Origin of the Species* in 1859. His theory of organic development by natural selection came at the same time as critical readings of the Bible were becoming popular. Christian opinion was divided on both. Most churchmen were able to incorporate evolution into the Christian doctrine of creation, while conservative groups (especially in North America) would later develop various responses collectively known as Creationism.

American awakening

Since 1800 open-air "camp meetings" and other revival events had contributed to a largely

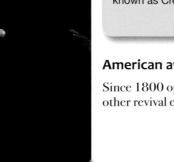

William Wilberforce campaigned for the end to slavery. Portrait by William Lane (1746–1819).

Presbyterian, student-led Second Great Awakening in the Northern and Eastern states of the USA. Similar effects were seen by Baptist and Methodist preachers in the West and South, making them the largest Protestant denominations in the US. These revived Christian energies were often channelled into creating new social agencies and voluntary organizations. By the 1830s, multiple Christian societies were in operation, disseminating religious literature, running colleges and Sunday schools, and advancing social reforms.

Antoinette Brown became the first ordained woman minister in 1853. Photograph taken c. 1900.

Antoinette Louisa Brown Blackwell (1825–1921)

The first woman to be ordained as a church minister, she was appointed to a Congregationalist church in 1853. Olympia Brown (1835–1926) was the first woman to graduate from a theological college, becoming a Unitarian minister in 1863. From 1880 US theological seminaries began to admit women for non-ordained ministries. Nine more Congregationalist women were ordained in 1893.

New religious movements

The Protestant emphasis on personal interpretation and heartfelt religion led to an explosion of new sects, especially in the United States. Many of these new movements departed significantly from creedal Christianity.

1814

Death of Joanna Southcott, English self-styled apocalyptic prophet who attracted a number of followers.

1827

Joseph Smith (1805–44) receives the revelation of *The Book of Mormon*, leading to the formation of the Church of Jesus Christ of Latter-Day Saints, based in Salt Lake City, Utah, since 1847.

1831

First meeting of the biblically literalist and sectarian Plymouth Brethren in England. Prominent Brethren preacher J. N. Darby (1800–82) sees success in America with his theory of dispensationalism, an apocalyptic scheme of biblical history promoting, among other things, a theology of the **rapture**, which teaches that all true Christians will be taken up into heaven at the **Second Coming** of Christ.

1844

The apocalyptic Seventh-Day Adventist movement persists in New England and Michigan, despite its failed prediction that the world would end on 22 October.

1875

Mary Baker Eddy (1821–1910) of Boston publishes *Science and Health,* the founding document for the Christian

Science movement, which denies the ultimate reality of sin, sickness, and evil.

1881

Charles Taze Russell (1852–1916) founds the Jehovah's Witnesses in Pittsburgh, USA, claiming that the Second Coming of Jesus ("the perfect man") had already occurred six years previously.

North and South

By 1830 the agricultural economy of the South was deeply dependent upon slavery at the same time that the abolitionist movement, led by people such as William Lloyd Garrison (1805–79) and Theodore Weld (1803–95), was gaining momentum in the North. Christians were not in agreement over the right response to slavery, and most of the various Protestant denominations divided along regional lines. The Presbyterians split in 1837. The Methodists split in 1845, as did the Baptists in the same year, with the creation of the pro-slavery Southern Baptist Convention. The victory of the North in the Civil War (1861–65) brought abolition, but racial segregation continued in the South, leading to deep ideological and cultural differences between US Christians.

African-American Christianity

The Evangelical awakenings and abolitionist movements led to the establishment of a number of independent African-American congregations and organizations.

1816

Foundation of the African Methodist Episcopal Bethel Church in Philadelphia with Richard Allen as bishop (see chapter 17).

1821

The African Methodist Episcopal Zion Church established in New York by James Varick (1750–1827).

1865–77

During the reconstruction period following the Civil War, a number of northern missionaries travel south to establish churches for former slaves.

c.1877

Bishop Henry McNeal Turner (1834–1915) and Alexander Crummell (1819–98) encourage black Christians to return to Africa as missionaries and immigrants.

1895

Formation of National Baptist Convention.

ORTHODOXY

In the nineteenth century the different religious groups living in the Ottoman empire were organized into **millets** (from *millah*, Arabic for nation). *Millets* were legally protected confessional groups enjoying a certain degree of autonomy. Under this system the patriarch of the Greek Orthodox Church was the highest authority, or ethnarch, exercising influence over all Orthodox Christians in the empire, including the Bulgarians, Albanians, Romanians, and Serbs. Armenian Christians comprised a separate *millet*, which also included the Coptic and Syriac Orthodox Churches.

Opposite: The celebrated author Fedor Dostoevsky included much autobiographical material in his novels. His characters wrestled with questions of violence and forgiveness, faith and atheism, and the search for truth. Portrait by Vasily Perov, 1872.

Orthodox nationalisms

In the nineteenth century the ferment of the French Revolution and the rise of nationalist movements in Europe led to a strong association between millets and national sovereignty for the disparate peoples living under Turkish rule. As well as agitating for political independence from the Ottomans, the different national churches would also achieve autonomy from the Greek church in this era.

For Greeks living under Ottoman rule, the Hellenistic national identity, language and culture had largely been preserved through association with the Greek Orthodox Church. These strong nationalist feelings led to an uprising, led by Alexandros Ypsilanti (1792–1828), in 1821.

Last of the New Martyrs

In 1821 Gregory V (1746–1821) was patriarch of the Greek church for the third time. Twice before the sultan had deposed the ethnarch, and Gregory was known to the Turkish authorities as a supporter of the Greek national cause. In order to avoid violent reprisals on the church in Constantinople, Gregory attempted to distance himself from Ypsilanti's rebellion. His attempts failed, and he was publicly executed as a revolutionary.

Church of Greece

After his martyrdom, Gregory's name became a rallying cry for the new independence movement. Eventually, with the aid of the English, French, and Russians, Greece was established as a free state in 1830. Following the political developments, in 1833 the Church of Greece asserted its independence from Constantinople and was recognized as fully autocephalous in 1850.

Encyclical of the Eastern patriarchs

In 1848 Pope Pius IX asserted Catholic universality with his *Epistle to the Easterns*. In response, Anthimus VI of Constantinople (1790–1878) and the other Orthodox patriarchs issued a public reply. Their encyclical strongly rejected papal supremacy, condemned Catholic missions in Orthodox lands and reiterated the objection to the *Filioque* clause (see chapter 5).

Church of Bulgaria

The transition to autonomy was rarely easy, as demonstrated by the events in Bulgaria. During the Ottoman period, until 1870, the Bulgarian church hierarchy was dominated by Greek churchmen and Greek culture. The Bulgarian nationalist movement was inspired in large part by earlier activists such as Neofit Bozveli (c.1785–1848), and led by Ilarion Makariopolski (1812–75) and Bishop Antim I (1816–88). The Turks recognized the Bulgarian church in 1870 as a separate entity. In 1872 Illarion and Antim led the call for a unilateral declaration of a Bulgarian Orthodox Church independent from Constantinople.

Against tribalism

The patriarchate of Constantinople resisted this move and the motives for creating the new church. In 1872 the Holy and Great Orthodox Synod, including the patriarchs of Alexandria and Jerusalem, and led by Ecumenical Patriarch Anthimus VI (c.1790–1878), excommunicated the Bulgarian nationalists on the charge of "phyletism". From the Greek *phyla*, meaning race or tribe, phyletism describes the heresy of confusing the church with a single nation and employing ethnic principles in church organization.

April uprising

The nationalist feelings fostered by the invigorated Bulgarian church were closely connected to agitation for political sovereignty. In 1876 a nationalist Bulgarian uprising against the Ottomans was severely repressed by Turkish soldiers. The ensuing massacres attracted international attention, turning North American and British opinion against the Turks and acting as the catalyst for the Russo–Turkish War (1877–78), which had as one of its aims the liberation of Balkan Christians and the reinstatement of Orthodox influence in Bulgaria.

Syrian Catholics

The ruling Ottomans recognized the Eastern Rite Syrian Catholic Church as a distinct body from the Syrian Orthodox Church in 1830, with the seat of the patriarchate in Beirut. An influential leading figure was Patriarch Ignatius Ephrem II Rahmani (1848–1929) who, in 1899, was responsible for the rediscovery and publication of *Lord's Testament*, an early liturgical text from the fourth century.

Slavophiles

In Russia in the 1830s, Christian nationalism manifested itself as the anti-Western, pro-Slavic movement known as slavophilism. The Orthodox Church was seen by many as the key institution to promote traditional Russian values and culture against "Western" innovations such as socialism, industrialization, and rationalism.

Fedor Dostoevsky (1821–81)

A Russian novelist, journalist, and slavophile revolutionary, Dostoevsky is also recognized as a theological thinker. Through novels such as *Notes from Underground* (1864) and *Crime and Punishment* (1866), and in the character of the Grand Inquisitor in *The Brothers Karamazov* (1880), Dostoevsky helped to articulate an existential Christian response to institutional religion.

The mystical community

An important slavophile theologian was Aleksei Khomyakov (1804–60). A philosopher and reformer, Khomyakov fought to abolish serfdom, believing that the common Russian people had access to truths denied to the materialist, individualist Western Protestants and Catholics. His theological concept of *sobornost*, which relates to the mystical community of Christian fellowship and simple faith, has had a lasting impact on Russian and Greek Orthodox theology.

Serfdom

Serfdom – the feudal system of bonded labour – was an important part of Russian life. By the nineteenth century agricultural peasants formed the majority of the population and there was much social unrest. As a conservative force in society, the Russian church tended to maintain the status quo, but occasionally Orthodox clergy spoke out on the issue. Some priests stressed the duties that Christian landowners had toward their indentured workers. Other clergy, such as Gregory, bishop of Kaluga, challenged the system itself. Gregory argued in 1858 that Christianity and the slavery of serfs were incompatible. Ultimately, however, it was fear of political revolution more than religious concerns which led to the great agrarian reforms of Tsar Alexander II (r. 1855–81) and the emancipation of the serfs in 1861.

Crimean War (1853–56)

This major conflict involved the Russians, the Ottomans, and most European powers, leading to massive casualties on all sides. One root of the conflict lay in Russia's claim, since the previous century, to be the protector of the Christians living in the Ottoman empire, a religious claim with political implications. In 1852, seeking a European alliance, the sultan granted France and the Roman Catholic Church guardianship of the holy places in Palestine. Russia's retaliation against the Ottomans soon drew in France, England, and eventually Austria on the side of the Turks, an event seen by the Russian Orthodox Church as the ultimate betrayal within Christendom.

Russian toleration

Another perennial issue was that of toleration for religions and Christian traditions other than Orthodoxy. In 1811–12 Tsar Alexander I (1801–25) and the Minister of Spiritual Affairs, Prince Alexander Golítsyn (1773–1844), introduced some toleration measures, as well as establishing the Russian Bible Society c.1813. However, the measures brought fierce resistance. Under the influence of the Orthodox monk Photius (born 1792), Alexander agreed to have Golítsyn ousted from office in 1824. The Russian Bible Society, which published Bibles and books of a non-Orthodox nature, was eventually suppressed in 1826. In 1863 further tension between Rome and the Orthodox Church arose over Russian treatment of Polish Catholic rebels.

Procurator Pobedonostsev

Constantine Petrovich Pobedonostsev (1827–1907) became procurator of the Holy Synod in 1880. Under his influence, Orthodox education of priests and lay people flourished, while persecution of people of other faiths, especially Jews, Protestants, and Catholics, became widespread. Constantine was probably the model for the character of Alexei Karenin in *Anna Karenina* by Leo Tolstoy.

Doukhobors

Tolstoy (1828–1910) was deeply involved in the struggle for religious tolerance, feeling a special affinity with the pacifist, agrarian Christian Doukhobor movement. When the Doukhobors were forced to leave Russia in 1895, their mass emigration to Canada was financed by proceeds from his novel *Resurrection*.

Auction of Serfs, 1910, by Klavdiy Vasilievich Lebedev.

Serafim of Sarov (1759–1833)

From 1794 the monk Serafim lived in seclusion. When he opened his doors in 1825 he received a stream of visitors, becoming a popular spiritual adviser (or *staretz*). His discipline, gentleness, and cheerfulness are celebrated throughout Russia.

The Twentieth Century

Some 2,000 years after its inception, Christianity remained in vigorous health, expanding worldwide, developing new ideas, and incorporating current cultural developments into its various theologies. Yet the modern era also gave rise to explicitly atheistic, totalitarian, and bloody regimes that posed the greatest challenges to followers of Christ. There were more martyrs in the twentieth century than at any other time in history.

Oppression and resistance

China

By the end of the nineteenth century most of China had been opened up to Christian missions, with a Protestant population estimated at between 40,000 and 75,000, and a Roman Catholic population upwards of 580,000.

The spread of Christianity was linked in the popular imagination with aggressive Western expansionist policies, and in 1900 nationalist feelings led to the Boxer Rebellion. Foreigners were expelled, Catholic and Protestant missionaries were killed, and close to 50,000 Chinese Christians were martyred.

Chinese recovery

The churches recovered in the period

Figures from the Monument to the People's Heroes by Lie Kai Qu. There has likely never been a more concerted effort to suppress Christianity than during the Cultural Revolution of Communist China.

following the Republican revolution led by Sun Yat-sen (1866–1925) in 1911. Churches and educational institutions flourished under the leadership of Protestants such as Cheng Ching Yi (1881–1939) and Timothy Tinfang Lew (1891–1947). Twenty-six Chinese Catholic bishops were consecrated in 1926. By 1927 there were an estimated 3 million Christians, four-fifths of whom were Roman Catholic. The rest of the population comprised mainstream Protestant denominations, as well as a number of independent, Evangelical churches keen to develop independently of foreign influence.

Communist China

Concurrent with the Chinese Christian revival was the rise of Chinese communism. Aggressively anti-religious, the communist revolution of 1948 and Chairman Mao's subsequent declaration of the People's Republic of China in 1949 drove the churches underground. By 1952 most foreign Protestant missionaries had fled or been expelled, and in the following decade Roman Catholic priests were forcibly removed. At this time the Chinese church was brought under the control of the government with the creation of the officially sanctioned Three-Self Patriotic Church. Chinese Catholics were forced to sever relations with Rome in 1957. Mao's Cultural Revolution of 1966 attempted to purge Chinese culture of much of its past and all of its religions, leading to the deaths of millions of Chinese citizens,

including many Christian martyrs. The events of 1966–67 are considered to be the most systematic attempt ever to eradicate Christianity from a state. However, through the official church, underground movements, and congregations meeting secretly in people's homes Christianity has survived in China, and even thrived in the face of growing discontent with Marxist ideology. In 2005 it was estimated that there were more Christians (80 to 100 million) than members of the Chinese communist party (70 million).

Armenian genocide

Still officially denied by the Turkish government, the systematic destruction of the Armenian population living in the Ottoman empire began in 1915 and continued until 1918. The massacres, confiscation of property, and destruction of religious artefacts all but eliminated the Armenian church, the oldest Christian culture in the world (see chapter 3).

The Spanish Republic

The Second Spanish Republic replaced the monarchy in 1931, instituting anti-clerical measures. The Catholic Church

Inset: The bodies of Armenian children who were massacred in Turkey during the First World War.

Opposite: A unit of Soviet soldiers march with their rifles in Red Square, Moscow, on the 70th anniversary of the Russian Revolution in 1987.

Below: General Franco, nationalist dictator of Spain. This signed photograph c. 1960 bears the inscription "Arriba Espana!"

was once again disestablished, education was secularized, civil marriage and divorce were legalized. Accordingly the church became closely identified with conservative opposition to the radical social and economic reforms of the Republic, with Pope Pius XI (r. 1922–39) siding with the perpetrators of a military coup in 1936. During the ensuing civil war between Republicans and Nationalists, Spanish clergy faced anti-clerical violence on a scale not yet seen in Western Europe, with hundreds of churches destroyed and over 7,000 priests killed. When the Nationalist general Francisco Franco (1892–1975) finally secured control in 1939 the church was re-established. The close alliance between the Catholic Church and the dictatorial state persisted relatively unchallenged for the next three decades. Under Franco, the minority Protestant churches in Spain were seen as Republican sympathizers and their activities were suppressed. By the time of the dictator's death in 1975, Spanish Catholicism had distanced itself somewhat from Franco's regime, following the social justice message of Pope John XXIII (r. 1958–63) and the results of the modernizing influence of the Second Vatican Council (1962–65; see below). Since the 1978 Constitution, Spain

had no state church, freedom of conscience has been enshrined, and legal restrictions on Protestantism have been relaxed.

Mexico

The Catholic Church was deeply involved in the political and economic affairs of the Mexican state. Following the revolution in 1911 and the establishment of the Constitution in 1917, church privilege was severely curtailed. Harsh anti-clerical measures were intensified under President Plutarco Elías Calles (1877–1945) in 1924, leading to fines and imprisonment for clergy. The church peacefully resisted for two years, but popular uprising against the government eventually led to the period of violence known as the Cristero War, with rebels fighting as "soldiers of Christ" from 1926. After considerable bloodshed to laity and clergy an uneasy truce between church and state was reached in 1929. However, Catholicism remains strong in popular Mexican culture, and diplomatic relations between Mexico and the Vatican were restored in 1992.

Communist Russia

Since 1721 the Russian church had been ruled by the Holy Synod – all twelve members of which were nominated by the tsar. In 1917 the patriarchate was finally restored following the abdication of Tsar Nicholas II (r. 1894–1917), with Metropolitan Vasil Belavin Tikhon (1866–1925) elected as its head. The same year that the patriarch took office, the Bolshevik

Revolution swept the communists into power and Tikhon was arrested. In 1918 Vladimir Lenin (1870–1924) banned the teaching of Christianity to people under the age of eighteen and made it illegal for churches to own property. A famine in 1921 led to the communist confiscation of church land and icons. Orthodox clergy who resisted were killed, imprisoned, or sent into exile. The League of the Militant Godless was founded in 1925. Jewish, Muslim, Protestant, Roman Catholic, and all other religious believers living in the Union of Soviet Socialist Republics (USSR) suffered severe persecution.

Georgi Gapon (1870–1906)

This Orthodox priest campaigned for workers' rights and better conditions for Russian peasants. In 1905 he led a procession to appeal to Nicholas II, but the protestors were stopped and attacked. This incident, known as Bloody Sunday, was a catalyst for the 1905 revolution. Father Gapon fell out with the Socialist Revolutionary Party and was killed by them in 1906.

Orthodox accommodation

During the Soviet era, Orthodoxy survived largely owing to a series of accommodationist policies. In return for granting

varying degrees of assent or allowing government control, the church was able to persist in truncated form, although persecution was never entirely absent. These compromise measures were controversial within the church, and led to much recrimination and mistrust after the communist era had passed. In the early 1920s the Living Church was established with Soviet blessing. This church, which was used to communicate the government's message, was not generally accepted and was considered schismatic by the wider Orthodox body. Tikhon was released from prison in 1923 after agreeing not to oppose Soviet rule. In 1927 Metropolitan Sergius I (1867–1944) reached a compromise with the ruling powers, but the agreement was not popular with the other bishops. In the late 1940s the Orthodox Church welcomed the state-sponsored incorporation of the Ukrainian Eastern Rite Catholic Church, and it supported the suppression of Protestantism and Catholicism. At an ecumenical conference held in Moscow in 1948 the Orthodox clergy took the party line, largely opposing rapprochement with the Western Protestant and Catholic churches. Often the Moscow patriarchate was forced to hide the extent of the persecution it was suffering.

The Stalinist purge

Persecution of all Christians reached its height under Josef Stalin (1879–1953) and during the Great Purge of 1934–37. Estimates for the total number of people killed under Stalin's regime range between 15 and 20 million. Christians were often a primary target for persecution. By 1939 state-sponsored anti-religious propaganda, church closings, murders, and mass exile had driven Christianity largely underground. Yet the faith was not eradicated and, when restrictions were relaxed for patriotic reasons in 1941 following the German invasion, thousands of churches were re-opened. It is estimated that in the Soviet Union between 1947 and 1957 roughly 90 million babies were baptized, about the same number as before the revolution in 1917, and more than were baptized in any Western European country during the same time.

Josef Stalin, leader of the Soviet Union. Despite a bloody campaign he failed to eradicate Christianity from Russia.

Albania

Persecution of Christians was especially strong under the communist dictatorship of Enver Hoxha (1908–85). Orthodox clergy were imprisoned and executed in 1949. That year Archbishop Kristofor Kisi was removed from office, tortured, and incarcerated. He died in prison in 1958. In 1967 Albania was declared an atheist state. All expressions of religion were outlawed, including street and family names derived from Christian tradition. Hundreds of clergy were killed, including Archbishop Damianos of Tirana in 1973. Following the collapse of communism, the church was officially re-established in 1991. Restoration continues.

Return of religious freedom

Between 1959 and 1964 persecution resumed in the USSR under Nikita Khrushchev (1894–1971), with Baptists and other Evangelicals especially targeted. The suppression of Christian activity continued until the appointment of Mikhail Gorbachev (born 1931) as Soviet leader in 1985. A new relationship with the state ensued, whereby, in recognition of Christianity's service to society, many Orthodox seminaries and monasteries were re-opened, new Protestant churches were built and, in 1989, the Eastern Rite Church was restored in the Ukraine. With the collapse of communism, between 1990 and 1993 laws restricting religious freedom were repealed. Freedom brought to light long-standing grievances, however, with mutual hostility being expressed between Catholic and Protestant groups on the one hand and the dominant Orthodox Church on the other. Internally, too, there was competition between the Orthodox Moscow hierarchy and those Orthodox groups living abroad who returned to Russia from exile in 1990.

Solidarity

The first non-communist trade union was established in Poland in 1980 under the leadership of the Catholic Lech Wałesa (born 1943). The Solidarity movement was profoundly influenced by Catholic social teaching, and received crucial support from Pope John Paul II (r. 1978–2005). In 1984 Jerzy Popieluszko, a Polish priest, was murdered for his public association with the movement. The election of Solidarity candidates in 1989 inaugurated peaceful anti-communist revolutions throughout the Eastern Bloc and led to the collapse of the Soviet Union.

Nazism

Following its defeat in the First World War, Germany had been forced into signing a humiliating and untenable peace, the Treaty of Versailles, in 1919. The population was in a state of disaffection, paving the way for the rise of Adolf Hitler (1889–1945). Hitler's Nazi party represented for Germans the possibility of making their country strong again; and it made the Jews a scapegoat for Germany's ills. The racist ideology of Nazism built on a history of European anti-Semitism. To this long-standing prejudice, Nazism also brought a nationalist, neo-pagan sentiment, celebrating (and largely inventing) the virtues of pre-Christian Norse culture and religion.

German Christians

In addition to the pagan German Faith Movement, Nazism sponsored the "German Christians". Equally nationalistic, this movement attempted to purge Christianity of the notion of original sin and of all Jewish elements, and it saw in Hitler the latest historical development of the law of God. Supported by theologians such as Emanuel Hirsch (c.1886–1954) and led by Ludwig Müller (1883–1945), the German Christians became the dominant group of the established Evangelical church in 1933.

Hitler receives the salute of the Columns in Adolf Hitler Platz, during the Reichs Party Congress in Nuremburg, Germany, 1 September 1938.

Confessing Church

The growth of the German Christians galvanized resistance from theologians and pastors in the Evangelical church. Led by Martin Niemöller (1892–1984), in 1934 the movement began to set up alternative parishes and administrative structures for those "Confessional" churches which rejected the nationalist theology of the German Christians. The Confessing Church served as a focal point for Christian resistance, especially before the outbreak of the Second World War in 1939. Many Confessing clergy and laity were conscripted into the army or sent to concentration camps; Niemöller himself was interned in Sachsenhausen and Dachau between 1937 and 1945.

Karl Barth (1886–1968)

This Swiss theologian and pastor served in Germany until forced to leave by the Nazi regime in 1935. Early readings of Kierkegaard and Dostoevsky led Barth to break with theological liberalism, inaugurating instead the method of dialectical theology, which emphasizes the concrete nature of truth as only revealed by Christ, the Word of God. His fourteen-volume *Church Dogmatics* has played a leading role in Protestant thought.

Barmen Declaration

Composed largely by Karl Barth and Dietrich Bonhoeffer (1906–45) at the Synod of Barmen in 1934, this declaration sets out the doctrinal foundation of the Confessing Church in opposition to Nazism: "We reject the false doctrine, as though the church could and would have to acknowledge as a source of its proclamation, apart from and besides this one Word of God, still other events and powers, figures and truths, as God's revelation."

Dietrich Bonhoeffer

As a pastor Bonhoeffer played a key role in the creation of the Confessing Church. As a committed opponent of the Nazi regime, he entered into a plot to assassinate Hitler. For this Bonhoeffer was arrested by the Gestapo in 1943 and executed two years later. Bonhoeffer's influential publications include *The Cost of Discipleship* (1937) and the posthumous *Letters and Papers from Prison* (1951).

The Holocaust

The Nazi programme to purge the German nation of all "undesirables" began in 1940. It led directly to the murder of an estimated 6 million Jews and another 5 or 6 million victims including homosexuals, communists, the physically and mentally disabled, black people, Slavs, Roma, and other ethnic populations. Christian groups were not the primary target of the Holocaust; however, Jehovah's Witnesses, Protestant dissidents, Catholic priests and citizens who tried to protect others were deported to the concentration camps.

With the end of the Second World War in 1945 the full extent of the horrors of the Holocaust (known in Hebrew as *Shoah*) became known, instituting a long process of internal examination within Christian circles that continues into the present day. "Post-Holocaust Theologians" such as Jürgen Moltmann (born 1926) with his *Crucified God* (1972) began to reconsider Christian notions of suffering and the nature of God. Recognition of the long history of Christian anti-Semitism has also prompted some groups to repair relations with Judaism through bodies such as the International Council of Christians and Jews, which was founded in 1947. In 1986 Pope John Paul II attended prayer at a Roman synagogue – the first ever recorded visit of a pope to a Jewish place of worship. In 1997 the Catholic Church in France offered a "Declaration of Repentance" for its silence during the deportation of French Jews to the camps during the Nazi occupation.

Innovation and Tradition

The twentieth century was the bloodiest time in the history of Christianity, but the era also saw spectacular growth. In this era the population base of Christianity definitively shifted from Europe and North America to Latin America, East Asia, and Africa.

African missions

From 1900 there was a rapid expansion of Christianity throughout Africa. Foreign missions continued apace, including outstanding work from the Anglican bishop Alfred Tucker (1849–1914), the Catholic White Father Archbishop Léon Livinhac (1846–1922) and the German Lutheran Dr Albert Schweitzer (1875–1965), who was awarded the Nobel Peace Prize in 1952. The majority of foreign missionaries at this time were North American, with conservative Evangelical missions established in Nigeria (1904), Chad (1909), Congo (1918), Upper Volta (1921), and the Ivory Coast (1935).

African Christianity

A central feature of twentieth-century African Christianity, however, was the growth of national churches, the increase in native clergy, and the rise of African prophetic movements. **Charismatic** preachers and healers such as Garrick Braid (active in Nigeria from 1909), Isaiah Shembe (a Zulu church leader in 1911), Sampson Opong (in Ghana from 1920), and Joseph Babalola (Sierra Leone, 1928) attracted followers independently of the mainstream foreign denominations. William Wade Harris (c.1860–1929), founder of the indigenous Harrist Church, was celebrated throughout the Ivory Coast and Ghana for his apocalyptic preaching,

African worshippers raise their hands in praise. The explosion of Pentecostal Christianity in Africa represents one of the most successful cultural movements of the modern era worldwide.

resistance to colonialism, and flamboyant opposition to local magicians and priests. Simon Kimbangu (c.1889–1951) faced opposition from Baptists, Catholics, and the Belgian colonial authorities for his healing ministry in Zaire. Kimbanguism, which incorporates elements of non-Christian African spirituality with charismatic Christianity, is thus strongly associated with national independence. One of the largest native African Christian movements, the Kimbangu Church was admitted to the World Council of Churches in 1969.

Janani Jakaliya Luwum (1922–77)

The Ugandan dictator Idi Amin came to power in 1971. One of the most outspoken opponents of Amin's brutal regime was the Anglican archbishop Luwum. In 1977 he was publicly accused of treason and arrested. Luwum's bullet-riddled body was discovered before he could go to trial, with some witnesses accusing Idi Amin of personally carrying out the murder. Luwum is commemorated as a martyr by the Anglican Church.

Desmond Tutu (born 1931)

In 1984 this Anglican priest, educator, and campaigner was awarded the Nobel Peace Prize for his work against apartheid in his native South Africa. In 1986 he became the first black African archbishop of Cape Town and in 1994 President Nelson Mandela appointed him chair of the Truth and Reconciliation Commission to help investigate and heal the abuses of some forty years of official segregation in South Africa.

Korea

1919

Korean Protestants are prominent in the movement for independence from Japan.

1950–53

During the Korean War many Christians are killed in the North. In the South there is an increase in Korean Catholic and other Christian aid activity.

1958

Foundation of the Assemblies of God Church, which will grow into the Yoido Full Gospel Church, boasting the largest single Christian congregation in the world.

1984

Pope John Paul II canonizes ninety-three Korean martyrs. This is the first canonization ceremony to take place outside the Vatican.

1991

Of Koreans who profess a religion, 34 per cent are Protestant, 10.6 per cent Catholic, 51.2 per cent Buddhist.

The social gospel

A number of new forms of Christian thought and practice rose to prominence in the twentieth century. Largely in reaction against the individualistic and quietistic nature of much North American Evangelical Christianity, various Protestant theologies with an emphasis on social justice arose in the years before the

First World War. The groundbreaking work of British "Christian Socialists" such as F. D. Maurice (1805–72) and Charles Kingsley (1819–75) was joined by that of Americans such as Washington Gladden (1836–1918) and Walter Rauschenbusch (1861–1918), whose 1917 *Theology for the Social Gospel* became a template for the movement. Social Gospel practitioners came from a variety of denominations, but they were generally united by a liberal theological emphasis on the natural goodness of mankind and by their critical views of capitalism's ability to create a just society.

Fundamentalism

This multi-faceted conservative movement rose to prominence in the USA in the 1920s. The name derived from *The Fundamentals*, a series of tracts published between 1910 and 1915 designed to defend "fundamental" Christian truths from liberal theology and higher-critical biblical research. Early leading figures included Princeton Presbyterian J. G. Machen (1881–1937). Soon, grievances against the political implications of the Social Gospel and against the teaching of evolution in schools became associated with the fundamentalist cause, especially following the trial of the Tennessee schoolteacher J. T. Scopes for teaching evolution in 1925.

Conservative Evangelicalism

By the 1950s, the fundamentalist

movement had acquired a reputation for divisiveness, prompting many American Evangelicals to seek alternative associations. Led by the likes of Harold John Ockenga (1905–85) and Carl F. H. Henry (1913–2003), these new Evangelicals retained much of the conservative theological and political ethos of fundamentalism, but strove to be more cooperative and intellectually respectable.

Billy Graham (born 1918)

A Southern Baptist and native of North Carolina in the USA, Billy Graham rose to international prominence for his evangelistic "crusades", stadium campaigns, and televised addresses. More people around the world have heard him than any other Christian preacher.

Billy Graham pictured in 1966.

The Great Reversal

The Evangelicals of the eighteenth and nineteenth centuries were at the forefront of cultural reform and led campaigns for social justice inspired directly by the ethical implications of biblical texts such as the Sermon on the Mount. Yet the new Evangelicals of the twentieth century as a rule tended toward political conservatism, shunning the radical social implications of their predecessors. This aversion to liberalism, an overriding concern with personal salvation (being "born again"), and a close association of conservative Christian culture with patriotic US values led to what Evangelical leader John Stott (born 1921) and others have called the "Great Reversal" in Evangelical social concern. This development within the dominant branch of Protestant Christianity has had a significant effect worldwide.

Moral Majority

In the United States, the latent political nature of Evangelical Christianity was mobilized to great effect in the 1970s and 1980s. The televangelist Jerry Falwell (1933–2007) established the Moral Majority movement in 1976. Rather than emphasizing social justice, the group's aim was to rally Evangelical support for politically conservative causes. The Moral Majority was a key player in the 1980 and 1984 presidential elections which returned Ronald Reagan. These successes led to a revived "Christian Right", which provided the electoral base for subsequent presidents George H. W. Bush (1988) and George W. Bush (2000, 2004). Internal divisions and dissatisfaction with the conservative political agenda in the last decades of the twentieth century have somewhat fragmented the Christian Right, leading to the rise of prominent centre or left-wing Evangelicals such as Rick Warren (born 1954), Tony Campolo (born 1935), and Jim Wallis (born 1948).

Pentecostalism and the charismatic renewal

The exercise of the spiritual "gifts" or "charismata" has long been a feature of Christian experience, dating back at least as far as the gift of the Holy Spirit to the disciples at Pentecost in Acts 2 and the community addressed by the apostle Paul in 1 Corinthians 12:8–11. The twentieth century saw a renewed interest in incorporating these gifts into regular church life, leading to some of the most controversial and also vibrant Christian traditions in existence today. It is estimated that Pentecostal and charismatic Christians represent a quarter of all Christians worldwide, with perhaps half of that population living in Latin America.

1901

Emergence of Pentecostalism in Topeka, Kansas, under the leadership of Bible-school teacher Charles Parham (1873–1929) and his student Agnes Ozman (1870–1937).

1906

African-American pastor William J. Seymour (1870–1922) presides over the Azusa Street Pentecostal revival in Los Angeles, California.

1908

Azusa Street Pentecostal missionaries active in China.

c.1910

Italian missionaries establish the first Pentecostal congregations in Brazil. The movement quickly spreads throughout South America, rivalling and often exceeding Roman Catholicism in numbers.

1914

Foundation of the Assemblies of God in America, now the largest affiliation of Pentecostal churches worldwide.

1960

Father Dennis Bennett (1917–91) is instrumental in bringing charismatic renewal to his Episcopal church in California.

1967

Growth in the charismatic movement among Roman Catholic university students.

1974

John Wimber (1934–97) helps to found the Vineyard Church movement with his teaching on "signs and wonders" at Fuller Theological Seminary.
Cardinal Léon Joseph Suenens (1904–96), a leading theologian of the Second Vatican Council, endorses charismatic renewal in the Catholic Church.

1990

Holy Trinity Brompton, a charismatic Anglican church in London, makes its introduction to Christianity course

available to other organizations. The "Alpha Course" has been used by Protestant, Roman Catholic and Orthodox churches, with an estimated 13 million participants worldwide.

1994

The charismatic revival at a Vineyard church in Toronto, Canada, results in the phenomenon of the "Toronto Blessing", receiving worldwide attention.

Liberation Theology

In the 1960s and 1970s a Roman Catholic theology was developed largely out of the context of political resistance to US and European foreign policy in Latin America and partly as a theological response to the conservative Evangelicalism that was seen as supporting that policy. "Liberation" theologians and activists objected to the exploitation of the poor that was occurring in the name of industrial development and Western capitalism. Encouraged by the atmosphere of progressive theology following the Second Vatican Council, two conferences of Latin American bishops (1968, 1979), the writings of the Peruvian Dominican priest Gustavo Gutiérrez (born 1928), especially *A Theology of Liberation* (1974), helped set the parameters of Liberation Theology. Taking the view that social structures can be inherently violent and oppressive, the movement emphasized that the church should have a "preferential option for the poor", that individual salvation can only come with social transformation, and that right belief (orthodoxy) can only come from right action (orthopraxis).

Catholic doctrine

1962–65

The Second Vatican Council, established by Pope John XXII, was in many ways a modernizing council. Major effects include: prescribing the use of the vernacular, rather than Latin, in the liturgy of the Mass; a thawing of relations with Protestants and Orthodox; and a renewed emphasis on issues of peace and justice, especially in the "Third World". Vatican II has continued to cause controversy between "traditionalist" and "progressive" parties within the church.

1965

Pope Paul VI (1963–78) and Ecumenical Patriarch Athenagoras (1886–1972) agree to retract the mutual excommunications of the Great Schism of 1045.

1968

Humanae vitae reaffirms Catholic opposition to birth control.

1970

Pope Paul VI reaffirms clerical celibacy as requirement and law of the Catholic Church.

Catholicism and liberation

In 1984 Cardinal Joseph Ratzinger (born 1927; Pope Benedict XVI from 2005) led the Sacred Congregation for the Doctrine of Faith in an examination of Liberation Theology. The findings endorsed the preference for the poor, but objected to the Marxist critique that most Liberation theologians used to analyse society. In 1986 the congregation issued the slightly more favourable *Libertatis conscientia*, and the following year Pope John Paul II publicly adopted Liberation language when addressing concerns for social justice.

Ordination of women

The Catholic and Orthodox churches do not ordain women, nor do many Protestant denominations. But in the twentieth century a number of Anglican and mainstream Protestant churches accepted women as priests and bishops.

1944

Florence Li Tim-Oi (1907–92) of Hong Kong becomes the first woman Anglican priest.

1956

In the US, the Methodists and Presbyterians ordain their first women ministers.

1977

The General Convention of the American Episcopal Church authorizes the ordination of women into the priesthood.

1989

Barbara Clementine Harris (born 1930) becomes the first female suffragen bishop in Massachusetts. Penelope Jamieson (born 1942) is elected bishop of Dunedin in New Zealand.

1994

The Anglican Church of England begins training women for ministry. By 2007 there are more women than men preparing for ordination.

Homosexuality

The Orthodox churches, the Roman Catholic Church and most Evangelical and Pentecostal denominations do not allow for the ordination of practising homosexual clergy or sanction the blessing of same-sex partnerships. In the twentieth century a number of Protestant churches opened the way for the full inclusion of gays and lesbians, including the United Church of Canada, the Lutheran churches in America, Germany, and Scandinavia, and many Presbyterian congregations. Within the Anglican communion, the Church of Canada (in 2002) and the American Episcopal Church (in 2003) have gone ahead with ordination and same-sex blessing, contravening the Lambeth Resolution of 1998, which reaffirmed that homosexual practice was incompatible with Scripture. The issue has led to deep internal divisions.

South American struggle

Liberation Theology has not been endorsed by Rome, and some priests have been forced to leave the clergy, such as the Brazilian Leonardo Boff (born 1938) in 1992. The willingness of some South American priests to engage in armed struggle and support revolutionary parties has not helped their cause within the church. Liberation communities in Brazil and El Salvador engage in political agitation and endorse political parties. The poet and priest Ernesto Cardenal (born 1925) actively supported the Sandinista guerrillas in Nicaragua, joining the revolution which overthrew the dictatorial government in 1979. Another priest, Camilo Torres Restropo (1929–66), was killed by the Colombian government while fighting for the National Liberation Army.

Oscar Arnulfo Romero (1917–80)

Originally appointed archbishop of San Salvador in 1977, on the strength of his opposition to Liberation Theology, Romero eventually changed his mind in the face of the corrupt dictatorship ruling El Salvador. He attracted severe opposition from the government and was assassinated while celebrating Mass in 1980.

Mother Teresa (1910–97)

An Albanian Catholic nun and admirer of Francis of Assisi, Teresa founded the Missionaries of Charity in Calcutta, India, in 1950. Her work with the orphaned and dying drew international attention (she was awarded the Nobel Peace Prize in 1979) and inspired a number of similar initiatives throughout India and in other countries.

The ecumenical movement

A noteworthy development in the history of Christianity is the rise and reach of the worldwide ecumenical movement in the twentieth century. The ecumenists strove for the unity of all Christians everywhere, regardless of denomination,

Opposite: The twentieth century was a time of much reconciliation between Christians. Here Pope Benedict XVI and Ecumenical Orthodox Patriarch Bartholomew celebrate Mass together at the Holy Spirit Cathedral in Turkey in 2006.

tradition, or variation of creed. Inspired by the interdenominational Evangelical revivals of the eighteenth and nineteenth centuries, the modern movement began in 1910 with the World Missionary Conference in Edinburgh, Scotland. In 1920 the patriarchate of Constantinople issued the first of its *Encyclical Letters by the Patriarchate of Constantinople on Christian Unity and the "Ecumenical Movement"* (completed in 1952). This major statement of doctrine urged full participation in forging closer links with separated Christians. It was not fully accepted by all the autocephalous churches, including Russian Orthodoxy. These bodies were thus absent from the first World Conference on Faith and Order in Lausanne, Switzerland, in 1927.

Worldwide

The World Council of Churches (comprising 147 members) formed in 1948 under the leadership of the Dutchman W. A. Visser't Hooft (1900–85). The Russians joined, with most of the other Orthodox churches, in 1961. Following a visit from the archbishop of Canterbury Geoffrey Fisher (1887–1972) to Pope John XXIII in 1960 (the first such visit since 1397) the Vatican also sent official observers to the council in 1961, although the Roman Catholic Church has not become a full member. By 1993 there were 322 participating churches of all denominations working together on matters of mission, social justice, and worship.

Epilogue

Two thousand years after its inception as a radical, persecuted sect, Christianity is now a truly international phenomenon, the most populous religion in the world with a wider variation of expressions than any other belief system on earth. Indeed, it has spread beyond the earth. On 20 July 1969 astronaut Edwin "Buzz" Aldrin (born 1930) celebrated Communion on the surface of the moon. While it will never be possible to tell the whole story of Christianity in all its detail, it is without a doubt true to say that the "obstinate atheists" who so troubled the governors of the Roman empire have come a long way.

SUGGESTED READING

Anderson, G. H., ed., *Biographical Dictionary of Christian Missions*, Grand Rapids: Eerdmans, 1998.

Bauckham, R., *Jesus and the Eyewitnesses: The Gospels as Eyewitness Testimony*, Grand Rapids: Eerdmans, 2006.

Cook, C., *Routledge Companion to Christian History*, London: Routledge, 2007.

Cross, F. L. and E. A. Livingstone, ed., *The Oxford Dictionary of the Christian Church*, Oxford: Oxford University Press, 2005.

Dalrymple, W., *From the Holy Mountain: A Journey in the Shadow of Byzantium*, London: Flamingo, 1998.

Douglas, J. D., ed., *The New International Dictionary of the Christian Church*, Carlisle: Paternoster, 1978.

Fergusson, E., ed., *Encyclopaedia of Early Christianity*, Chicago: St James Press, 1990.

Hart, D. B., *Atheist Delusions: The Christian Revolution and its Fashionable Enemies*, New Haven: Yale University Press, 2009.

Jenkins, Philip, *The Next Christendom: The Coming of Global Christianity*, New York: Oxford University Press, 2002.

Kung, H. and J. S. Bowden, *Women in Christianity*, London: Continuum, 2005.

MacCulloch, Diarmaid, *A History of Christianity: The First Three Thousand Years*, Harmondsworth: Allen Lane, 2009.

Quash, B. and M. Ward, *Heresies and How to Avoid Them: Why It Matters What Christians Believe*, London: SPCK, 2008.

Stevenson, J. and W. H. C. Frend, ed., *A New Eusebius: Documents Illustrating the History of the Church to AD 337*, London: SPCK, 1987.

Ware, T., *The Orthodox Church*, Harmondsworth: Penguin, 1993.

Williams, C., *Descent of the Dove*, Vancouver: Regent College Publishing, 2001.

Glossary

Anabaptists: from the Greek *anabaptizein* ("to baptize again"). Various strands among radical sixteenth-century European Reformers rejected infant baptism in favour of the baptism of adults. These people would already have been baptized as babies but were now making a conscious profession of faith. Most Anabaptist groups tended toward pacifism and the strict separation of church and state. The Anabaptist tradition continues to the present day.

anchorite: a person who takes vows in order to triumph over temptations and pursue a life of contemplation and prayer. Anchorites may be solitary hermits, or live as solitaries in organized communities. They typically live in confined, uncomfortable quarters and practise rigorous discipline.

apocalyptic: from the Greek *apokalyptein* ("to reveal"). The belief in the future destruction of the world, or at least of the present world order. It looks forward to the foundation of a new heaven and a new earth and God's triumph over evil. The Apocalypse is the name given to the last book in the Bible, also called the book of Revelation.

Apocrypha: early religious writings not included in a particular canon of Scripture. Roman Catholic and Orthodox Bibles contain Hebrew books not accepted by Protestants as part of the Old Testament canon. The term also applies to early Christian works of doubtful authenticity or theology that were not accepted for inclusion in the New Testament.

apostasy: the abandonment of Christianity, usually public, and usually in the face of persecution.

autocephalous: this term usually refers to those Orthodox churches governed by their own national synods. They are in communion with other Orthodox churches, but are not under the superior authority of another patriarch or metropolitan.

baptism: the application of water to the head, or full immersion of the body. The ceremony is a sacrament representing the purification of sin and entry into the community of Christians.

bishop: a chief or senior member of the clergy who oversees several congregations in a diocese or bishopric. Some Christian traditions do not have bishops. Cardinals, archbishops, popes, patriarchs, and metropolitans are all gradations of the office in different traditions.

bull, papal: an official document issued by the pope, relating to matters of high importance to the church and wider society.

canon: an official list of rules, saints, or biblical books considered authentic and standard. Within Roman Catholicism and Anglicanism, a canon is also a member of a group of senior priests in a church or parish. Canon law is the code of law laid down within a church.

cardinal: high-ranking Catholic clergyman, traditionally attached to a parish in Rome. Cardinals administer the church and are the pope's immediate counsellors. The right of electing a new pope is exclusive to them.

Catholic: from the Greek meaning "universal". The word on its own or in lower case usually refers to all Christians everywhere (the "universal church"). After the schism between the Eastern and Western empires, the Western church adopted this label, while the East took "orthodox". Following the Reformation, "Roman Catholic" has been used to describe the church that aligns itself under the pope, as opposed to the Protestant groups that do not recognize the priority of Rome.

charismatic: from the Greek *charisma* ("gift of divine grace"). The term generally refers to that which in Christianity has to do with gifts given by God to individuals for the good of the church, such as described in 1 Corinthians 7 and 12. The term has come to describe those Christian movements that emphasize works of the Holy Spirit and the personal religious experience of healing, prophecy, and speaking in tongues.

Christology: that aspect of theology which deals specifically with the work and person of Jesus Christ. It is often associated with Trinitarian formulations and tracing the implications of the lordship of Jesus for Christian life and thought.

coenobite: a member of a religious community who has taken vows. Coenobites may undertake to live in silence or poverty in common with others.

Communion of both kinds: the reception of both bread and wine during the eucharist. Historically, various church traditions have sometimes reserved one of the elements for the clergy, and given only bread or wine to the congregation.

concordat: a formal agreement between the pope and the government relating to the regulation and organization of the church in a particular state.

deism: from the Latin *deus* (God), deism is a movement of thought that has its roots in eighteenth-century rationalism and is opposed to Christianity. Deists affirm the existence of a supreme being who created the universe, but they deny any personal dimension, supernatural intervention or divine revelation to this being. Many Enlightenment philosophers were deists, as were key leaders in the French Revolution and most of the American Founding Fathers.

dialectical theology: a mode of theology set against both liberal optimism and conservative dogmatism. It emphasizes the limits of what humans can know about God by stressing the transcendence of the divine, our need for revelation, and the inherent tensions and paradoxes of existence. Key figures include Søren Kierkegaard and Karl Barth.

diaspora: the term usually refers to Jewish communities living outside the Holy Land. The label also applies to large populations of other peoples exiled from their traditional homelands.

docetism: from the Greek *dokeein* (to seem), this is the view that Jesus only appeared to be human. Docetists denied the importance of the body and the doctrine of the incarnation. As a "pure spirit", Jesus had no physical form and thus only seemed to suffer and die. It was condemned as a Gnostic heresy by the early Church Fathers, but the ideas persisted until the medieval era among the Albigensians.

dogma: from the Greek *dokein* (to think). Dogmas are statements and ideas that are to be accepted or obeyed by all Christians. The early Christian era designated as revealed truth the teachings of Christ and his apostles. Later traditions expanded the role of the church in defining and interpreting dogma; however, the distinction is always preserved between the teaching of Christ and the teaching of others.

ecumenical patriarch: the patriarch of Constantinople and the highest official of the Orthodox Church.

encyclical: originally a circular letter sent to multiple recipients, the term now refers to official papal documents. Unlike papal bulls, which have a general audience, encyclicals are addressed to bishops and archbishops of the Roman Catholic Church.

end times: *see* apocalyptic and eschatology.

eschatology: from the Greek *eschatos* (last). This aspect of theology addresses the nature and destiny of creation and the implications of the kingdom of God preached by Jesus. It considers the matters of death, resurrection, immortality, divine judgment, salvation, and the future state of the world. It is related to apocalyptism but not synonymous with it.

ethnarch: the ruler of an ethnic group or kingdom. The Muslim Ottoman empire established ethnarchs over the minority religious national communities (called millets) living under its influence.

eucharist: from the Greek *eukharistia* (thanksgiving). The eucharist is the central act of Christian worship, also called Holy Communion, the Lord's Supper, the Blessed Sacrament, the Divine Liturgy, or Mass according to tradition. The rite celebrates the Last Supper of Jesus with his disciples (Mark 14 and parallels) and is one of Christianity's earliest institutions (see 1 Corinthians 11). The taking of bread and wine in commemoration of Jesus giving his body and blood has been a source of much controversy as to the exact nature of the elements and their meaning. For Orthodoxy and Roman Catholicism, at the point of consecration the bread and wine undergo a metaphysical transformation (called transubstantiation by Roman Catholics) and become the body and blood of Jesus Christ. For Lutherans and many Anglicans the event signifies the real presence of Jesus in the elements, but without transformation. Other Protestant groups see it as a memorial event of symbolic significance. All Christian traditions regard the eucharist as an important event in the communal life of the church.

excommunication: the formal exclusion of a person from the communion of the church. A person so excluded cannot lawfully administer or receive the eucharist, and any action they carry out on behalf of the church is rendered invalid.

Gnosticism: from the Greek *gnosis* (knowledge). The term refers to the family of heretical beliefs emanating from pre-Christian pagan, Jewish and early Christian sects that placed a high value on obtaining secret knowledge about creation and the spiritual realm. Gnostics looked to the release of the pure soul from the prison of physical matter and usually claimed that the world was created by a demon (or demiurge) who should be distinguished from the true God. Gnostics denied the bodily incarnation, crucifixion and resurrection of Jesus Christ. Many of the apocryphal books rejected from the New Testament canon such as the Gospel of Thomas and the Gospel of Mary Magdalene were Gnostic in origin.

heresy: the formal denial and maintained opposition to any defined doctrine of the Christian faith.

homoousios: a Greek technical phrase meaning "of one substance". First used at the Council of Nicea (325) in order to describe the relation of the Son to the Father. This Trinitarian formulation was deliberately intended to exclude the followers of Arius.

Immaculate Conception of the Virgin Mary: in Roman Catholicism the dogma that from the first moment of conception, Mary the mother of Jesus was kept free from original sin.

incarnation: the Christian doctrine that in the person of Jesus Christ, the divine took on human flesh. Christ is both fully God and fully man. The doctrine was formally defined at the Council of Chalcedon in 451 but its roots go back to the earliest Christian beliefs about Jesus, such as those found in Galatians 4, Matthew 11, and John 1.

indulgences: the traditional practice of remitting the penalty for sins by drawing on the merits of Christ and the saints. In the Middle Ages this took the form of granting indulgences to those who took part in crusades, or selling certificates of remission issued by the church.

lay investiture: the practice of a king (or other non-ordained ruler) appointing bishops and other key church officials, granting them the symbols of their authority, and sponsoring their time in office.

liturgy: in the Orthodox Church, the liturgy primarily refers to the rite of the eucharist. More generally within the Christian traditions, liturgies are prescribed forms of public worship, in contrast to private and informal practices.

Mass: *see* eucharist

Mennonites: originally followers of the Dutch Anabaptist Reformer Menno Simons, the movement is known for its non-violence and simplicity of life.

metropolitan: in Orthodoxy, this is the title for the bishop who exercises provincial jurisdiction, enjoying a rank just below the patriarch. In Roman Catholicism the metropolitan is the archbishop with provincial powers who oversees suffragan (or assistant) bishops.

millets: *see* ethnarch

mysticism: the practice of seeking immediate knowledge of the divine through personal meditation, religious experiences, and spiritual disciplines such as fasting and asceticism.

nonconformists: British Protestant dissenters who refused to conform to the doctrines and authority of the established Church of England.

ordinand: a person who is preparing for admittance into the ministry of the church as a priest or minister.

original sin: in Christian theology the phrase describes the state of corruption or tendency toward evil innate in all people, a state inherited as a consequence of the sinfulness of the first humans. The idea is articulated by the apostle Paul in Romans 5 and was accepted in some form by most of the early Church Fathers. A later key figure in the formulation of the doctrine was Augustine of Hippo.

orthodoxy: right belief. As a technical term, the word refers to correct Christian doctrine as opposed to heresy. As a label, 'Orthodox' or 'Eastern Orthodox' applies to the family of churches originally affiliated to eastern Christendom and Constantinople.

parousia: from the Greek *parousia* ("presence" or "arrival"). The eschatological doctrine of the return, or Second Coming, of Christ to judge the living and the dead and to inaugurate a new age.

paschal: from the Hebrew *Pesach* (Passover). The word is used to describe anything to do with the Christian celebration of Easter. Christ is often called the Paschal Lamb in reference to the lamb sacrificed during the Jewish Passover.

patriarch: the title given to the bishops of the five main sees of early Christendom: Alexandria, Antioch, Jerusalem, Rome, and Constantinople. More recently, it is also given to the head of the autocephalous Orthodox churches.

penance: a sacrament of the Orthodox, Roman Catholic, and some other churches. Penance is a formal system of confession, repentance, and reparation for sins committed, usually administered by a religious authority. In the Middle Ages, acts of public penance were occasionally demanded of kings and rulers who had been excommunicated by the pope.

pope: from the Latin *papa* and the Greek *pappas* ("father"). In the West the title is now reserved exclusively for the bishop of Rome, the leader of the Roman Catholic Church. The Orthodox and Coptic Churches formerly used the title for the patriarch of Alexandria. During the early years of the church it referred to any bishop.

presbyter: the earliest organization of church leadership was that of a board of presbyters, or elders (see Acts 14). Early church presbyters oversaw the teaching and administration of local congregations, ranking below bishops. Later traditions retained the office as a senior minister. Presbyterianism describes those denominational structures that have no bishops or appointed leaders, but instead are governed by elders popularly elected to their posts.

Protestant: *see* **Reformation**

purgatory: in Roman Catholic teaching, the souls of people who have died in a state of grace yet who still have need of further purification enter a condition or time of spiritual purging before attaining the final state of blessedness. Prayers for the dead can aid the soul's purification, as can indulgences and acts of penance carried out by the living. Orthodoxy holds to prayers for the dead and a time of purification but is less explicit about the details of purgatory. The doctrine was a main target of the Reformer's attack and is rejected by all Protestant traditions.

rapture: the literal transportation of believers into heaven at the Second Coming of Christ. Variations of the belief are prevalent among some Protestant groups. The idea mainly derives from eighteenth-century Puritan theology and there is no early church tradition of the doctrine. Many Protestant denominations, and the Anglican, Roman Catholic, and Orthodox Churches do not accept it.

Reformation: the term denotes the various movements in Western Europe that sought to reform (sometimes radically) the religion, institutions, and political practices of medieval Christendom.

Roman Catholic: *see* **Catholic**

sacraments: Christian rites believed to be a means or a visible form of grace. The Orthodox, Roman Catholic, and some Protestant churches hold to the seven rites of baptism, confirmation, eucharist, penance, anointing the sick, ordination, and marriage. Anglicanism distinguishes baptism and eucharist (which were ordained by Jesus) from the other five. Other Protestant traditions hold only to these two.

Second Coming: see *parousia*

schism: the serious and formal breach of union within one church tradition.

see: the official seat of residence of a bishop.

simony: the purchase or sale of spiritual things. The term especially applies to the practice of paying to be ordained or to attain a position in the church. The word derives from the story of Simon Magus in Acts 8.

syncretism: the combining of two different religious systems. The practice of presenting Christianity using the rites and concepts of other religions became especially controversial following Roman Catholic missions to east Asia in the sixteenth and seventeenth centuries.

synod: church council of clergy. Lay delegates sometimes meet with clergy in a general synod.

tonsure: the shaving of all or part of the head as a mark of religious observance and the renunciation of worldly values. Traditionally it was practised by all Roman Catholic monks and clerics. Some modern Catholic orders retain variations of the practice, as do Orthodox clerics.

transubstantiation: *see* **eucharist**

Trinity: the central Christian doctrine that the one God exists in three Persons and one substance, Father, Son and Holy Spirit.

Index

PEOPLE

Abelard, Peter 90–91
Absalon, Archbishop 85
Acacius, patriarch of Constantinople 38
Adolphus, Gustavus II, king of Sweden 136
Adrian, patriarch of Moscow 148
Aethelbert, king of Kent 43, 48
Aidan 49
Aistulf, king of the Lombards 56
Alacoque, Margaret Mary 138
Alaric, king of the Visigoths 34
Alban 25
Alberic II, duke of Spoleto 69
Albuquerque, Alfonso 133
Alcuin 58, 60
Alexander I, tsar of Russia 176
Alexander II, tsar of Russia 176
Alexander III, Pope 89–90
Alexander V, antipope 110, 117–18
Alexander VI, Pope 123
Alexis, tsar of Russia 146
Alexius Comnenus, Eastern Roman emperor 81
Alexius I, Eastern Roman emperor 83
Alfonso, king of Portugal 86
Alfonso VI, king of Castile 80
Alfred "the Great", king of Wessex 67
Alighieri, Dante 107
Alopen 50
Ambrose of Milan 32
Amin, Idi 187
Andrew II, king of Hungary 93
Anghel, Atanasie, Metropolitan 37

Anna, Princess 73
Anselm, archbishop of Canterbury 79, 88
Anskar, archbishop of Hamburg and Bremen 66
Anthimos, metropolitan of Wallachia 150
Anthimus VI, Ecumenical Patriarch 174–75
Anthony of the Desert (Anthony of Egypt) 24, 29
Antim I, Bishop 174
Antoninus Pius, Roman emperor 14
Aquinas, Thomas 101, 116
Arcadius, Eastern Roman emperor 32
Aristides of Athens 14
Aristotle 101
Arius 28–29, 198
Arminius, Jacobus 140
Arthur, King 71
Athanasius the Athonite 71
Athanasius, bishop of Alexandria 29–30
Athenagoras, Ecumenical Patriarch 191
Attila "the Hun" 34
Augustine, archbishop of Canterbury 43, 48, 79
Augustine, bishop of Hippo 16, 31
Avvakum, Archpriest 146
Babalola, Joseph 186
Balmes, Jaime Luciano 162
Baradaeus, Jacob 41
Barlaam 112
Barth, Karl 184–85
Basil (Vasili) III, grand prince of Moscow 124–25
Basil I, Eastern Roman emperor 65
Basil II, Eastern Roman emperor 73
Basil "the Great" 29, 71
Basiliscus 38
Batu Khan 99–100
Baur, F. C. 167
Becket, Thomas, archbishop of Canterbury 88–89
Bede 58
Bekkos, John, patriarch of Constantinople 97
Benedict of Aniane 66
Benedict of Nursia 45, 47
Benedict VI, Pope 69

Benedict XIII, Pope 117–118
Benedict XIV, Pope 156–57
Benedict XVI, Pope 191–92
Bennett, Dennis 190
Berengar II, king of Italy 69
Berenguer, Ramón IV, count of Barcelona 86
Bernard de Sedirac, archbishop of Toledo 80
Bernard of Clairvaux, Abbot 91
Bertha, queen of Kent 43
Beza, Theodore 140
Bilderdijk, Willem 168
Bismarck, Otto von, Prince, chancellor of Germany 162–63
Blandina 15
Boehler, Peter 152
Boethius 40, 59
Boff, Leonardo 192
Bohemond, Prince 83
Bolívar, Simón 163
Bonaparte, Napoleon, emperor of France 160–61
Bonhoeffer, Dietrich 185
Boniface (Wynfrith), archbishop of Mainz 57–58
Boniface of Montferrat 95
Boniface VIII, Pope 102, 104, 107
Booth, William 171
Boris, king of Bulgaria 65
Braid, Garrick 186
Breakspear, Nicholas see Hadrian IV
Brown, Antoinette Louisa 172
Brown, Olympia 172
Bunyan, John 143
Caecilian, bishop of Carthage 26
Calles, Plutarco Elías, president of Mexico 180
Callistus I, Pope 16
Callistus II, Pope 88
Callistus III, Pope 120
Calvin, John 129, 136–37, 140–42, 144–45, 155, 168
Campolo, Tony 189
Canisius, Peter 132
Canute IV "the Holy", king of Denmark 81

Canute VI, king of Denmark 85
Canute, king of England 75
Cardenal, Ernesto 192
Carey, William 154
Carpini, Giovanni da Plano 98
Carranza, Pedro, Bishop 139
Carroll, John, Bishop 163
Casas, Bartolomé de las 200
Castro, Matheus de 139
Catherine "the Great", empress of Russia 149, 157
Catherine of Alexandria 26
Catherine of Aragon, queen of England 131
Celestine I, Pope 34–35
Celestine III, Pope 85
Cesarini, Julian, Cardinal 115–116, 119
Chantal, Jane Frances de 136
Charlemagne, king of the Franks and Western Roman emperor 54, 58–61, 66
Charles I, king of England 143
Charles II, king of England 143
Charles III, king of Spain 158
Charles of Anjou, king of Naples and Sicily 97, 101
Charles VII, king of France 120
Cheng Ching Yi 179
Christian III, king of Denmark 128
Chrysostom, John, patriarch of Constantinople 32
Chu Munmo 157
Clare of Assisi 94
Claver, Pedro 139
Clement I, Pope 9, 12
Clement II, Pope 76
Clement III (1080–1100), antipope 78
Clement III (1187–91), Pope 86
Clement of Alexandria 17
Clement of Ochrid 65
Clement V, Pope 105
Clement VI, Pope 108
Clement VII, Pope 110
Clement XI, Pope 156–58

Clement XIV, Pope 158
Climacus, John 111
Coke, Thomas 152, 155
Collete, Abbess 94
Columba 44
Columbanus 45, 47
Columbus, Christopher 123
Commodus, Roman emperor 16
Conrad III, king of Rome 84–85
Constantine IX Monomachos, Eastern Roman emperor 78
Constantine V, Eastern Roman emperor 54, 62,
Constantine VI, Eastern Roman emperor 55–56
Constantine, Roman emperor 26–29, 56
Constantius, Roman emperor 25–26, 30
Cornelius, Pope 21–22
Cortés, Hernán 133
Cortés, Juan Donoso 162
Cosmos 72
Cranmer, Thomas, archbishop of Canterbury 131
Cromwell, Oliver 143
Crowther, Samuel Ajayi 171
Cyprian, bishop of Carthage 16, 22–23
Cyril of Alexandria 34–35, 37
Cyril V, Ecumenical Patriarch 150
Cyril, "apostle to the Slavs" 64–65
D'Ailly, Pierre 117
Da Costa, Isaak 168
Damasus, Pope 30
Damianos, archbishop of Tirana 183
Dandolo, Enrico, doge of Venice 95
Dante see Alighieri, Dante
Darby, J. N. 172
Darwin, Charles 171
Decius, Roman emperor 21–22
Denys (Dionysius), bishop of Paris 21
Descartes, René 151
Diaz, Rodrigo see El Cid 80
Diderot, Denis 158
Diocletian, Roman emperor 24–25

Dionysius, bishop of Paris
  see Denys
Dionysius, Pope 24
Dmitri, Prince 113
Dominic 93–94
Domitian, Roman emperor 9
Donatus Magnus 26
Dositheus, patriarch of
  Jerusalem 146
Dostoevsky, Fedor 174–75,
  183
Dunstan, abbot of
  Glastonbury and
  archbishop of Canterbury
  70–71
Eck, Johann 127
Eddy, Mary Baker 172
Edgar, king of England 71
Edward "the Confessor",
  king of England 81
Edward I "Longshanks", king
  of England 102
Edwards, Jonathan 154–55
Edwin, king of Northumbria
  48
Eichhorn, Johann 166
El Cid (Rodrigo Diaz) 80
Eliot, John 144
Elizabeth I, queen of England
  142
Elizabeth of Hungary 93
Elphinstone, Bishop 121
Erasmus, Desiderius 108,
  126–27, 129
Erik II (Horik), king of
  Jutland 66
Erik IX, king of Sweden 85
Eudes, John 138
Eudoxia, Empress 32
Eugenius III, Pope 83, 91
Eugenius IV, Pope 115,
  119–120
Eusebius of Caesarea 15
Eustochium 30
Eutyches 37–38
Falwell, Jerry 189
Felicitas 18
Felix III, Pope 38
Ferdinand II, Holy Roman
  emperor 136
Ferdinand V, king of Aragon
  122
Filaret, patriarch of Moscow
  146
Finan 49
Fisher, Geoffrey, archbishop
  of Canterbury 193

Florence Li Tim-Oi 191
Formosus, Pope 69
Fox, George 143
Francis of Assisi 94, 192
Franco, Francisco, General
  180
Frederick I "Barbarossa",
  Holy Roman emperor 86
Frederick II, Holy Roman
  emperor 93
Frederick IV, king of
  Denmark 153
Frelinghuysen, Theodore
  154
Fulbert, canon of Notre
  Dame 90
Gallienus, Roman emperor
  23
Gapon, Georgi 181
Garrison, William Lloyd 173
Gennadius II, patriarch of
  Constantinople 116
Germanus, patriarch of
  Constantinople 54
Germogen, patriarch of
  Moscow 146
Gerson, Jean 117
Ghazan Khan 100
Ghengis Khan 98–99
Giovanni of Monte Corvino
  99
Gizurarson, Gissur, bishop of
  Iceland 74
Gizurarson, Isleifur, bishop
  of Iceland 74
Gladden, Washington 188
Godfrey of Bouillon, Duke
  82
Golitsyn, Alexander, Prince
  176
Gorbachev, Mikhail 183
Graham, Billy 188
Grant, Charles 154
Gratian 91
Gregory II, Pope 57
Gregory III, Pope 54
Gregory IX, Pope 100
Gregory of Nyssa 111
Gregory of Sinai 111
Gregory I "the Great",
  Pope 42
Gregory the Illuminator 28
Gregory V, patriarch of
  Constantinople 69, 174
Gregory VI, Pope 76
Gregory VII, Pope 77–78,
  102

Gregory VIII, antipope 86
Gregory X, Pope 97
Gregory XI, Pope 109–110
Gregory XII, Pope 118
Gregory XIII, Pope 125
Gregory XV, Pope 138
Gregory XVI, Pope 164
Gregory, bishop of Kaluga
  176
Groote, Geert de 108
Grundtvig, N. F. S. 168
Gutenburg, Johannes 121
Guthrum, king of East
  Anglia 67
Gutiérrez, Gustavo 190
Hadrian I, Pope 55
Hadrian II, Pope 65
Hadrian IV, Pope 88
Hadrian, Roman emperor 14
Harald Bluetooth, king of
  Denmark 73
Harald, king of Jutland 66
Harris, Barbara Clementine
  191
Harris, William Wade 186
Hastings, Selina, countess of
  Huntingdon 153
Hegel, G. W. F. 167–68
Helena 26–27
Héloïse 90
Henry "the Navigator",
  Prince 122
Henry I, king of England 88
Henry II, king of England 89
Henry III, Holy Roman
  emperor
Henry IV, Holy Roman
  emperor 88
Henry V, Holy Roman
  emperor 88, 121
Henry V, king of England
Henry VIII, king of England
  7, 131
Henry, Carl F. H. 188
Heraclius, Eastern Roman
  emperor 50–51
Hermes, Georg 165
Herod Agrippa, king of
  Judea 8
Hideyoshi 134
Hilda, abbess of Whitby 49
Hildebrand *see* Gregory VII
Hildegard of Bingen, Abbess
  91
Hippolytus 20
Hirsch, Emanuel 184
Hitler, Adolf 183–85

Hohenzollern, Albrecht von,
  archbishop of Mainz 127
Honorius I, Pope 48, 51
Honorius, emperor of the
  Western Roman Empire
  32
Hooft, W. A. Visser't 193
Hooper, John 131
Hoxha, Enver 183
Humbert, Cardinal 79
Hume, David 151
Hus, Jan 119
Hutter, Jacob 129
Ignatius of Loyola 131–32
Ignatius, bishop of Antioch
  12
Ignatius, patriarch of
  Constantinople 62
Innocent I, Pope 34
Innocent III, Pope 92–93,
  95–6, 100, 102
Innocent IV, Pope 97–98
Innocent X, Pope 136, 138
Irenaeus, bishop of Lyons 15
Irene, empress of the Eastern
  Roman empire 54–55
Isabella I, queen of Castile
  122–23
Ivan III "the Great", grand
  prince of Russia 116
Ivan IV "the Terrible", tsar of
  Russia 125
James I, king of England
  (James IV of Scotland)
  130, 143
James, the apostle 67
Jamieson, Penelope, Bishop
  191
Jansen, Cornelius Otto 137,
  158
Jeremias II, patriarch of
  Constantinople 125
Jerome 29–30
Jesus Christ 11, 20, 28,
  35, 37, 81, 111–112,
  131, 151–52, 157, 165,
  167, 172–73, 195–99
Joan of Arc 120
Jogaila, Grand Duke 112
John IV, Pope 51
John of Antioch 35
John of Damascus 54, 91
John of Jandun 107
John of the Cross 132
John Paul II, Pope 164, 183,
  185, 187
John "the Faster",

Ecumenical Patriarch 42
John Tzimisces, Eastern
  Roman emperor 71
John V Palaeologus, Eastern
  Roman emperor 111
John VIII Palaeologus,
  Eastern Roman emperor
  115
John VIII, Pope 64–65, 68
John X, Pope 69
John XII (955–63) 69
John XIV, Pope 69
John XV, Pope 69
John XXII, Pope 106–107,
  191
John XXIII (1410–15),
  antipope 117–118
John XXIII (1958–63),
  Pope 180
John, king of England 93
Jonas, metropolitan of Kiev
  116
José I, king of Portugal 157
Joseph I Galesiotes, patriarch
  of Constantinople 97
Joseph of Arimathaea 71
Joseph of Constantinople
  115
Joseph of Volokolamsk 124
Joseph, bishop of Edessa 30
Julian of Norwich 109
Julian, emperor of Rome 31
Julius Caesar, Roman
  emperor 125
Julius II, Pope 127
Justin I, Eastern Roman
  emperor 39
Justin Martyr 14–15
Justinian I, Eastern Roman
  emperor 39–41
Justinian II, Eastern Roman
  emperor 52
Justus, bishop of Rochester
  48
K'ang Hsi, emperor of China
  157
Kaleb, king of Ethiopia 43
Kant, Immanuel 151, 165
Keble, John 168
Kempis, Thomas á 108, 118
Khomyakov, Aleksei 176
Khrushchev, Nikita 183
Kierkegaard, Søren Aabye
  168
Kimbangu, Simon 187
Kingsley, Charles 188
Kino, Eusebio Francisco 139

Kirill (Cyril) III, metropolitan of Kiev 101
Kisi, Kristofor, Archbishop 183
Knox, John 142
Kublai Khan 7, 99
Kuyper, Abraham 168
Lacordaire, H. D. 165
Lalibela, Gebre Mesqel, emperor of Ethiopia 87
Lammenais, Félicité Robert de 165
Langton, Stephen, archbishop of Canterbury 93
Latimer, Hugh 131
Lazar, prince of Serbia 111
Leander, bishop of Seville 43
Lee Sung-hun 157
Lenin, Vladimir 181
Leo III, Eastern Roman emperor 53
Leo III, Pope 54
Leo IV, Eastern Roman emperor 54
Leo IV, Pope 63
Leo IX, Pope 76
Leo I "the Great", Pope 34
Leo V "the Armenian", Eastern Roman emperor 61–62
Leo V, Pope 69
Leo X, Pope 127, 131
Leo XIII, Pope 164
Lessing, Gotthold 166
Licinius, Roman emperor 26–27
Liele, George 155
Livingstone, David 169
Livinhac, Léon, Archbishop 186
Locke, John 151
Lombard, Peter 56, 90–91
Louis "the German", king of the East Franks 64
Louis I "the Pious", Western Roman emperor 66
Louis IV, Holy Roman Emperor 107–108
Louis IV, landgrave of Thuringia 93
Louis VII, king of France 85
Louis XIV, king of France 158
Louis XV, king of France 157
Louis XVI, king of France 158

Lucar, Cyril, Ecumenical Patriarch 144–45
Luther, Martin 105, 127–31, 136–37, 140–41, 168, 186, 192
Luwum, Janani Jakaliya, Archbishop 187
Macarius of Corinth 125
Macarius, metropolitan of Moscow 151
Machen, J. G. 188
Makariopolski, Ilarion 174
Mandela, Nelson 187
Mani of Persia 20
Manuel Comnenus, Eastern Roman emperor 86
Mao Tse-Tung 179
Marcia 16
Marcian, Eastern Roman emperor 37
Marcion of Sinope 13
Marcus Aurelius, Roman emperor 14
Mark, the evangelist 197
Maron 85, 166
Marsiglio of Padua 107–108
Martel, Charles, ruler of the Franks 53, 57–58
Martensen, Hans Larsen 168
Martin I, Pope 51
Martin of Tours 29
Martin V, Pope 110, 118
Marx, Karl 179, 191
Mary I, queen of England 202
Mashtots, Mesrob 33
Mather, Cotton 154
Maubant, Pierre 164
Maurice, F. D. 188
Maurice, prince of Orange 144
Maximilla 19
Maximus "the Confessor" 111
Medici, Catherine de' 130
Mellitus, bishop of London 48
Mendizábal, Juan Álvarez, prime minister of Spain 162
Menezes, Alexis, archbishop of Goa 134
Methodius, "apostle to the Slavs" 64–65
Methodius, patriarch of Constantinople 62
Michael Cerularius, Ecumenical Patriarch 78

Michael II, Eastern Roman emperor 62
Michael III, Eastern Roman emperor 62, 64
Michael VIII Palaeologus, Eastern Roman emperor 97
Michael, tsar of Russia 146
Michelangelo see Buonarroti, Michelangelo
Mieszko I, prince of Poland 73
Miltiades, Pope 28
Mindaugas, king of Lithuania 112
Moffat, Robert 169
Mogila, Peter, metropolitan of Kiev 145
Mohammed II, Ottoman sultan 115–116
Moltmann, Jürgen 185
Montaigne, Michel de 130
Montanus 19
More, Thomas 131
Moreno, Gabriel García 163
Morosini, Thomas 95
Muhammad 41
Müller, Ludwig 184
Müntzer, Thomas 129
Murad I, Ottoman sultan 111
Murad II, Ottoman sultan 114
Murad IV, Ottoman sultan 145
Mutimir, prince of the Serbs 65
Mynster, Jakob Pier, Bishop 168
Neale, J. M. 73
Nemanja, Stephen, prince of Serbia 98
Nero, Roman emperor 9
Nestorius, patriarch of Constantinople 35, 37–38
Nevsky, Alexander, Prince 99–100
Newman, John Henry 168
Newton, John 152, 171
Nicephorus II Phocas, Eastern Roman emperor 71
Nicephorus of Mount Athos 111
Nicephorus, patriarch of Constantinople 62
Nicholas I, Pope 62

Nicholas II, tsar of Russia 180–81
Nicholas III, Pope 101
Nicholas IV, Pope 99
Nicholas of Cusa 108, 120
Nicholas V (1328–30), antipope 107
Nicholas V (1447–55), Pope 121
Nicodemus of the Holy Mountain 150–51
Niemöller, Martin 184
Nikon, patriarch of Moscow 146–48
Ninian 36
Nobili, Robert de 139
Nóbrega, Manuel de 133
Nogaret, Guillaume de 104
Novatian 22
Ntsikana 170
Ockenga, Harold John 188
Odilo, abbot of Cluny 70
Odo, abbot of Cluny 70
Odoacer, king of Italy 38
Olaf I Tryggvason, king of Norway 74
Olga of Kiev, Princess 73
Ōmura Sumitada 133
Opong, Sampson 186
Orestes 38
Origen 20–21, 35
Orleans 105
Oswy, king of Northumbria 49
Otto I, Holy Roman emperor 69
Otto IV, Holy Roman emperor 94
Ozman, Agnes 189
Pachomius 29
Padilla, Juan de 133
Palamas, Gregory 111–112
Palladius 36
Parham, Charles 189
Pascal, Blaise 138
Patrick 71
Paul III, Pope 131–32
Paul of Samosata 64
Paul VI, Pope 191
Paul, the Apostle 8–9, 128, 189, 198
Paula 30
Paulinus, bishop of York 48
Pelagius 31
Pelagius II, Pope 42
Penn, William 144
Pepin "the Short", king of the Franks (Pepin III) 56, 58

Perpetua 18–19
Peter of Castelnau 96
Peter "the Great", tsar of Russia 146, 148
Peter "the Hermit" 82
Peter "the Venerable", abbot of Cluny 91
Peter, metropolitan of Kiev 113
Peter, the apostle 8–9, 12
Peter, tsar of Bulgaria 72
Petrarch, Francesco 105–106
Petri, Laurentius 128
Petri, Olaus 128
Philip I, king of France 77
Philip II of France 86
Philip IV "the Fair", king of France 101–102, 105
Philotei of Athens 127
Philotheus 124
Phocas, Nicephorus 71
Photius, patriarch of Constantinople 42, 62–64
Photius, the monk 176
Pius IX 165–66, 174
Pius VI, Pope 159–60
Pius VII, Pope 160–62
Pius XI, Pope 180
Plato 79
Plessis, Armand-Jean du see Richelieu, Cardinal
Pliny the Younger 11
Plütschau, Heinrich 153
Pobedonostsev, Constantine 177
Petrovich 177
Polo, Marco 99
Polycarp, bishop of Smyrna 14
Pomare II of Tahiti 170
Popieluszko, Jerzy 183
Porga, duke of Croatia 51
Pothinus, bishop of Lyons 15
Priscilla 19
Prokopovich, Bishop 148
Pusey, Edward 168
Rainalducci, Pietro see Nicholas V
Ratzinger, Joseph, see Benedict XVI
Rauschenbusch, Walter 188
Raymond du Puy 84
Reagan, Ronald 189
Recared I, king of the Visigoths 42

Reimarus, Hermann 166
Restropo, Camilo Torres 192
Ricci, Matteo 134–38, 157
Richard I "the Lionheart", king of England 86
Rahmani, Ignatius Ephrem II, patriarch of Beirut 175
Richelieu, Cardinal 136
Ridley, Nicholas 131
Romanovich, Daniel, Prince 101
Romanus III, Eastern Roman emperor 81
Romero, Oscar Arnulfo 192
Romulus Augustus, Western Roman emperor 38
Rousseau, Jean-Jacques 151, 158, 165
Rudolf I, Holy Roman emperor 102
Ruggieri, Michele 134
Russell, Charles Taze 173, 203
Saladin 85–86
Sales, Francis de 136
Sancho III "the Great", king of Navarre 79
Sava (Sabas) 99
Schleiermacher, Friedrich 151
Scholarius, George, see Gennadius II 116
Scholastica 45
Schwartz, Christian Friedrich 153–54
Schweitzer, Albert 186
Scopes, J. T. 188
Septimius Severus, Roman emperor 17–20
Serafim of Sarov 177
Sergius I, Metropolitan 182
Sergius II, Pope 68
Sergius III, Pope 69
Sergius 113
Sergius, patriarch of Constantinople 51
Seton, Elizabeth Ann Bayley 163
Sewall, Samuel, Judge 156
Seymour, William J. 189
Sharp, Granville 170
Shembe, Isaiah 186
Shenoutte 29
Sigismund, Holy Roman emperor 118–119
Simeon I, khan of Bulgaria 65, 72

Simons, Menno 129, 198
Sixtus IV, Pope 122
Sladich, Theodore 150
Smith, Adam 151
Smith, Joseph 172
Smyth, John 144
Sophronius of Jerusalem 51
Sorsky, Nil 124
Soubirous, Bernadette 165
Southcott, Joanna 172
Spener, Philip Jakob 141
Stalin, Josef 182
Stephen I, Pope 22
Stephen II, Pope 56t
Stephen IX, Pope 76
Stephen Nemanjich, king of Serbia 99
Stephen VI, Pope 69
Stephen VIII, Pope 69
Stephen, king of Hungary 73, 75
Stephen, martyr 8
Stott, John 189
Strauss, David Friedrich 167
Suenens, Léon Joseph, Cardinal 190
Suidger see Clement II
Suleiman "the Magnificent", Ottoman sultan 76
Sun Yat-sen 179
Sviatopolk, Prince 65
Sviatoslav, prince of Kiev 73
Sylvester I, Pope 28
Sylvester II, Pope 75
Sylvester III, Pope 76
Taewongun, Prince Regent 164
Tarasius, patriarch of Constantinople 55
Tashfin, Yusuf ibn 80
Taylor, J. Hudson 170
Telesphorus, Pope 14
Tengo Jabavu 170
Tennent, Gilbert 154
Teresa of Avila 132
Teresa of Calcutta, Mother 192
Tertullian 16, 19
Tetzel, Johann 127
Thecla, abbess of Kitzingen 58
Theodora (died c.867), Empress 61–62
Theodora (c.500–48), Empress 41
Theodore of Mopsuestia 40
Theodore of Studios, Abbot 61–62

Theodore of Tarsus, archbishop of Canterbury 49
Theodoret, bishop of Cyrrhus 41
Theodosius I, Roman emperor 31–32
Theodosius II, Eastern Roman emperor 34–35
Theophilus, Eastern Roman emperor 30, 62
Theophylact, patriarch of Constantinople 72
Thomas of Cana 30
Thomas, the apostle 30, 50
Thornton, Henry 170
Tikhon of Zadonsk 149
Tikhon, Vasil Belavin, patriarch of Moscow 180–82
Tile, Nehemiah Xoxo 170
Timothy Tinfang Lew 179
Tiridates III, king of Armenia 28
Tiyo Soga 170
Tolstoy, Leo, Count 177
Torquemada, Tomás de 122–23
Tournon, Cardinal de 156
Trajan, Roman emperor 11–12
Tucker, Alfred, Bishop 186
Turner, Henry McNeal, Bishop 173
Tutu, Desmond, archbishop of Cape Town 187
Tyndale, William 131
Tzimisces, John 71
Ulyanov, Vladimir Ilyich, see Lenin
Ulfilas, Bishop 30
Urban II, Pope 81–82
Urban IV, Pope 95
Urban VI, Pope 110
Urban VIII, Pope 136, 139
Valentinian III, Western Roman emperor 34
Valerian, Roman emperor 22–24
Valerius Diocletanus see Diocletian
Varick, James 173
Varlaam, metropolitan of Moscow 125
Venn, Henry 170
Vicelin 86
Victor Emmanuel, king of I

Italy 166
Victor I, Pope 17
Victor IV, antipope 89
Vieira, Antonio 139
Vigilius, Pope 41
Viseslav, Prince 64
Vladimir, prince of Kiev 73, 78, 101–102, 181
Voltaire 158
Waldo (Valdes), Peter 90
Wałęsa, Lech 90
Wallis, Jim 189
Warren, Rick 189
Weld, Theodore 173
Wenceslas, duke of Bohemia 72–73
Wesley, Charles 152, 170
Wesley, John 141, 152, 155, 170
Weyer, Johann 130
Whitefield, George 130
Wilberforce, William 171
William "the Pious", duke of Aquitaine 70
William I, king of England 77
William I, king of Holland 168
William of Ockham 107
William of Rubruck 99
Williams, Roger 144
Wimber, John 190
Winthrop, John 144
Władysław (Vladislaus) III, king of Hungary and Poland 115
Wycliffe, John 109, 118, 121
Xavier, Francis 133–34
Ypsilanti, Alexandros 174
Za'ra Ya'qob (Zara Jacob) 117
Zangi 83
Zeno, Eastern Roman emperor 38
Ziegenbalg, Bartholomaeus 153
Zinzendorf, Count 141, 152
Zosima 149
Zumárraga, Juan de, Bishop 133
Zwingli, Huldrych 129

PLACES

Aachen 60, 66
Abyssinia 37, 117

Aberdeen 121
Acre 86, 97
Aegean 71, 149
Africa 16–17, 22, 26, 29, 31, 52–53, 56, 79, 96, 122, 139, 152, 155, 169–70, 173, 185–87, 189
Agincourt 120
Al-Andalus 79
Albania 28, 150, 173, 183, 192
Alcalá 127
Alexandria 10, 12–13, 16–17, 20, 23, 26, 28–29, 32, 34–35, 43, 52, 54, 60, 78, 150, 175, 199
Algeria 31
Amazon 139
Angamale 138
Anglia 67, 201
Angola 169
Antioch 8, 12, 23, 29, 32, 35, 52, 54, 60, 78, 82–83, 199
Arabia 8, 36, 41
Aragon 122–23, 131
Arizona 139
Armenia 28, 33, 39, 43, 52, 56, 94, 173, 179
Asia Minor 8, 17, 72, 81, 87
Austria 164, 176
Avignon 105–107, 110, 160
Axum 43
Azusa Street Church 189–90
Baghdad 36
Baja California 139
Balkans 34, 72, 78, 87, 115
Baltimore 163
Barcelona 86
Basle 119–20, 127
Bavaria 57, 107–108, 135
Beijing (Peking) 100
Beirut 175
Belarus 137
Belgium 162, 187
Bengal 154
Bethlehem 23, 27–28, 30, 145
Birka 66
Bithynia 11, 61
Bobbio 45, 47
Bogotá 133
Bohemia 64, 72–73, 118–119, 136–37, 152

Bolivia 133, 163
Bologna 91–92, 105
Bosporus 56
Boston 172
Brandenburg 128
Brazil 133, 139, 163, 190, 192
Britain 47, 66, 84 153
Brunswick 128
Buenos Aires 139
Bulgaria 62, 64–65, 68, 72, 87, 97, 102, 115, 149, 173–75
Burgundy 45, 70
Byzantium see Constantinople 12, 28, 52, 56, 87, 96, 111 112, 115, 195
Caesarea 15, 23, 27–29, 32, 60
Calabria 112
Calcutta 192
California 139, 189–90
Cambridge 127
Canada 155–56, 177, 190, 192
Canterbury 43, 48–49, 71, 79, 88–89, 94, 131, 193
Cape Colony 169
Caribbean 132, 139
Carthage 12, 16–18, 22–23, 32, 52, 60
Castile 122–23
Catalonia 86
Cathedral of Quito 163
Cathedral of the Assumption (Dormition Cathedral), Moscow 113
Cathedral of the Holy Wisdom (Kiev) 40, 80
Cellia 29
Ceylon 153
Chad 186
Chiapa 133
Chicago 4, 195
China 4, 20, 36, 47, 50, 100, 108, 132, 134, 138, 147, 157, 170, 178–79, 190
Church of St John Lateran 28
Church of St Peter, Rome 28, 70
Church of St Geneviève 160
Church of the Holy Sepulchre 28, 80
Church of the Holy Wisdom

40 (Constantinople) see Hagia Sophia
Church of the Nativity 28
Civetot 82
Cluny Abbey 70
Cohin 134
Colombia 133, 139, 163, 192, 205
Congo 186
Constantinople 23, 28, 31–35, 38–44, 47, 50–53, 55–56, 60–62, 5, 68, 72–74, 78–79, 81, 83, 85, 87, 96–98, 104, 110–111, 112, 114–116, 120, 124–25, 144–45, 150, 174, 193, 197–99
Copenhagen 121, 145
Cordoba 12, 23, 32, 60, 78–79
Corinth 8 12, 32, 151, 189, 196–97
Corsica 23, 32, 56, 60
Crimea 51, 176
Croatia 51, 64
Cuba 133
Cusa 12, 16, 108, 120, 130
Cyprus 8, 32, 36, 60, 94
Czech region 64–65, 72–73, 118–119, 152
Dachau 184
Damascus 12, 32, 54, 60, 78, 85, 92
Denmark 66, 81, 86, 94, 128, 136, 145, 168
Divar 139
Dome of the Rock 146
Dominican Republic 123
Dunedin 191
Ecuador 163
Edessa 12, 23, 30, 32, 36, 41, 52, 60, 82–83, 85
Edinburgh 193
Egypt 13, 15–17 20, 24, 29, 37, 43, 50, 56, 63, 78, 96–97
El Salvador 192
Elisabethkirche 94
Ely Monastery 67
England 43–44, 48–49, 57–58, 60, 67, 70–71, 75, 77–79, 81, 86, 88, 95, 103, 108–109, 120, 130, 131, 140, 142–44, 147, 152–53, 155–56, 166, 168–72, 176, 191, 198

Ephesus 8, 12, 14, 23, 32, 35–36, 38, 60
Estonia 86
Ethiopia 37–39, 43, 87, 117
Ferrara 120
Fiji 170
Florence 104, 107, 114, 116–117, 120, 123, 191
Florida 133
France 22, 29, 44, 51, 56, 70, 72, 77, 78, 82, 86, 88, 94–95, 97, 102–106, 110, 120, 129–30, 136–37, 140, 147, 158–62, 165–66, 176, 185
Fritzlar 57
Fulda 57–59
Fuller Theological Seminary 190
Gaeta 102, 166
Galicia 79
Gaul 29, 32, 48, 56
Geismar 57
Geneva 110, 129–30, 136
Genoa 97
Georgia 28, 32 60, 99, 149–50
Germany 57–58, 66, 77–78, 86, 88–89, 97, 102, 129–31, 135–36, 140–41, 151–52, 156, 162–63, 183–84, 192
Ghana 186
Glastonbury 70–71
Goa 132–34, 139, 183
Gran 75
Granada 123
Greece 34, 71, 115, 127, 174
Greenland 152
Guadalupe 133
Hagia Sophia 40, 116
Haiti 123
Hedeby 66
Herrnhut 152
Herzegovina 99
Hesse 58, 128
Hilandar Monastery 99
Hippo 20, 23, 31, 198
Holland 129, 136, 140, 144
Holy Land 27, 82–84, 86, 96, 150, 197
Holy Trinity Brompton 190
Hong Kong 191
Hungary 73, 75, 87, 94, 102, 115, 126, 140–41

Iberia 74, 79–80, 86
Iceland 74–75
Illyria 56
India 30, 36, 39–50, 100, 108, 122, 132–34, 138–39, 147, 152–54, 156–57, 170, 192
Iraq 36, 50
Ireland 36, 39, 44–45, 67, 163
Istria 56
Italy 26, 30, 34, 38–39, 44–45, 54, 56, 61, 68–69, 70, 72, 78, 82–83, 94–95, 97, 102, 104, 108, 110, 112, 162, 164
Ivory Coast 71, 186
Jamaica 155
Jamestown 144
Japan 132, 134, 138, 165, 187
Jerusalem 8–9, 12, 23, 28, 32, 50–52, 54, 60, 63, 78, 80–83, 85–86, 96–97, 126, 145–46, 150, 175, 199
Jutland 66
Kansas 133, 189
Karakorum 100
Karelia 146
Kiev 73, 78, 80, 100–102, 113, 116, 145
Kitzingen 57–58
Korea 147, 157, 164, 170, 187
Kulikovo 113
La Isabella 123
Labrador 152
Lalibela 87
Languedoc 66, 97
Latvia 86
Lausanne 193
Lavra 71
Lebanon 85, 166
Leipzig 141
Lepanto 126
Ligugé 29
Lima 133
Lindisfarne 48–49, 60
Lisbon 86
Lithuania 86, 112–113, 137
London 12, 23, 48, 60, 78, 121, 131, 152, 171, 190, 195

Los Angeles 189
Lourdes 165
Luxeuil 45, 47
Lvov 137
Lyons 15, 17, 23, 32, 60, 98
Macao 134
Macedonia 64, 71
Madura 156
Mailapur 138
Mainz 58, 91, 127
Malabar 30, 156
Malaya 134
Manzikert 81
Marburg 94
Maritza River 111
Marmara, Sea of 61, 111
Marmoutier 29
Massachusetts 144, 156, 191
Mecca 41, 126
Mexico 122, 133, 139, 164, 180
Michigan 172
Mogilëv 149
Monastery of the Holy Trinity 113
Mondego 79
Monte Cassino 45, 70
Monte Corvino 100
Montreal 157
Moravia 64–65, 73, 129, 152, 156
Moscow 100–102, 113–114, 116, 124–25, 146–47, 149, 180, 182–83
Moshtanica 150
Mount Athos 71, 99, 111–112, 150
Mount Sinai 111
Mozambique 169
Mysore 156
Nagasaki 134
Naples 23, 32, 60, 98, 110
Narenta valley 65
Navarre 79
Netherlands 140, 168
Neva, River 101, 110, 129–30, 136
New Mexico 139
New York 144, 173
New Zealand 170, 191
Nicea 17, 29–31, 38, 55, 99, 111, 198
Nicaragua 133, 192
Nigeria 170, 186

Nineveh 50
Nisibis 32, 36, 60
North Africa 16, 22, 26, 29, 31, 52–53, 56, 79, 96
North America 129, 133, 139–41, 143–44, 154–55, 158, 163–64, 171, 185–87
North Berwick 130
North Carolina 188
North Korea 187
Norway 88
Notre-Dame Cathedral 160
Nova Scotia 139
Novgorod 31, 78, 101
Orléans 120
Oxford 4, 67, 90–91, 105, 127, 152, 168, 195
Palestine 6, 176
Pamplona 79
Pannonia 65
Papal States 43, 53, 56, 62, 68–69, 118, 160–61, 164
Paraguay 139
Paris 21, 49, 57, 67, 78, 90–92, 102, 105, 110, 129–30, 133–34, 148, 158–60, 164, 196
Pecherska Lava (Monastery of the Caves) 80
Peipus, Lake 101
Peking see Beijing
Pennsylvania 144
Persia 20, 23, 30, 32, 34, 36, 47, 50–52, 78
Peru 163, 190
Perugia 105
Piacenza 77
Pisa 110, 117
Pittsburgh 173
Plombariola 70
Poitiers 29, 56–57
Poland 73, 75, 101, 113, 115, 131, 137, 141, 156, 183
Pomerania 86
Portugal 79, 86, 94, 122–23, 157, 163
Prague 72, 78, 118–119, 136
Princeton 188
Providence 144
Prussia 73, 102, 153, 156, 162
Przemysl 137
Quebec 139, 156–57

Ravenna 18, 33, 38, 40, 56, 61
Regensburg 57, 64
Rhode Island 144
Roha 87
Romania 27, 137, 141, 145, 173
Rome 8, 12–15, 21, 23–36, 38–39, 41–45, 49, 54, 56–57, 60, 62–65, 68–69, 76–81, 85, 90, 94–95, 98–99, 101–102, 105–108, 110, 116, 118–120, 124, 126–28, 131, 134, 137, 144, 149, 160–61, 163, 166, 168, 176, 179, 192, 196, 199
Rostov 113
Russia 7, 68, 73, 78, 93, 100–102, 104, 112–114, 116, 124–26, 135, 145–51, 153, 156–57, 161–62, 174–77, 180–83, 193
Saccudion 61
Sachsenhausen 184
Salamanca 105
Salem 144, 156
Salonica see Thessalonica 12, 23, 32, 60, 64, 112
Salt Lake City 172
Salzburg 45
Samoa 170
San Salvador 192
Santa Fé 139
Santo Domingo 123, 132
Sardinia 16, 23, 32, 56, 60
Saxony 128, 152
Scandinavia 61, 66, 75, 88, 110, 141, 192
Scete 29
Schleswig 66
Scillium 16
Scotland 36, 39, 44, 49, 60, 110, 129–30, 140, 142, 156, 170, 193
Seleucia-Ctesiphon 36
Serbia 64–65, 87, 89–99, 111, 115, 146, 150
Shandong 157
Shrine of St James 67
Sicily 6, 23, 56, 60, 78, 98, 110
Sierra Leone 155, 170, 186
Sistine Chapel 8, 126
South Africa 152, 169–70, 187

South America 85, 123, 139, 163–64, 192
South India 133, 153
South Korea 164
Spain 42, 50, 56, 67, 78–81, 83, 86, 94–95, 110, 122–23, 127, 136, 140, 142, 162–63, 180
Spice Islands 134
Sri Lanka 39, 134
St Gall 45
St Peters Church in Rome 127
Studios 61, 71
Subiaco 70
Sutri 76
Sweden 66, 86, 88, 128, 130, 136
Switzerland 129, 140, 151, 193
Syria 15, 24–25, 29–30, 35, 37, 41, 43, 47, 50, 81, 85, 97, 134, 173, 175
Tahiti 170
Tanjore 153
Tanzania 152
Tarsus 8, 23, 49
Temple of Jerusalem 9, 13, 31, 84
Thessalonica 12, 23, 32, 60, 64, 112
Thrace 72
Tiflis 99
Toledo 23, 32, 42, 60, 63, 80
Topeka 189
Toronto 190
Tranquebar 153
Transylvania 75, 137, 140
Trichinopoly 153
Tripoli 14, 82, 126
Tübingen 125, 167
Tunis 16, 57
Uganda 187
Ukraine 101, 137, 183
Union of Soviet Socialist Republics (USSR) 181, 183
Upper Volta 186
Utah 172
Valencia 80, 86
Varna 115
Vatican 76, 102, 121, 166, 180, 187, 190–91, 193
Velehrad 65

Venaissin 160
Venetia 56, 96, 115
Venezuela 139, 163
Venice 25, 68, 83, 89, 96
Vienne 15, 23, 105
Virginia 144
Vladimir 73, 78, 101–102, 181
Wàdi n' Natrùn 29
Wales 144
Wallachia 115, 149–50
Waterloo 162
Wessex 57, 67
West Indies 139, 152
Westminster Abbey 81
Windesheim 126
Wittenberg 127–28, 130
Worms 77, 88–89, 128
Würzburg 45
Yarmuk 52
Yoido Full Gospel Church 187
York 23, 26, 32, 48–49, 60, 67, 144, 173
Zadonsk 149
Zaire 187
Zurich 129
Zwolle 118

EVENTS/PEOPLES/IDEAS

abolition of slavery 143, 152, 154, 171, 173
accommodation 134, 156, 181
Act of Supremacy 131
Act of Uniformity 143
Aeiparthenos 41
African-Americans 155, 173, 189
Alans 38
Albigensians 64, 72, 94–95, 97, 105, 197
Almoravids 80
Alpha Course 190
Amazing Grace 152
American Civil War 173, 180
American War of Independence (American Revolution) 154–56, 158
Americanism 164
anchorites 196
Anglo-Catholics 168, 171

Anthropotokos 35
Antiphonary of St Benigne 70
antipope 88, 107, 110, 117, 196
anti-Semitism 183, 185
apartheid 187
Apocrypha 30, 196, 198
apologetics 14, 102
apostates 18, 21–22
apostolic vicariate 164–65
Arabs 8, 32, 36, 41, 50, 52, 60, 75, 79, 105, 117, 132, 173
Arianism 28–30, 38, 40, 42–43, 137
Arles, Council of 23, 28
Armenian genocide 28, 33, 43, 56, 173, 179
Arminianism 140–41, 152, 155
Athanasian Creed 29
atheism 11, 15, 21, 151, 158, 174, 183, 194–95
Augsburg Confession (Luther) 125, 141
Aztecs 133
Babylonian captivity of the church 105–106, 120
Baptist Missionary Society 154
Barmen Declaration 185
Bartholomews Day Massacre 113, 130, 134, 192
Basle, Council of 119–120, 127
Battle on the Ice 101
Bavarians 57, 107
Bechuana 169
Benedictines 45, 58, 66, 70–71, 91
Berbers 79–80
Black Death 108–109
Black Friars see Dominicans
Bloody Sunday 181
Bogomils 72, 97
Bohemians 73, 119, 136, 152
Book of Common Prayer 131, 143
Book of Mormon 172
Bourbons 136
Boxer Rebellion 178
Brethren of the Common Life 108
British and Foreign Bible Society 154, 176

Buddhism 50, 134, 187
Burgundians 38
calendars 17, 125
canon 13, 15, 25, 30, 196, 189
Canon Law (Nomocanon) 91, 102, 196
Capuchinesses 95
Capuchins 95, 131, 156
Caribbean Catholic Synod 139
Carmelites 132
Carolingian Renaissance 58, 60
catechumens 17–18, 20
Cathars 72, 94, 97, 100
Catholic League 136
Catholic social teaching 183
celibacy 52, 76, 121, 191
Celtic Christianity 32, 39, 43–44, 47–49, 53, 60, 70, 74
Chalcedon, Council of 37–38, 41, 43, 50–51, 198
charismatic renewal 186–87, 189–90, 196
Childrens Crusade 97
China Inland Mission 170
Chinese Rites 157
Christotokos 35
Chronicle of Seert 30
Church Fathers 16, 18, 42, 91–92, 97, 197–98
Church Missionary Society 154, 170
Cistercians 85, 90
Clapham Sect 154, 170–71
Codex Alexandrinus 145
coenobites 24, 29, 71, 196–97
College of Cardinals 77, 110
College of Spiritual Affairs 148
Colletines 95
communism 165, 178–83, 185
Conciliar Movement (Conciliarism) 117, 119, 126
Concordat (1801) 160–62
Concordat of Worms 88–89
Confessing Church (Germany) 184–85
Confession of Faith (Lucar) 145
conservatism 155, 161–63,

166, 168, 171, 176, 180, 186, 188–90, 197
Constance, Council of 110, 117–119, 166
Constantinople, sack of 96
Constantinople, Second Council of 41
Constantinople, Third Council of 51
Constitutional Act (Canada) 156
Conventuals 95, 106
Coptic (language) 24, 56
Council of the 100 Chapters see Moscow, Council of
Counter-Reformation 131–32, 136–37
Creationism 171
creed 25, 29, 37, 38, 42, 51, 62, 98, 117, 125, 172, 193
Creed of Chalcedon 37
Crimean War 176
Cristero War 180
Crusade of Kings 86
Crusade, First 6, 81–82
Crusade, Fourth 86, 93, 96–97
Crusade, Second 83, 85
Crusade, Third 86
Cultural Revolution (China) 178–79
Cyrillic alphabet 65, 72
dark night of the soul 132
Declaration of Repentance 185
Declaration of the Rights of Man 159
Decree of the Holy Great Church of Christ (Cyril V) 150
Defender of the Faith 131
Definition of Chalcedon, see Creed of Chalcedon
demiurge 13, 198
Destruction of the Indies (de las Casas) 133
dialectical theology 90, 168, 184, 197
Diamper, Synod of 134
dispensationalism 172
docetism 13, 197
Doctors of the Church 25
Dominicans (Black Friars) 95
Donation of Constantine 56, 69

Donatists 26, 28
Dort, Synod of 140
Druze 166
Dyophysites 37
East India Company 154
Easter 17, 30, 48–49, 125, 198
ecumenical movement 39, 42, 79, 144, 150, 175, 182, 191–93, 197
Ecumenical Patriarch 39, 42, 79, 144, 150, 175, 191, 197
Edict of the Three Chapters 41
Edict of Toleration (Gallienus) 41
Eighteen Articles see Jerusalem, Synod of
Emancipation Act 171
end times 142, 197
English Civil War 142–43
Enlightenment 147, 149, 151, 158, 197
Ephesus, Council of 35–36
Epistle to the Easterns (Pius IX) 174
Ethiopic (language) see Geéz
ethnarch 173–74, 197–98
eucharist 12, 20, 94, 129, 132, 197–99
Evangelical Alliance 171
evolution 171, 188
existentialism 168, 175
Feast of Orthodoxy 62
Fifth General Council 52
Fifth Lateran Council 126
Filioque 42, 62–63, 79, 98, 137, 174
Finns 32, 60, 86
First World War 179, 183, 188
flagellation 179, 183, 188
Florence, Council of 114, 116–117
Fourth Lateran Council 94, 97
Franciscans 93–95, 99–100, 106–107, 113, 131–32, 134, 146, 163
Frankfurt, Synod of 60
Franks 30, 53, 57, 200–203
Free African Society 155
French Academy 136
French Revolution 158, 160, 174, 197

Frisians 57
fundamentalism 188
Gallicanism 128, 158
Geéz (language) 43, 117
German Christians 184
German Faith movement 184
Germanic peoples 30, 34, 38, 43, 53, 57
Germanicum, Synod of 58
Gnosticism 12–13, 15, 17, 20, 197–98
Golden Horde 100, 113
Goths 30, 32, 34, 38, 40, 42–43, 50, 94
Great Awakening 154–55, 172
Great Captivity 114, 116
Great Persecution 24–27, 157
Great Purge (Stalin) 182
Great Reversal 188–89
Great Schism 78, 110, 117, 120, 126, 191
Gregorian calendar 125
Gregorians 43, 70, 125
Gunpowder Plot 142
Hail Mary 132
Hammer of Witches 122
Hapsburgs 136
heresy 28, 51, 72, 97, 105, 119, 175, 197–98
Hessians 57
hesychasm 111–112
Hieria, Synod of 54–55
higher criticism 166
Hildebrandian reforms 77
Hinduism 133, 138–39, 153, 156
Holocaust 185
Holy and Great Orthodox Synod 174
Holy Roman Empire 53, 130, 159
Holy Synod 148–49, 177, 180
homoousios 29, 198
homosexuality 185, 192
Hottentots 169
Huguenots 129–30, 144
Humanae vitae (Paul VI) 191
humanism 106, 120, 160, 165
Hundred Years War 120
Iberian Crusade 86
Iconoclasm, First 54

Iconoclasm, Second 61–62
icons 53–56, 61–62, 181
Ilkhanids 100
Immaculate Conception of the Virgin Mary 165, 198
indulgences 94, 118, 127, 198–99
Inquisition 97–98, 122–23, 139, 162
Inuits 152
investiture 77–78, 88, 198
Islam 36, 41, 56, 72, 80, 83, 86, 92, 96, 100, 111, 116, 123, 166
Jansenists 137–38, 158
Jassy, Synod of 145
Jerusalem, Synod of 145
Jesuits 131–34, 138–39, 147, 149, 156–58
Jesus Prayer 111–112, 151
Jews 6, 8–9, 12–13, 16–17, 50, 52–53, 63, 67, 82–83, 85, 123, 177, 183–85
Judaism 8, 18, 92, 123, 185
Julian calendar 125
Khazars 64
King James Authorized Version 143–43, 191
kingdom of God 6, 8, 197
Knights Hospitaller 84
Knights of Malta 84, 126
Knights of the Order of the Hospital of St John 84
Knights Templar 84, 105
koinobios 29
Korean War 187
Kuchuk Kainarji, Treaty of 187
Kulturkampf 162
labarum 26–27
Lambeth Resolution 192
Lateran Synod 77
League of the Militant Godless 181
liberal Catholics 165
liberal Protestantism 167
Liberalism 59, 161–62, 164–68, 171, 184, 188–89, 197
Liberation Theology 190–92
Lindisfarne Gospels 48–49
Living Church (Russia) 182
Lollards 121
Lombards 38, 43, 45, 56, 89

Lyons, Second Council of 15, 17, 23, 32, 60, 90, 98
Magyars 60, 72
Malabar Christians 30
Malabar Rites 156
Manichaeism 20, 53
manifest destiny 164
Manzikert, battle of 81
Maoris 170
Marian devotion 32, 133
Marranos 123
martyrdom 6–9, 11, 14–16, 18–22, 24–26, 51, 54, 58, 62, 73, 81, 88–89, 119, 121, 127, 133, 146, 150, 174, 178–79, 187
Marxism 179, 191
Medicis 130
Messiah 6, 8
Milan, Edict of 27
Milvian Bridge, battle of 26
Ming dynasty 100
modernism 165, 168
Monastic Agreement 71
Monastic Rule (Columbanus) 29, 44–45, 47
monasticism 24, 29–30, 45, 67–68, 70
Mongols 32, 36, 60, 93, 99–102, 104, 113–114, 116
Monoenergism 51
Monophysites 37–38, 40–41, 43, 51, 53, 81
Monothelitism 51–52
Montanism 219, 40, 166
Moors 56, 58, 63, 79–80, 83, 86, 123
Moral Majority 189
Moriscos 172
Moscow, Council of 125
National Baptist Convention 173
National Liberation Army (Colombia) 192
nationalism 38, 104, 110, 117, 135–36, 156, 161–62, 165, 168, 174–75, 178, 180, 183–84
Nazism 183–85
Neo-Catholics 162
New Martyrs 19, 127, 150, 174
New Testament 8–9, 13, 15,

30, 100, 127–28, 131, 153, 167, 196
Nicea, First Council of 17
Nicea, Second Council of 55
Nicene Creed 29, 42, 62, 98
Nicopolis, battle of 111
Ninety-five Theses Against Indulgences (Luther) 127–28
Nobel Peace Prize 186–87
Nomocanon see Canon Law
Normans 74, 78, 83, 89
Northern Crusades 86
Novatianists 22
Oak of Thor, the 57
Oak, Synod of the Observants 32, 57
Old Believers 146, 149
Order of Preachers see Dominicans
Order of the Visitation 136
Ordinances (Torquemada) 122, 129
ordination of women 191
Organic Articles (Napoleon) 161
original sin 31, 184, 198
Orthodox Confession (Mogila) 145
Ostrogoths 38, 40
Ottomans 40, 105, 111, 114–116, 125–27, 144–45, 149–50, 161, 173–76, 197
Ottonian Privilege 69
Our Lady of Guadalupe 133
Oxford Movement 168
Palais Royal 136
papal infallibility 164, 166
papal primacy 56, 166
Paris Missionary Society 164
Parlement 158
Parthians 15
Passion of Perpetua and Felicitas, The 18
Pastoral Care (Gregory the Great) 43
Paulicians 63–64, 71–72
Peace of Szeged 115
Peace of Wedmore 67
Pelagianism 31
Penitential (Columbanus) 20, 47
Peoples Crusade 82
philosophes 158, 165
phyletism 175
Pilgrim Fathers 143

Pisa, Council of 117
Poitiers, battle of 29, 56–57
Polyglot Bible 127
Poor Clares 95
Pragmatic Sanction of Bourges 120
predestination 140
preferential option for the poor 197
presbyter 12, 19–20, 22, 142, 199
purgatory 98, 107, 127, 199
Quartodeciman 17
Quinisext Council 52
Quran 92
Raskolniki see Old Believers
rationalism 14, 151, 158, 160, 165, 175, 197
rebaptism 22, 129
Reconquista 79, 86
Reformation 44, 71, 75, 90, 102, 105, 110, 114, 117, 119, 121, 126, 128–29, 131–32, 135–37, 140–42, 144, 151, 158, 196, 199
Remonstrance (Arminians) 140–41
Renaissance 53, 58, 60–61, 106
Roma 185
Romanians 137, 173
Romanovs 146
Rome, sack of (AD 410) 34
Rule of Benedict 45, 47
see also Benedict of Nursia; Benedictines
Russian Bible Society 176
Russian Revolution 180
Russo–Turkish War 149, 175
sacraments 22, 98, 150, 196–99
Sacred Heart 138, 165
Sacred Heart of Mary 138
Saint Thomas Christians 30
Sandinistas 192
Sanskrit 139
Santiago de Compostela, pilgrimage of 67, 81
Saracens 63
Saxons 48–49
schism 35, 38–39, 41, 43, 53, 41, 43, 53, 62, 78, 89, 98, 104, 110,

117–117, 120, 126, 131, 191, 196, 199
schismatics 22, 26, 90, 135, 146, 182
Scillitan martyrs 16
Sechwana 169
Second Coming 172–73, 198–99
Second Great Awakening 172
Second Vatican Council 180, 190–91
Second World War 184–85
Secularism 148
Seljuks 81, 85
Serbs 64–65, 72, 87, 98–99, 111, 115, 146, 150, 173
serfdom 148, 161, 176–77
Shepherd of Hermas 13, 43
Shinto 134
Shinyu persecutions 157
Sian-fu Stone 50
simony 55, 76–77, 102, 199
Singulari nos (Gregory XVI) 165
Sisters of Charity 163
Six Chapters see Jerusalem, Synod of
Sixth General Council, see Constantinople, Third Council of
slavery 13, 15–16, 18, 36, 66, 132, 139, 143, 152, 155, 161, 164, 170–71, 173, 176
Slavic (language) 64, 72
slavophilism 175–76
Smalcald Articles 141
sobornost 176
Social Contract (Rousseau) 158
social gospel 187–88
socialism 162, 165, 175, 181
Society for the Propagation of the Gospel 154
Society of Jesus see Jesuits
Soissons, Council of 58
Solidarity 183
Southern Baptist Convention 173
Spanish Civil War 180
Speyer, First Diet of 128
Speyer, Second Diet of 128
Spiritual Franciscans 106–107

States General 159
suttee 154
Swiss Reformation 129
Symbolical Books 63
Synaxarium 24
Synodicon 62
Tamils 153, 156
Teutonic Knights 101, 102, 112
Theatines 131
Theotokos 35, 37, 41
Third Estate 159
Third Rome 116, 124, 149
Thirty Years War 135–36
Tiguez 133
Time of Troubles 146
Tokugawa Shogunate 138
Toledo, Council of 23, 32, 42, 60, 63, 80
toleration 23, 27, 128, 149, 165, 176
Tongans 170
Tordesillas, Treaty of 123
Toronto Blessing 190
traditores 26
translations of the Bible 20, 49, 65, 121, 127, 131, 142, 145, 151, 153, 169
transubstantiation 94, 109, 121, 132, 197, 199
Treatise Concerning Religious Affections (Edwards) 155
Treatise on Laws (Gratian) 91
Trent, Council of 132
Truce of God (treuga Dei) 70
Truth and Reconciliation Commission 187
Ultramontanism 166
Umayyads 79–80
Union of Brest-Litovsk 101, 137
Unitarianism 177
university 6, 65, 83, 90–92, 95, 105, 110, 118–119, 121, 127, 138, 140, 151, 167, 169, 190, 195
Urbanists 95
Vandals 34, 38
Varna, battle of 115
Vatican I see First Vatican Council
Vatican II see Second Vatican Council
Vatican Library 121

Venetians 96, 115
Venice, Treaty of 89
Versailles, Treaty of 183
Vicar of Christ 93
Vienne, Council of 105
Vikings 53, 60–61, 66–67, 74, 78, 81
Virgin Mary 32, 35, 85, 132–33, 165, 198
Visigoths 32, 34, 38, 42, 50
Vladimir, Council of 102, 105
Vulgate Bible 30, 132
Waldenses 90
wars of religion 135
Waterloo, battle of 162
Wends 86
Westphalia, Treaties of 136
Whitby, Synod of 49
White Monks see Cistercians
Windesheim, Congregation of 126
witchcraft 120, 122, 130
World Conference on Faith and Order 193
World Council of Churches 187, 193
World Missionary Conference 193
Worms, Diet of 128
Xhosa 170
Yes and No (Abelard) 90–91
Yoruba 170
Zoroastrians 34, 47, 50
Zulus 186

CHURCHES AND DENOMINATIONS

Abyssinian (Ethiopian) Church 117
African Methodist Episcopal (AME) Church 155
African Methodist Episcopal Bethel Church 173
African Methodist Episcopal Zion Church 173
American Episcopal Church 191–92
American Methodist Church 152, 155
Amish 129
Anabaptists 129, 196, 198
Anglicans 121, 131, 142–44, 153, 155–56, 165, 170, 186–87, 190–92, 196–97, 199
Armenian Church 28, 179
Assemblies of God 187, 190
Assyrian Church 50
Baptists 143, 155–56, 173, 183, 187
Bohemian Brethren 152
Bulgarian Orthodox Church 72, 174
Calvinists 129, 136–37, 140–42, 144–45, 152, 155, 168
Catholicism 12, 15, 19, 29, 38, 42, 53, 78–79, 81, 95, 100–101, 104, 110, 112, 117, 119–120, 122–23, 125, 128–39, 142–47, 149–51, 153, 154, 156–66, 168–69, 171, 174–83, 185–87, 190–93, 196–99
Christian Reformed Church 168
Christian Scientists 172
Church of Jesus Christ of Latter-Day Saints 172
Church of the East 50
Congregationalists 143–44, 155, 172
Coptic Church 24, 37, 199
Countess of Huntingdons Connexion 153
Danish Peoples Church 168
Doukhobors 177
Dutch Reformed Church 141, 168
Dutch Reformed Presbyterian Church 144
Eastern Rite Catholic Church (Uniate Church) 101, 182
Eastern Rite Maronites 166
Eastern Rite Syrian Catholic Church 175
Ethiopian Church, see Abyssinian Church 117
Evangelicalism 128–29, 147, 151–55, 169–71, 173, 183–84, 186–90, 192–93
Harrist Church 186
Hussites 119–20, 136
Hutterites 129
Jacobites see Syrian Orthodox Church 37
Jehovahs Witnesses 173, 185
Kimbangu Church 187
Lutherans 128, 136–37, 140–41, 156, 168, 186, 192, 197
Maronites 95, 166
Mennonites 129, 144, 155, 198
Methodists 141, 143, 152–53, 155–56, 171–73, 191
Moravians 64, 129, 152, 156
Nestorians 30, 35–37, 41, 99–100
nonconformists 143, 198
Orthodoxy 29, 61–62, 72, 79, 98–99, 101–102, 111–114, 116, 135, 137, 144–51, 173, 176, 181, 190, 193, 197–99
Pentecostalism 186, 189–90, 192
Pietism 141, 152–53
Plymouth Brethren 172
Presbyterian Scottish Kirk 142
Presbyterians 142–44, 154–56, 169–70, 172–73, 188, 191–92, 199
Protestants 29, 90, 105, 117, 119, 125–32, 134–38, 140–47, 150–54, 156, 158, 161 62, 164, 164, 166–67, 169–70, 172–73, 176–85, 187, 189–92, 196–99
Puritans 149, 142°44, 154, 199
Quakers 143–44, 155–56
Religious Society of Friends see Quakers
Romanian Orthodox Church 173
Russian Orthodox Church 93, 101, 145, 176
Ruthenian Catholics 137
Salvation Army 171
Serbian Orthodox Church 99
Seventh Day Adventists 172
Southern Baptists 173, 188
Swiss Brethren of Zurich 129
Syrian Catholic Church 175
Syrian Christians 47, 85
Syrian Orthodox Church 37
Tembu Church 170
Thomas Christians 30, 134
Three-Self Patriotic Church 179
Transylvanian Greek Catholic Church 137
Ukrainian Eastern-Rite Catholic Church 182
Uniate Church see Eastern Rite Catholic Church
United Church of Canada 192
United Native African Church 170
Vineyard Church 190

Acknowledgments

Alamy: pp. 10–11 The Art Archive; pp. 12br, 66 Interfoto; p. 57 Andrew Davies; p. 134 Michele Falzone; p. 150 Globuss Images; p. 165 Dinodia Images

Corbis: p. 3 Thierry Brésillon/Godong; p. 7 Mimmo Jodice; pp. 8–9 Gian Berto Vanni; p. 11bl The Art Archive; p. 18l Dave Bartruff; p. 28 Hulton-Deutsch Collection; p. 33 (box image) Atlantide Phototravel; p. 49 Stapleton Collection; p. 51 David Lees; pp. 54, 127 (box image) The Gallery Collection; p. 65r Marco Cristofori/Robert Harding World Imagery; pp. 74–75 Arctic-Images; p. 76 David Turnley; p. 107 Patrice Thomas/Hemis; p. 113 Dallas and John Heaton/Free Agents Limited; p. 123 Stephanie Colasanti; p. 135 Armin Weigel/dpa; p. 147 Dorothy Burrows/Eye Ubiquitous; p. 155 (box image) Bob Sacha; pp. 178–79 Jim Richardson; p. 181 Peter Turnley; p. 188 (box image) Bettmann; pp. 194–95 Lewis Kemper/Aflo Relax

Getty: pp. 34l, 119, 128, 129, 132, 151, 164 (box image), 179 (box image), 182; p. 8br Raphael; p. 19 Cris Bouroncle/AFP Images; p. 26 (background) Antoine Jean Baptiste Thomas; p. 39 DEA/A. De Gregorio; p. 40 Travelpix Ltd; p. 41 Nabeel Turner; pp. 44ml, 44b Macduff Everton; p. 48 John Woodworth; p. 50 Tim Graham Images; p. 71 (foreground) Medioimages/Photodisc; pp. 71 (background), 126 Grant Faint; p. 72 Otto Stadler; p. 87 Gavin Hellier; p. 118 Guy Vanderelst; pp. 124–25 Bruno Morandi; p. 130 DEA/G. Dagli Orti; p. 133 Renaud Visage; pp. 137, 167 SuperStock; p. 141, 184 Time & Life Pictures Images; p. 142 John Decritz the Elder; p. 145 Inti St. Clair; p. 146 Cosmo Condina; p. 153 India Today Group Images; pp. 156, 186, 193 AFP Images; p. 169 Herman du Plessis; p. 171 After John Russell; p. 175 Vasili Grigorevich Perov; p. 177 Klavdiy Vasilievich Lebedev

Photolibrary: p. 63 www.photolibrary.com

Sonia Halliday: p. 37

The Art Archive: p. 8bl Collegiate Church of San Martino Treviglio/Gianni Dagli Orti; pp. 13, 60 (box image) Bibliothèque des Arts Décoratifs Paris/Gianni Dagli Orti; pp. 17 (foreground and background), 64 (foreground and background), 70, 83, 84l, 103, 163 Gianni Dagli Orti; pp. 21, 82 Neil Setchfield; p. 22 Musée du Louvre Paris/Gianni Dagli Orti; p. 24 Nicholas J. Saunders; pp. 35, 36, 38, 55, 61 (foreground), 104 Alfredo Dagli Orti; pp. 26 (foreground), 136 National Gallery London/Eileen Tweedy; p. 27 Moldovita Monastery Romania/Alfredo Dagli Orti; p. 31 (foreground and background) Roger Cabal Collection/Gianni Dagli Orti; p. 42 Vezzolano, Italy; p. 45 Abbey of Monteoliveto Maggiore Siena/Alfredo Dagli Orti; p. 59 Musée du Louvre Paris/Alfredo Dagli Orti; p. 61 (background) Culver Pictures; pp. 65 (box image), 100 Bodleian Library Oxford; p. 67l Ashmolean Museum Oxford/Eileen Tweedy; pp. 68, 69r Stephanie Colasanti; p. 75 (box image) Private Collection/Gianni Dagli Orti; p. 80 Science Academy Lisbon/Gianni Dagli Orti; p. 84r Kharbine-Tapabor/Collection LOU; pp. 85, 115 (foreground) Galleria degli Uffizi Florence/Alfredo Dagli Orti; p. 89 Canterbury Cathedral/Jarrold Publishing; p. 91 (box image) Biblioteca Civica Lucca/Gianni Dagli Orti; p. 92 Bibliothèque Mazarine Paris/Kharbine-Tapabor/Coll. Jean Vigne; p. 93 San Francesco Assisi/Alfredo Dagli Orti; p. 95 Museo Civico San Gimignano/Alfredo Dagli Orti; p. 97 Bibliothèque de l'Arsenal Paris/Kharbine-Tapabor/Coll. Jean Vigne; p. 105 Galleria d'Arte Moderna Rome/Alfredo-Dagli Orti; p. 106 (box image) Galleria Sabauda Turin/Gianni Dagli Orti; p. 109 Bibliothèque Nationale Paris; pp. 114–15 Moldovita Monastery Romania; p. 121 Private Collection/Philip Mould; p. 122 National Palace Mexico City/Gianni Dagli Orti; p. 140 Bibliothèque Universitaire Geneva/Gianni Dagli Orti; p. 148 Russian Historical Museum Moscow/Alfredo Dagli Orti; p. 149 Miramare Palace Trieste/Alfredo Dagli Orti; p. 159 Musée Carnavalet Paris/Alfredo Dagli Orti; p. 161 Musée du Château de Versailles/Alfredo Dagli Orti; p. 162 Culver Pictures; p. 180 Private Collection/Marc Charmet

The Bridgeman Art Library: p. 35 (foreground and background) Richard and Kailas Icons, London, UK; pp. 53, 96, 160 Giraudon; p. 172 Schlesinger Library, Radcliffe Institute, Harvard University

Topfoto: pp. 14, 16, 18br, 20, 34r, 81, 99, 117, 152 (box image) The Granger Collection; p. 15 Spectrum Colour Library/HIP; p. 33 Roger-Viollet; pp. 46–47 2006 Alinari; p. 52 (foreground and background) World History Archive; p. 67r E&E Image Library/HIP; p. 69l The Print Collector/HIP; pp. 73, 101 RIA Novosti

Maps

Richard Watts Total Media Services: pp. 12bl, 23, 32, 60, 78

Lion Hudson

Commissioning editor: Kate Kirkpatrick
Project editor: Miranda Powell
Designer: Jude May and Nick Rous
Picture researcher: Jessica Tinker
Production manager: Kylie Ord